" He stumbled through, with the cracking echoes of the shot in his ears, half carrying, half dragging Julia."   *Chapter XXXII*

From the painting by John Cassel

Beyond the Law

By

Miriam Alexander

❊

G. P. Putnam's Sons
New York and London
The Knickerbocker Press
1912

The Knickerbocker Press, New York

CONTENTS

iv . Contents

Beyond the Law

BEYOND THE LAW

CHAPTER I

ETHNA LISRONAN

"YOU have no news of how affairs are going in
England, I suppose, Owen?"

Owen D'Arcy roused himself. He recognised
that the question had its origin in a desire to turn
the conversation into a fresh channel and that he
ought to be grateful for it. When a man has proposed to a woman for the fifth time in three years,
and for the fifth time been very gently but very
firmly refused, it is only right that his mind should
be directed to other matters, however little interest
the other matters may hold for him at the moment.
And in truth they had little.

Wanting Ethna Lisronan as he had never
wanted anything before in life, it seemed to Owen
bitterly hard that all his efforts, all his devotion,
should count as nothing against her loyalty to a
memory. He looked across almost angrily to
where she sat, distressed at heart but calm to out-

ward appearance, under the blue-green shadow of the old yew.

A straight shaft of sunlight had made its way through the black branches and fell full on her, finding golden threads in the bunches of satin-smooth dark-brown curls that clustered about her ears. Her narrow black eyebrows were drawn together in a little frown, her long lashes cast a shadow on the delicate line of her cheek. She looked infinitely less than her twenty-eight summers and, to the eyes of the man who might not win her, infinitely sweet.

He cursed the dead man who had had her love—who still held it.

"I—I am anxious about the boy," she went on in the sweet minor voice that was not the least of her charms. "I fear—nay, I know not exactly *what* I fear; but things have been so bad for us—so terribly bad—and 't is whispered that they may be so again."

Owen D'Arcy shook his head, but rather dubiously.

"If the treaty Sarsfield made is held to—" he began, and then left the sentence unfinished.

Ethna glanced up. "That is what I am afraid of," she said very low, looking across at him with a shadow of fear clouding her soft eyes, which held all the light and laughter of a sunlit stream in their liquid dark-grey depths.

Owen was silent for a moment, then, "I served under the Prince of Orange," he said. "He is a

man whose word may mean much—or little—
according to his needs."

"So I have heard. And he—hates us. He
would wipe every Catholic out of existence if
he could."

D'Arcy frowned. He was not particularly fond
of the elder faith himself, nor of those who pro-
fessed it, and just now he had an idea that their
difference in religion widened the gulf between
Ethna and himself. He suspected old Father
Moran, her confessor, of a bias against a heretic.

"Remember what Holland suffered at the hands
of Spain," he said rather drily.

The shadow in Ethna's eyes deepened.

"Owen," she said passionately, "I can remember nothing but what my own people suffered
because they were loyal and faithful to the Church.
Not for worlds would I hurt you or seem to slight
your religion, but—but——"

"Go on, Ethna."

Lady Lisronan smoothed out the embroidery
on her lap with nervous fingers.

"We Irish Catholics are as Ishmael," she faltered
after a pause. "No one lifts hand or voice in our
defence. No one remembers, for our justification,
the bitter, horrible wrongs inflicted on us. Think
of the scores and scores of our women who were
sold—shipped and sold—to the Algerines by Cromwell's men. Nay, two of my own father's sisters
went amongst them. Think of that terrible 1st
of May, forty-three years ago, when every Catho-

lic, high and low, who remained in his home—on land inherited from his forefathers—was put to the sword without heed for age or sex. The whole three kingdoms ring with execrations should any injury be wrought on an Irish Protestant, but if a hundred of us be slaughtered in cold blood who denounces it? Who bears it in mind in later years when some poor wretch is moved to savage reprisals? I am not saying unjust or untrue things, am I, Owen?"

"No—more's the pity! But why think of the matter at all, dear? Those times are past, we hope. Let them lie buried."

"Aye, but are they past, Owen? If I could only feel sure of it! There was so much talk of them in my childhood that I cannot forget them, try as I may. You never heard my grandfather speak of what befell him—of how he stood, bound hand and foot, while two of Broghill's men stripped his wife naked, and hung her by the heels until she died—or of what they did to the child, my father's brother—I pray you never may. I wake now at night sometimes, thinking I hear his voice again— and see his face. He had been through a worse hell than any that lies beyond the grave—and my terror is that Dermot may some day know the same."

Her voice sank to a whisper and Owen D'Arcy was conscious, hot as the day was, of a sudden shiver.

"'T is a nightmare to me," she went on after

a second's silence, "and has been ever since
the first whisper of the Revolution. I played
a coward's part—lying close at home, letting
none of mine lift hand for either side, lest the
boy should suffer. There are times when I grow
hot thinking of it—I, the wife and daughter of
soldiers—but there are other times, times when
I remember my grandfather's words, and then
I 'm glad! It 's a hard thing to be a woman,
Owen, and a——"

"Alone in the world," had been the words in her
mind, but she remembered in time. "And a
mother," she finished lamely with a sudden
wave of pink in her cheeks.

"I think your fears are really groundless," said
D'Arcy slowly. He had guessed the unspoken end
of the sentence and winced, not so much at it as
at the strong and shadowy barrier between them
of which it was a symbol. "None of Dermot's
name took any side in the fight—and the boy's
age is sufficient warrant for his neutrality, were
warrant needed. Even if the treaty is violated,
I cannot see how his property could be touched,
save through some inconceivable villany. I think
in fretting as you do, that you cross a ford you
may never meet."

"I pray you are right—but I am the veriest
coward where Dermot is concerned."

To this D'Arcy made no immediate response
and another silence fell between them. Both
sat looking away beyond the shadow of the old

yew across a stretch of sunlit daisy-spangled grass
which sloped to the river.

Lisronan House stood in a little oasis of culti-
vation snatched from the bog. Eagles and ravens
harried its fowl-yard, grey wolves, out of the
wooded glens beyond Monadarrig, came on winter
nights to nose about its sheep-pens. Outside the
limit of a few fields—a farm or two—lay mile upon
mile of brown bare land, honeycombed with little
lakes, seamed by deep ravines.

The major part of the large and valuable Lisronan property lay in northern Munster, but its late
owner had preferred the wide spaces, the far silver
horizons, dear to his youth—and his widow held
sacred all that he had loved.

Owen broke the silence at last.

"I shall travel into England next month," he
said, "to London. It was my luck once to serve
the Prince of Orange signally—and though I misdoubt me that it will please him to remember it,
yet for very shame he cannot deny the one favour
I shall ask. 'T will be a promise that happen
what may in his lifetime no harm shall befall
Dermot. I'll have it in writing—Kings' memories are short—and the Prince is a Stuart in that
respect. That should set your mind at rest,
Ethna."

"Owen! 'T would be too good of you—too
good!" she cried with the smile that had years
before made him her slave. "I can never thank
you enough."

"Do you think I want thanks?" he asked rather bitterly. "Thanks for any service for you! Surely you know better than that!"

A poignant regret that it was beyond her power to give what he so well deserved stabbed Ethna, not for the first time.

"I know that you are the best friend I have ever had—or shall have, Owen," she said in her gentlest tones.

A faint sound of splashing broke the silence that followed. Both glanced instinctively to where the wide amber river ran glittering over the shallows half a mile away. A black pony was splashing his way across in a rain of diamond drops, followed by two dark specks, each of which cleaved a slate grey arrow-head in the silver water.

"Dermot," said Owen. "Faith! But he seems in a hurry!"

As Dermot's mother laid down her embroidery to watch the pony's scampering rush up the long field with the deerhounds at his heels there was a light in her eyes that even the first Dermot had never seen. She had all the traditional attributes of her race, and the maternal instinct is the strongest the Irish woman knows.

Dermot pulled up when he got near the yew, slipped off, and leading the pony walked decorously up to where his mother sat.

He was a slim, brown-faced, small-featured boy of eleven, with the same fine grey eyes, the same straight brows, and the same long black lashes that

distinguished Ethna. To a superficial observer
the likeness between mother and son was very
marked, but Owen had discovered the one great
difference years before and sometimes wondered
idly how two pairs of eyes so alike in colour and
beauty could differ so utterly in the message they
gave to the world.

Sorrow had been powerless to subdue the lurking
laughter in Ethna's. They laughed even when
her face was grave; their mirth was as irrepressible
as the mirth of a Connacht bog-stream leaping
seaward down the mountain on a silver March
morning.

Dermot's on the contrary, with the same brilliance and the same liquid depths, had a fated
look which nothing dispelled—that shadow of
profound grief, or brooding resentful melancholy,
that haunts so many Irish eyes.

Even now when he stood panting before them,
with hair ruffled by the gallop, and white teeth
gleaming, to outward appearance as happy a little
animal as the deerhound pup at his heels, it was
present—and Owen, being Irish and therefore
given to sudden fancies, wondered all at once
whether Ethna's fears might not be, after all,
prophetic.

"There's a gentleman, Madame, at the ford,"
said the boy breathlessly. "His mare hath broken
her knees and he craves permission to leave her in
the stable here. There he comes!"

He turned as he spoke and pointed across the

river to the wide slope of bog-land on the farther side, down which a figure, followed by a limping horse, came slowly.

Ethna began to fold her work.

"We must find him another horse—or perhaps he would prefer to lie the night here," she said.

"I misdoubt we 've a horse to carry him," answered Dermot. "'T is a very big man—huge —and very red in the face," he added reflectively, as though this must in itself involve additional weight.

"Big—red in the face," repeated D'Arcy frowning, "sounds like—but, no—that could hardly be."

"He has a foreign way of speaking and he was swearing to himself in a strange tongue," put in Dermot.

"French?" asked his mother quickly.

"No, Madame—one I have not heard before. He names himself Van—? Van—? Van der Wynykt."

D'Arcy looked annoyed.

"Gad, then it is Albrecht Wynykt!" he said. "He has added the 'Van der' since our last meeting. If I may advise, Ethna, I would not bid him to lie the night here. The inn at Lisronan is good enough for him."

"You know him then?"

"Yes—knew him in the Low Countries. He 's a swaggering underbred brute—a man unfit to sit in any lady's company. He got his troop solely because when the Prince of Orange wanted money he was ready to lend on better terms than the Amsterdam Jews."

Ethna glanced nervously at Dermot.

"It might be unwise to offend him, Owen," she murmured.   "Men with money to lend often have the ear of higher powers.   He may wish to stay."

"In that case——"

"Well?"

"Oh, 't was only that—an' it pleased you, I 'd stay too."

The shadow went out of Ethna's face.

"Of course it would please me, Owen," she said eagerly.   "Dermot, when you have taken Toby to the stable, run and tell Anne to prepare the green chamber and the brown for guests."

CHAPTER II

THE COMING OF THE DUTCHMAN

L ISRONAN was not in any way a typical Irish
house. It had been built in the first years of
Charles II's reign by an English architect and on
a Tudor model, with no thought for defence and
no heed to the Irish storms. The living rooms
possessed wide, latticed casements—in themselves
a novel innovation—and opened out of a long
gallery hung with weapons and armour, which
had in by-gone days gleamed in the vaulted hall
of the Lisronans' old home.

Ethna was proud of her house and its belongings; her homespun linen, her dairy, her pot-
pourri, the few bits of china—rare in Ireland then
—the oak furniture that gleamed with dark lights
when the sunlight shone on it.

She rustled about the withdrawing room this
June evening, a ghostly figure in the dusk, moving
a bowl of roses here, setting straight a chair there,
tidying away her embroidery. But for once her
heart was not in the work. Though she settled
things from force of habit, her thoughts were

centred on her Dutch guest. Her dislike for him already outdid Owen's.

She had crossed herself furtively when his back was turned, and had hoped, even in the first moment of meeting, that it might please him to pass on. To sit at the same table with him seemed to her almost beyond endurance.

But it had not pleased the Dutchman to pass Lisronan. On the contrary, he had asked permission to stay the night and now was in the dining-room finishing dinner. Ethna had shirked the meal. Owen was there to play host and Owen had approved her absence.

Lady Lisronan, listening to a loud guffaw which echoed even through closed doors, felt that she had done right. She stood a second irresolute, her nose wrinkled with disgust, and then slipped out of the withdrawing room into the gallery. This was a long narrow chamber which ran the whole length of the house and had at its eastern end eight wide stone steps leading down to the entrance door, and at its western a flight of stairs.

The arched outer door stood open to-night, framing a vista of crystal clear sky, the colour of lavender and spangled here and there by a point of diamond light. Darkness lay heavy under trees themselves dim and vague of outline. Bats swooped eerily out of one dim spot into another. The moon was as yet hardly above the eastern horizon and a pink gleam of sunset lingered on the wide parts of the river.

Ethna, having come down the stone stairs and stood a second on the threshold, turned her steps to her own rather untidy little garden, where shadows were growing long and flowers yielding up their evening incense.   It was a fragrant, peaceful place, with its high medieval walls of dark green yew and its old oval well ringed by a low fern-grown parapet—fit haunt for fair, peaceful women-folk.   The well, deep and clear as crystal, made a mirror that in May reflected a swaying pink-blossomed apple-branch, and in September an overhanging white lavender bush and the whiter butterflies that haunted it.   Moonlight turned the water into a silver shield, sunset into an opal. This June night it gleamed like a dark jewel between velvet snapdragon flowers and emerald tongues of fern.

The spot had that indefinable atmosphere of sanctity which clings round a place where for many years men and women have come in their more exalted moods.   Memories hung about it like a spell—the memories of vows whispered there, of tales told to eager children in by-gone summer twilights, of fair faces smiling down at the pictured face on the water.

Ethna never came to it without something of the same reverence that touched her when she made her genuflexion to the High Altar; never saw it without a thought of the hours she had spent there with Dermot's father—that other Dermot who had had all her heart.

She was thinking passionately of him this evening as she paced slowly along the worn flagged path and sat herself down on the parapet in a space between the snapdragons. The sunlight lingered still, reddening the top of the yew hedges and the brooding purple mountains that rose beyond them, and even here in the shadow an aftermath of the golden glow seemed to linger like the dying echoes of music.

Ethna sat very still among the crimson and lemon-coloured flowers, her lavender-blue skirt sweeping the flags, her hands crossed in her lap. D'Arcy, who had been following noiselessly, paused where he could see every detail of her— the curls massed in warm brown waves upon the whiteness of neck and forehead, the straight brows, the long sweeping lashes which looked so very black against her clear skin. For a long minute he remained silent, too gratified by the picture she made to move. Then, as she raised her eyes, he came forward.

"Owen!" she said with a little smile, "I never noticed you! Have you been walking behind me long?"

"Five minutes mayhap—I saw you leave the house." Ethna glanced first over one shoulder and then over the other.

"I—I don't like my guest," she said very low.

"Nor I—I am sorry that he should be your guest."

Lady Lisronan nodded.

"He frightens me," she murmured. "If you were not here I should be horribly frightened. I think he has the evil eye."

"I think there's precious little of him but is evil," answered her companion drily. "'T was an ill chance brought him to Lisronan."

Ethna picked a young fern and nibbled at the stalk thoughtfully with small, very white teeth.

"I have never had so great a horror of any one," she went on. "Is it a warning, Owen?"

D'Arcy laughed. "A warning of what?" he asked, with a slightly contemptuous note in his voice and an anything but contemptuous glance at the fair face raised to his.

"Of—of danger. Oh, you may smile, but I have had warnings ere this. I had one when Dermot brought home that sorrel mare—the mare that afterwards—you remember?"

Owen nodded. Ethna had never before, even to him, alluded to the accident which had made her a widow, and he gauged by this fact the extent of her present fear.

"I heard him—Meinherr Van der Wynykt— talking to the boy," she went on, dropping her voice nervously. "They were walking outside my window as I changed my gown. He was asking Dermot questions anent the property—what rent roll it carried, and how many tenants and how far it extended. Now, why should it interest him?"

"He's an underbred hound, and the underbred

are ever curious," answered Owen, but there was a note of uneasiness in his voice, a shadow on his mobile face—and Ethna watching him very closely saw it.

"Owen, I 'm not such a coward as you think," she said quietly. "If you apprehend danger— and I think you do—pray, pray tell me of it. I shall then beg your advice, and follow it whatever it be."

D' Arcy glanced quickly at her. She was leaning a little forward, one slim hand resting on the wall among the snapdragons, the other hanging over her knee. He realised suddenly that if he were to impress on her the fact that Dermot's safety could only be compassed by marriage with him—a Protestant and an avowed adherent of the new King—there was a chance, nay almost a certainty that she would consent. Her love of the boy would override all else.

He looked away to the deepening shadows under the yew hedge, beset suddenly by a fierce temptation. He had cared for her ever since that day— twelve years ago now—when he had first seen her, a bride of sixteen, sitting just where she now sat and in just the same attitude. The curious tenacity of purpose and the utter faithfulness of the Irish race were his to an unusual degree. He knew, had known always, that he could make her happy; and now—now at last—a hope almost dead but never quite abandoned, raised its head again for a second.

He had heard whispers—nay, most persistent rumours—that the treaty given to the Irish would eventually be broken.   That the Irishmen now in power would use any means, however dishonourable, to force the Mother Parliament into a betrayal of their compatriots was common talk. Already they were showing signs of that complete absence of moral rectitude which was to make the century of their ascendency the blackest in Ireland's history.

It might well be, that Ethna, alone, unprotected, avowedly "Papist," and therefore presumably Jacobite, ran great risks—or again it might not. Owen, torn between sentiment and scruple, found the decision bitterly hard.

He was silent so long that Ethna put out a hand and caught his sleeve.

"Owen! You *do* fear some danger," she said imperatively.   "Nay, don't deny it! I read it in your face.   I heard it in your voice when you first saw this man."

"What you heard was anger at the thought of such a brute coming near you.   As for the danger, there would undeniably be danger were the treaty violated; but the treaty holds—at present."

Ethna drew a long breath.   "I' faith, the ink is hardly dry on it yet," she said.   "For very shame it must be kept a little while—but you know what the peasants say: 'Beware of the head of a bull, the heels of a horse, and the smile of an Englishman.'"

2

Owen D'Arcy smiled, but angrily.

"Egad and they 've reason!" he answered with more vehemence than usual, adding in a quieter tone, "though in this case—as in most others of our history—Ireland's worst enemies are inside her own gates."

Ethna slipped her hand off his sleeve. Like most of her sex, a matter so impersonal as the wrongs of her country interested her little. In her eyes the Treaty of Limerick had been framed solely to protect Dermot.

"Should I have come to dinner, Owen?" she asked suddenly, flitting to another topic in the little inconsequent way she had. "I felt I could not sit at meat with that—Dutch savage."

Owen made a grimace.

"You showed discrimination," he answered. "Never have I felt more desire to see a man's food choke him!"

Lady Lisronan gave a little ripple of laughter.

"La! You too!" she said. " 'T was the knowledge that I should feel the same kept me from the table. And yet—conceive it—he has a wife. What kind of creature can she be?"

"A Dutch savage, doubtless—of the female sex."

"No—no. Irish—he told me so—and his own mother was Irish too."

"We are honoured!" said Owen drily. "Was he—er—talking about his mother with you, Ethna?"

"He mentioned that she had been a country-woman."

D'Arcy reflected that there was little else about the lady which could have been mentioned with advantage.

"But indeed I spoke as sparely with him as I might," added Ethna. "Odious creature! He——"

Owen's hand on her arm cut short the sentence.

"Here is the brute," he muttered disgustedly. "Mucabus too! Will you slip away, Ethna, while I attract his attention?"

Ethna got up hastily. She had a horror of drunkenness exceedingly out of place in that age. Not the least of Owen D'Arcy's virtues in her eyes lay in the fact that he took no part in the swinish orgies of the county and had never appeared before her as too many of her acquaintances did.

It took her a second to free her satin skirt from a projecting stone in the old wall, and before she could start Albrecht Van der Wynykt had come lumbering through an arch in the yew hedge into her holy of holies—profaning it for ever by his mere presence.

He was, as Dermot had said, a huge man—red-haired, red-faced, and coarse in build as a bull. Sensuality was written in every line of his heavy vicious features, cruelty looked out of his light treacherous eyes.   Even the least sensitive must have shrunk from him with the instinctive recoil of a sane mind confronted by the abnormal.

Ethna, standing straight and slim with her skirts

twisted round her, made no effort to keep the horror she felt out of her face.

Van der Wynykt was, in point of fact, less drunk than Owen D'Arcy had imagined. He could carry an incredible quantity without becoming more than excited. He stood now just inside the arch and leered at Lady Lisronan.

"D—d fine place," he said loudly. "D—d fine —very fitted to a pretty woman like your ladyship."

Ethna cast a glance of agony at Owen, who held out his arm to her.

"Not going, are you?" asked the Dutchman, as the couple moved towards him, Ethna almost hidden by Owen. "Vy the devil should you go, my lady? Nice garden—nice company—d—d nice company!"

He ended the sentence by a laugh that made Lady Lisronan shiver. She did not bid him good evening when she passed; did not even look at him.

She and D'Arcy had gone a hundred yards from where he stood before she even spoke. Then:

"Oh, Owen! Oh, if you were n't here!" she whispered tremulously, clinging to his velvet sleeve. "If I were alone with that — that monster!"

D'Arcy's arm tightened on her hand.

"You won't be—so why think of such a thing?" he returned in the nervous soothing tone of a man who fears a scene.

He had piloted her away from the garden and

out on to the dim sweep of lawn before the house, the eaves of which rose sharp and dark against the clear violet sky.

"I'll to my own chamber," said Ethna, stopping for a second to lift her skirt off the dew-soaked grass.

"Please, Owen, whatever that dreadful man may do or say, do not get angry with him. 'T is borne in on me that he will work some of us a mischief yet—so please, please, give him no cause for malice."

Owen D'Arcy laughed. "Oh, you little coward," he retorted, but very gently. "How can I get angry with the brute, when an evil fate has put me in the position of his host? I should like to stand him on his head in the river."

"Oh, 't would pollute it—and kill all the fish for sheer horror. Now here we are at the house, so I will wish you good-night."

She slipped her fingers from his arm as she spoke and went lightly up two shallow steps to a rose-wreathed open door. On the threshold she paused, turned, held out both hands to him like a child.

"Good-night, you best of friends," she said.

He looked hard at her for a second through the twilight before he bent in the stately fashion of the day to kiss her fingers; looked and thought bitterly that "friend" was the worst title in the world from woman to man. Then without a word he turned and walked away.

Ethna stood for a second watching his lean active little figure cross the grass.

There was a sigh on her lips and at her heart as she went indoors. Things would be so simple if only she could care for him as he cared for her— or even, since that was impossible, if she could forget those few and long past years of passionate happiness, and the man who had taken her love over with him into the far dark country.

She went upstairs slowly, and across her own room to the little one beyond it where Dermot slept.

Usually at this hour he was represented by a slight ridge of bedclothes and a small brown head burrowed deep in the pillow, but to-night she found him wide awake and very restless.

"I saw you go to the garden, Madame—and Meinherr Van der Wynykt follow," he began excitedly, sitting up as she came rustling softly over the boards. "I hope he will travel hence to-morrow."

"You ought to be asleep, Dermot."

Dermot ignored this truism.

"I hope the Meinherr will take himself away to-morrow," he repeated, putting out a brown little claw to tweak at a bracelet on his mother's wrist. "He hath me wearied with his questions," he added.

"I trust you answered politely. He is your guest, remember."

Dermot desisted suddenly from his fiddling,

lifted his long black lashes, and stared solemnly at Ethna.

"Then why don't you like him, Madame?" he demanded with the painful directness of childhood. "You signed yourself when he came up."

Lady Lisronan took refuge in the tottering fortress known as parental authority—a building she seldom dared to enter.

"You should not ask questions, Dermot," she said, sitting down on the small bed. "I 've told you that before—and Father Moran has told you so too."

"Father Moran should speak to Meinherr Van der Wynykt then," returned the boy. "There was no question he did n't plague me with—rude questions, too."

"I heard him."

"You, Madame! How?"

"Through the open window."

Dermot appeared to reflect.

"Yes. We saw you—and Anne too. She was tiring your hair," he said suddenly. "And the Meinherr asked if that was your room and how one came at it from inside."

A wave of most unwonted carmine flew into Lady Lisronan's cheeks, and then ebbed again, leaving them paler than before.

"Go to sleep, my son," she said, getting off the bed. "See, we have awoken Cuconnacht."

She waved her hand at Dermot's deerhound, who had been sleeping on a mat under the window,

and who now lifted his head and thumped a languid
tail on the floor.

"I 'll nearly not go to sleep to-night," said
Dermot firmly—and in pursuance of this plan he
turned on his side and lay looking through the door
into his mother's room, where Anne, the tire-
woman, had lit half a dozen candles.

Ethna's undressing was a leisurely process.
Like Dermot she was not in the least sleepy. She
sent Anne away and sat in front of the glass, a
slim white figure, with bare feet and a mane of
brown hair rippling down to her waist.

Her reflection, lit by two candles, made a picture at which she might excusably have glanced.
But she did not. She sat instead looking across
the room—a wide low chamber panelled and ceiled
with dark oak. Like the old garden, it was one of
those hallowed places of the earth wherein people
had been happy—and in some intangible way it
conveyed the fact even to a new-comer.

A faint scent of dried lavender hung in the air,
overwhelmed at present by the strong sweet breath
of roses, which Ethna an hour earlier had tucked
hastily into a bowl on her dressing-table.

The night was so hot and still that both the
latticed casements stood open, and a chevron of
pale moonlight slanted across the deep window
seats, straight on to the carved posts of the bed,
awaking twisted blue reflections in each dark curve.

Ethna's crucifix, which hung above her *prie-dieu*
caught the silver glow and seemed to stand out

from the panelled wall like a thing alive—and it was at this she looked, though without intention.

All her fears had come back to her now that Owen was no longer present to laugh at them. They surged round her like a flood of water—chill, fathomless, terrifying.

The chime of the big clock in the hall striking twelve roused her at last. She straightened herself stiffly, shook back her hair, and stretched her hand out for a ribbon with which to tie it.

The moonlight, waxing ever stronger, had by now travelled from the bed to the door, making visible the little nails which studded it and the scrolls of carving upon its upper panels. Ethna, as she plaited her hair, stared absently at it, listening the while to the harsh self-vauntings of a corn-crake and the distant murmur of the river.

So absorbed was she in thought that she failed to notice a step in the passage outside, until the sound of her door being tried made her jump like a nervous horse.

"Who is it? Who is there?" she called.

The question went unanswered; but another furtive push on the old woodwork brought her to her feet with a heart thumping so loud that it deafened her to all else.

"'T is locked! Who wants me?" she called again, this time louder than before, to cover the fact that she was tiptoeing to the door.

Again the creak of strained timber and the sound of heavy breathing was the only reply.

She knelt down and peeped through the keyhole.

"The Dutchman—and drunk!" she whispered to herself with a terrified glance round the room. Six inches of oak seemed scant protection against this irresponsible monster.

"You have made a mistake, Meinherr," she said, in as steady a voice as she could command. "Your chamber is farther down the passage—the third door."

For a second there was silence. Then Van der Wynykt laughed.

"Mistake be d—d!" he answered, obviously putting his great mouth down to the keyhole. "The mistake 's yours, my lady. Open to me!"

Ethna glanced across to the closet where her tire-woman slept. She lost her head easily in emergencies.

While she was wondering in terror how best to answer the brute outside, a second step echoed down the passage. She heard the shuffle of turning feet, and then Van der Wynykt's voice saying hastily:

"I have made a—er—a mistake."

"You have," returned Owen, in his grimmest tone.

"I—I have mistook the door," continued the Dutchman. "Any man might in zis rabbit varren ot a 'ouse."

"I will show you your own."

"Thank you, sir."

Two pairs of steps went away down the passage.

Ethna, blessing Owen fervently, remained by the door. She was still cold and shaking, and to put out the cheerful candle-light and face silence and the shadows of the night-lamp seemed impossible just yet.

She had not long to wait. In less than a minute Owen was back.

"I've locked him in, Ethna," he whispered through the keyhole, "and I'll see that he takes the road before you are about to-morrow."

CHAPTER III

OWEN D'ARCY sat in his cousin Morgan's lodging in Gray's Inn Lane, London, recalling bitterly the fears Lady Lisronan had confessed to him under the yew tree six weeks before. This evening, on which the text of the new law against Catholics was made for the first time public property, proved how well founded those fears had been.

A man with any patriotism could scarcely bear to contemplate the havoc that this statute must work in his native land—the utter ruin of the older aristocracy, the handing over of Ireland to men who were what the men who leave their own country for a foreign soil usually are—ne'er-do-weels, wastrels, unscrupulous adventurers—men at best ignorant of the people, inimical to them, and without the traditions so essential to a governing class; at worst, brutes whose crimes would breed crime for centuries to come; but Owen as yet had hardly considered this aspect of the matter. He was thinking entirely of Ethna and the hopeless

28

barrier that the State had raised between them. Even to assist her in her social and financial ruin was almost beyond his power. She had become, by reason of her faith, a pariah—a creature outside the law.

"Any fresh news?" he asked, glancing up at his cousin Morgan D'Arcy, who had just come in and now stood before him, his sword and gloves under one arm and his wide-leaved hat on the back of his head.

"Yes—of sorts," answered Morgan. "D' you call to mind a half-bred Dutch swine named Wynykt who was in St. Omer in '77? A low fellow, a bit worse than most? You do. Then mayhap you 've heard that he lent the King fifteen thousand pounds five years ago, and has been pestering him ever since he came to the throne. 'T is said this afternoon that he has got a grant of the Lisronan estates—and will turn out the pretty little Papist widow. 'T will be a d—d shame if so—and I had it on very good authority."

Owen sat for a second as stiff as a setting dog.

"He can't—she has taken the oath," he said after a second, in a hard tense voice.

"He can—if she does n't conform—or even if she does—with the King behind him," answered Morgan, glancing curiously at his cousin, whose face was eloquent of dismay.

"Who told you, Morgan?"

"Randal Beresford—and no later than an hour ago."

Owen got up and paced once down the length of the room like a man driven by an intolerable thought. The red sunset light fell fiercely on him as he passed the casement, lightening his snuff-coloured coat with its square pockets and deep cuffs, catching the long lace ends of his cravat, gleaming in his heavy peruke.

He looked ten years older when he turned to snatch up a paper which lay near him on the table, a copy of the new law—seed that in years to come was to bear such black and bitter harvest for betrayer and betrayed alike.

After a minute he began to read out paragraphs. Wrapped though they were in the abstruse phraseology of the law, their meaning was terribly clear. They denied to every member of the Church of Rome—four-fifths of Ireland's population—the common right of man: the right to work, to read, to worship God. The lowest prostitute of the Dublin streets who chose to call herself Protestant would henceforward be of more account than the Catholic daughter of O'Conor or Geraldine; the most infamous cut-throat might plead, with absolute certainty of acquittal, that his victim had been "a Papist." The code embraced even such trifles as the carrying of a sword or the possession of a horse.

"Merciful God!" cried Owen as he read. "And they call this justice!"

Morgan D'Arcy gave his shoulders a slight shrug.

"As to that, 't is framed on the French laws against the Huguenots," he returned.

"I know! I know! A mighty outcry we made on these same French laws that we now copy! That we now would enforce not on a handful but on a whole nation! God! Sarsfield should turn in his grave at this!"

Morgan D'Arcy laughed.

"Did you ever think the Treaty of Limerick would be held to?" he asked.

"Yes—as did Sarsfield himself."

"Sarsfield, you see, worked on Grace's principle, 'a gentleman does not betray his trust,'" answered the other, drily. "The men he had to deal with—especially the Irishmen—held an entirely opposite opinion. You may thank your stars your father conformed and bred you up in his ideas, Owen, for egad! the Papists are like to have a mighty bad time of it henceforward."

Owen made no answer. He was wondering desperately if it would be possible to induce Ethna to change her religion.

"I should like to know whose personal gain is behind this damnable treachery?" he demanded at last, savagely.

"Whose gain? Faith, the gain of those scurvy half-Irish plantation men and undertakers, who see a rare chance in the ruin of the upper class. 'T was their representatives framed the code, and its object is to fill their pockets under pretext of protecting England's interests!"

"And the King?" cried Owen D'Arcy angrily. "The King, whose cry was ever religious liberty?"

"Religious liberty was a good card in those days!" returned Morgan with a sneer. "Persecution of the Papists is doubtless a better one now. The King plays for his own hand, and not the least part of his genius is knowing what card will serve him best."

He paused, and then, finding that Owen remained silent, and having that strong predilection for the sound of his own voice which usually afflicts Irishmen, went on:

"The King does denounce the whole scheme—or pretends to—but 't is generally whispered that the matter has his sanction. He has laid himself under obligation to several, and though he may be willing to forget it, they are not; so, since a sop had to be found for them, what better sop than the properties of the 'mere Irishry'—the Papist Irishry, of course! Put the Papists beyond the law, and the thing is done! Hence that."

He pointed to the parchment.

After his words silence fell between the cousins. They had little in common save their religion and those ties of blood to which expatriated men cling.

Morgan, the younger son of an impoverished squire, had some years earlier given his services to William of Orange, and haunted the Court now in hope of recompense. He was an idle, kind-hearted scamp, with the good looks that had been denied Owen, and an infinite capacity for wine,

woman, cards, and gossip—the last man to win
notice from the cold, crafty soldier whom England
had chosen as her king.   But he had not yet quite
ceased to hope; and Owen knowing no better way
turned to him now when he wished for an inter-
view with his old chief.

"I must have speech with the King, Morgan,"
he said, suddenly breaking the silence.

Morgan yawned and ran a hand over his peruke.

"Faith then, I don't know how you 'll manage
it," he answered, sitting himself down in a straight-
backed chair, with due consideration for the long
skirts of his coat.

"I thought you——"

"I?   Egad, it would n't suit the King to remember my existence at present, and I 'll lay a guinea
't won't suit him to remember yours either,
Owen—besides——"

"Well?"

"Well, if your design is to aid my Lady Lisronan,
't is a d—d dangerous one.   Read that law,
and you 'll see how Protestants who assist Papists
are to fare.   She 's a ruined woman unless she
conforms, and why add——"

Owen D'Arcy cut short the speech with a gesture
of utter impatience.

"Hang it, Morgan—I know all that!" he said
irritably.   "I must have speech with the King—
I don't care how I come by it.   Any backstair
method will do if it brings me face to face with
him.   What of Randal Beresford?   He 's con-

3

nected with some one at Court. Surely he could work it? Good God, if I thought Albrecht Wynykt would ever go to Lisronan!"

He flung out his hand in a gesture of desperation, then let it drop to his side and left the sentence unfinished.

"Don't count on being able to stop him, Owen," put in Morgan, drily. "Much as I esteem the Prince of Orange as a general, I know—we all know—that he keeps faith with only one man in this world and considers only one—the Prince of Orange."

"I have a claim on his consideration, Morgan."

"So much the worse for you! Well, I 'll do what I can. I 'll sound Randal Beresford. He may be able to procure you an audience—but don't count on it."

.   .   .   .

"What are you going to say to the King, Owen?" asked Morgan D' Arcy in a low voice, two days later, as the cousins walked together up the old Tudor staircase of Hampton Court—Wolsey's Hampton Court, for the newer portions were hardly completed yet.

Owen shook his head.

"It depends," he answered.

"Well, for God's sake, keep your temper—I have known you——"

Morgan left the sentence unfinished except for a dubious glance, and a thought of the red light that flamed in Owen's eyes whenever he spoke of Van der Wynykt.

"He may not even see us," he muttered.

Owen stopped dead.

"Faith! you said he *would*," he exclaimed, crossly.

"There 's a vast deal between saying and doing in a Court," retorted Morgan. "Come on into the ante-room—we can't stand arguing here. Hullo, there 's Beresford! Well, Randal, how goes it? You remember Randal Beresford, Owen?"

Owen did not, but he had been given to understand that the young man had done much to procure him his audience with the King—and he greeted him accordingly.

"We 'd better go in," said Beresford, marshalling them over the threshold into the ante-room, a small chamber rich and subdued in tint, but unfurnished save for a few carved chairs against the tapestried wall.

There were two other groups—one of three men and one of four—awaiting his Majesty's pleasure. The dull afternoon light gleamed on their perukes and sashes when they moved, and sent ripples of colour down their long coats. All seven wore that air of monumental importance common to those whose life is spent in magnifying trifles.

Beresford looked at them with hardly concealed amusement.

"Come into the window," he said, taking Morgan by the elbow. "I weary of the stares of these

clods.   One has come from Lincolnshire to consult
his Majesty about a right of way, if you 'll believe
me; and another desires it be known that he sus-
pects his neighbours of having mass said in their
cellar of a Sunday night.   They 'll go in before
you, though."

"Why?" asked Morgan D'Arcy.

"Because his Majesty happens to remember
your cousin here.   'Owen D'Arcy,' quoth he last
night, looking mighty black, 'the man who was
at Cassel?'   'The same, sir,' says Bentinck, who
was with him.   Then the King whispered something to Bentinck, and Bentinck nodded.   Now
you know all I know—save that this morning
't was intimated to me that his Majesty would
see you."

"Did Bentinck tell you this?" said Owen.

Beresford laughed.   "Lord, no!" he answered.
"'T was his page-in-waiting.   Bentinck!   Why,
Bentinck 's the King's right hand—his *âme damné*,
as the Jacks say.   No man learns aught from
Bentinck, I promise you."

"Then, frankly, do you think my chances——?"

"Frankly, I think your chances are d—d bad,
Mr. D'Arcy.   You 'll forgive my asking if 't is
about the Lisronan property you 've come?"

Owen looked slightly startled.

"Morgan told you, then!" he said.

"Morgan dropped a hint," answered Beresford.
"'T is a bad subject, I 'm afraid.   The King is
indebted to Wynykt, and since the Dutchman

won't let him forget the debt he would discharge
it as lightly as he may. Then, too, he holds
Wynykt a suitable man to send to Ireland. No
danger of his showing mercy, you see, and his
Majesty, being of a frugal nature, would not
encourage any clemency save what may be turned
to profit. There, we are to go in now."

Owen put his hand instinctively on his sword-
hilt and then, conscious of the absurdity of the
action, snatched it away again. His habitual
coolness had deserted him. He was consumed
by anxiety. No previous crisis of his life had
found him other than calm and collected; but then,
on no other occasion had so much been at stake.

The King's closet, into which they were shown,
was panelled with dark wood and lighted by two
deep-set windows. There was a peculiar stillness
about it, as if the silence of years, during which
people had waited for a monarch's word, had
woven itself into the very atmosphere.

A shower beat noisily against the casement and
ran in weeping drops down the glass, and a little
flame purred amongst the logs on the hearth; but
neither sound seemed to break the stillness; if
anything, they intensified it.

William of Orange sat by the hearth staring
into the flames. His haggard face wore the look
of a man who has sacrificed all to one end, has
found that end profitless, and yet is bitterly determined to pursue it while life lasts. There was
knowledge of suffering in his cold green-hazel eyes,

a knowledge tempered by cruelty and by the
infinite selfishness of his mother's race.

Owen D'Arcy, looking at the wizened motionless
figure as he walked up the small room, realised
how little prosperity had softened the man, and
his heart sank.

Bentinck stood behind the chair and eyed the
King's visitors askance. Owen had known Bentinck well in the old days, and had shared rations
with him once when rations were short, but the
favourite's face now was like a stone.

Morgan D'Arcy, having kissed the King's hand,
passed on, and it was his cousin's turn.

He, too, bent the knee, touched the King's
hand perfunctorily with his lips, and then rose
and stood before him, so obviously waiting that
words were almost forced from the reluctant
monarch.

"Vell?" he asked sharply in a weak voice.
"Vot 'ave you to say—I onderstand you 'ave
some request?"

His tone was antagonistic; his face, always hard
and crafty, wore a look almost of hatred.

"Your Majesty does not remember me?"

"No—I 'ave never seen you before."

"Not at Cassel in '77, sir?"

For a moment their eyes met, contempt in one
pair, guile in the other, then:

"Cassel! Bah! It is alvays de same," said
the King, curtly. "You 'ave come to beg—
comme toujours."

The colour rushed into Owen D'Arcy's face. There is no aristocracy on earth so arrogant as the Irish, and he was in himself a proud man. Only for Ethna's sake would he have condescended to remind the King of his obligation.

"Beg!" he repeated fiercely. "No, sir, I have come to claim a promise your Majesty gave to me that day."

"I tell you I 'ave not seen you dat day—or any day."

"And I most respectfully submit that your Majesty did see me that day—that I had the honour to save your Majesty from—from death——"

The colour was in his Majesty's face now.

"Soh—you give me de lie!" he said grimly. "It is enough—Bentinck——"

He looked up at his lieutenant and then at the door.

Bentinck made a step forward, but Owen did not budge. He was conscious of Morgan gaping in the background; of Randal Beresford making frantic signals; of the general stir in the room.

"Your Majesty gave me this token—mayhap you will remember it," he said, pulling a coat-button out of his pocket—a silver button engraved with the arms of Holland.

"I remember nodings," returned William, very shortly.

He put his thin hands on the arms of his chair and got up.

Randal Beresford came forward, crimson with agitation, and took his countryman by the elbow. But Owen shook his hand off. He was fast losing both his presence of mind and his temper.

"Sir—what I had to ask you was about the Lisronan estate," he cried desperately, still standing before the outraged King. "You have granted it to a scoundrelly bastard named Wynykt. The lady to whom it belongs is loyal—is——"

"A Papist!" snarled William—and all the venom of his nature seemed to concentrate in the hated word.

For the fraction of a second they stood facing one another, no longer King and subject, but two men bitterly antagonistic, and each resolved that his own will should prevail.

"I'll pay Wynykt the money," said Owen hoarsely, "if your Majesty will revoke the grant. Nay, sir, let me have five minutes alone with you—for God's sake!"

William of Orange looked at the door.

"Go—and be d—d to you!" he said, losing his temper suddenly, as was his way.

Before the words were said, Owen's sword flashed out of its scabbard, and every man in the room jumped, save the man who stood nearest the bare steel.

Bentinck sprang forward, but before he could seize D'Arcy, the Irishman had snapped the blade across his knee.

"''T was a bad day for Ireland when I brought you off from the French!'' he said in a low, vehement tone, flinging the pieces at William's feet. "For myself, I 'll no longer serve a Prince who knows neither truth nor honour!''

He turned as he spoke and walked off, blind with fury, towards the door by which he and Morgan had come in.

It opened before he reached it, and he saw straight in front of him, blocking the narrow space, the gigantic form and coarse face of Albrecht Van der Wynykt.

It was the final touch. For a second Owen "saw red." He walked straight up to the Dutchman, waving him aside imperiously, and then, when Van der Wynykt hesitated, flung up his right hand and struck him full in the face.

Van der Wynykt swore. "Vot the devil you mean?" he howled, regardless of the wide-eyed, staring spectators, of Bentinck's outraged exclamation, even of the King's presence.

"You know quite well what I mean, you misbegotten coward!" retorted D'Arcy, shaken from head to foot by the blind, unreasoning passion of the Celt.

The Dutchman rubbed his cheek.

"You—you—vould insult me!" he said.

Owen laughed. "That 's for you to decide," he said.

By this time Bentinck, Morgan, and Randal Beresford were upon the infuriated couple, and

Bentinck was shutting the door literally against their bodies.

"My God, such an affair—under his Majesty's very eyes!" he exclaimed, as they backed away from the threshold.

"For God's sake, Owen, come away!" said Morgan D'Arcy, seizing his cousin's arm. "'Fore God, man, you've made trouble enough as it is!"

"Dere vill be more yet," said Van der Wynykt furiously. "'E 'ave insult me—I demand satisfaction!"

"You shall have it!" returned Owen. "Name a friend."

The Dutchman looked at Bentinck, who had come out and was holding the door against them; but the favourite shook his head contemptuously. Though he had, as King William's right-hand man, to do things that went against his sense of honour, he drew the line higher than the Prince he served.

"Mein friend—Hendrik Steen, den," said Van der Wynykt, unwillingly. "He may be found at de House of Orange Inn in de Haymarket."

"Very well—my cousin will wait on him immediately. The less delay there is in settling the affair the better," answered Owen, and then turning on his heel he walked away down the long room.

Morgan stood a minute to speak in a very low voice to Bentinck, who, however, made no response. He was watching the small, snuff-coloured figure—and when it had disappeared through the dark doorway and past the red coats of the guard, he swung round without a word and reopened the door of the King's closet.

Wynykt caught at his cuff.

"Dey should be laid by de heels—arrested— dese Irishmen," he muttered in a low voice.

Bentinck shook off the Dutchman's hand.

"They will be—within the hour," he said curtly.

CHAPTER IV

"A SHADOW . . . BROAD AS A MAN'S GRAVE"

ETHNA LISRONAN lay with her arms spread before her, staring across the room. She could not sleep—had not in fact slept all night—and now the uncurtained window was beginning to glimmer greyly in the dark wall.

Fear lay upon her like a heavy garment—a more definite fear than the vague terror which held all Catholic Ireland. She had heard nothing from or of Owen for two months, and of late—during the last week—a curious feeling that he was very near had so possessed her, awake and asleep, that every hoof-fall on the avenue brought her to the window, and at every step in the hall her heart leaped.

To-night the feeling was stronger than ever, but tinged by a strange cold undercurrent of horror. To lie and face it alone taxed all her maternal powers of self-abnegation, for Dermot awakened, Dermot staring solemnly at her out of wide bright eyes and asking unanswerable questions, would have been an infinite relief.

44

She sat up at last with a restless backward toss of her hair, determined at all costs that the child should be spared. The room was still utterly dark, save for the one grey patch, but she glanced round it in that feverish hope of detecting the first evidences of daylight that come only of a sleepless night.

And then—quite suddenly—standing near the foot of her bed she saw Owen D'Arcy. He was looking full at her with an expression she had never seen before, an expression of such passionate despair, such unutterable regret and pain, that almost involuntarily it wrung a cry from her.

"Oh, Owen!" she cried, holding out her hands to him. "Owen, what is it? What has happened?"

Before the words were spoken he had gone. The blackness hung before her again like a curtain, and with it came a sudden realisation of facts overlooked a second earlier. That there had been no sound of steps, that her door was locked, that even if Owen had done so unheard-of a thing as to walk unbidden into her room at dawn, she could not without light have seen him.

On top of these thoughts, or rather hand in hand with them, ran a chill, nameless, overwhelming terror, which seemed to seize her whole soul in its ice-cold grasp.

Instinctively she signed herself, touching forehead and breast with trembling fingers. Owen was dead—so much she knew. Nothing else seemed to matter for the moment—not even the desire which had been strong enough to bring his spirit back through "the Gate of many feet."

. . . .

Dermot, waking some seconds later strangely terrified, though why he could not tell, heard the sound of stifled sobs in his mother's room, and after a little time spent in wrestling with a desire to slip under the bedclothes, got up and crept to the door.

He knew what he would see. Once before, in a faint autumn dawn, the anniversary of his father's death, he had waked to find his mother kneeling at her *prie-dieu*, shaken by passionate grief, but on that occasion she had heard the patter of his bare feet and had turned and called him to her.

This time—well, this time Dermot did not wait to be called. Fear, an intangible, horrible fear, suddenly got the upper hand—he ran back quivering to his bed and pulled the blankets over his head.

. . . .

Ethna sat on her cob, looking away over the bog-land to a misty blue horizon. At the earliest hour possible she had had horses saddled and had ridden with Dermot to Owen's house, Pouldarrig, and now she was waiting the confirmation of the knowledge which lay so far between herself and her soul.

Dermot eyed her from time to time curiously—

as her household had done—but he had no inkling.

Ethna knew how unfitted the land which lies east of the moon and west of the sun is for children's feet; .knew that they see its mist-haunted peaks sometimes, and that they have always— how, who shall say?—a certain vague consciousness of those black and fathomless abysses which lie amongst them.

She would not tell the boy, would not even look at him now, as he stood waiting for the answer to their summons under the arched doorway of Pouldarrig, lest he should read her face too clearly.

Owen's home stood high on a hill above a sweep of red bog, with a narrow, noisy trout stream which had once been penned in a moat washing its southern wall and leaping away from it down a slope into a little hollow full of birch.

The D'Arcys' enemies had come against the place in old days in vain—had wasted fire-balls and broken battering rams on the tower's broad base, and been defied from its crown by jeering men-at-arms. It breathed defiance still, as it stood up, square and grey and bare, overlooking wide wild lands which had belonged to D'Arcys for five hundred years. Not a fruitful heritage, perhaps, but one which a man born thereunto might love with a greater love than any ever awakened by fat pasture lands and peaceful vales.

Ethna, sitting slack in her saddle, looked at it all and saw nothing of it. Owen's face, eloquent of a despair that passed human comprehension, was perpetually before her, and she could think of little else. She set her teeth at the sound of steps on the stone-flagged hall. Suddenly it seemed to her that to hear in so many words that Owen was dead would be more than she could bear.

She kept her head averted while Dermot greeted and was welcomed by Owen's old butler, Eoin, a friend of many years' standing. With strained ears she waited for the vital question. It came at last.

"Was Mr. D' Arcy back from England yet—and what news had Eoin of him?"

Eoin, it appeared, had none. His honour had not written for a long time, but he might ride up any day. Uncertain he was always in his comings and goings. And would n't her ladyship come in and rest?

Ethna found her voice with difficulty. Dermot, much vexed, was told to remount his pony at once, in spite of the fact that Eoin had a new hawk to show him if he could but wait.

"You will send me news on the instant, Eoin, when you have any of Mr. D' Arcy," said Ethna. "Late or early. Do not forget. Come, Dermot."

She touched her cob with her heel as she spoke, and rode off, leaving Dermot half on and half off his fidgety pony—a most unusual action in a woman who generally watched every movement of her son's with more or less anxious eyes.

The boy was destined by after events to remember that ride for the rest of his life; but at the

time it was marked by only two things—vexation
that he had not seen the hawk, and a wonder what
had happened to that best of comrades, his mother.
She would not even race him along the mile of
short grass where they always raced, and when
Cuconnacht put up a pack of grouse, neither
noticed them nor echoed his frantic regret that
they had not thought of bringing the new peregrine
falcon.

.   .   .   .

Later that same forenoon Ethna took pen and
paper and wrote to her half-sister, Esmée de
Louysnes, imploring her to journey forthwith from
her French home to Lisronan.

It was a more entirely self-centred letter than
Ethna had hitherto composed, but she felt certain
of Esmée's sympathy. Madame de Louysnes,
from the seniority of her fifteen years, had never
failed to mother the only child of her own mother's
second marriage with the most attractive, happy-
go-lucky, and impecunious gentleman who ever
sailed out of Galway port.

The voyage would not deter her. She would
forget its hardships when she learnt Ethna's
soul-chilling, intangible fears.

Lady Lisronan made haste to seal her letter and
despatch it by a trusted messenger. She even
watched the man out of sight, shivering at thought
of the fortnight which must elapse before he
could reach Paris.

4

Owen had come to warn her—but of what?

She whispered the question to herself, as she turned to go indoors again—but found no answer save the heavy premonitions of her own heart.

CHAPTER V

BY RIGHT OF MIGHT

LADY LISRONAN sat over a dying wood-fire, holding out her hands to the faint warmth. Opposite her, on the other side of the hearth, Dermot lay in the depths of a high-backed chair, asleep.

It was long past his bed-time, but Ethna lacked courage to sit alone. Everything frightened her to-night—even the sizzling of the languid, rainbow-hued flames. Outside, a low sad wind made moan now and again round the silent house, and then departed with a sigh.

Each time the long sough drew near she found herself waiting almost involuntarily for some other sound, though what that sound was she could not have told. Owen D'Arcy's continued silence terrified her. It was a fortnight since the night of her vision, and still no letter came, no hint of how he fared in London. Presentiment had her soul in its cold grasp this evening. If Owen had walked in at the door, she would from sheer relief have promised to marry him.

51

More than once her fingers crept towards the silver bell which would summon a servant, but shame always stayed them at the last moment. Yet she shivered quite visibly as she sat, one hand still on her idle spinning-wheel, the other held out to the fire. Its light gleamed in the white curves of her neck, in silver threads woven through the green and white stripes of her brocade gown, in the rings she wore.

After a time she forced herself to glance round the long narrow room. There were reflections of candles in the polished floor, and gleams of golden light on the low beamed ceiling and in the furniture, but shadows lay everywhere. And Ethna had so great a horror of shadows to-night that the prettiness of the mellow half-light made for once no appeal to her. A high screen of painted leather near the door became a menace. Even the vase of white roses which she had herself set on top of an *armoire* frightened her, when it caught her eye, by its likeness to a human face.

She was turning back to her wheel again, angry with herself for this last folly, when a sound drifted in to her from the night—a laugh.

"Dermot!" she cried sharply, and then again: "Wake up, Dermot!"

Dermot sat upright with a start, blinking like an owl.

"Your pardon, Madame," he said gravely. To fall asleep in his mother's withdrawing room was, he felt, a grave misdemeanour.

Ethna held up her hand. "Listen!" she whispered.

Dermot listened. "Horses outside—a whole lot of horses," he said. "Who can it be, Madame? May I look through the casement?"

Before Ethna could answer, there came a thump of waddling feet from the gallery and Anne Regan, the tire-woman who had been Lady Lisronan's nurse, burst ponderously into the room.

"Oh, my lady!" she panted, clasping herself about the middle. "Oh, my lady—that gentleman —that Dutch Meinherr! He has come back. He is downstairs—and a hundred ruffians with him!"

For a second the room seemed to sway round Ethna like a ship at sea.

"Meinherr Van der Wynykt!" she said in a frozen whisper.

Dermot, who had slipped to his feet, came across the hearth and stood beside her.

"Tell him he cannot come in, Anne," he said. "Nay, I 'll tell him myself."

He would have dashed off, but Ethna caught his arm.

"No, Dermot, no!" she cried vehemently, "*I* will see Meinherr Van der Wynykt. Mayhap he only wants a night's lodging."

Anne began to sniffle.

"The dear knows what the like of him would want," she said. "Let yez not go near him, my lady. Sure Antony and meself have him told you 're away to Dublin—an' it 's best so."

Ethna stood a moment looking helplessly round the room. Danger had brought back her courage —such as it was—and her one thought was for Dermot.

"Take him out to the stable the back way, Anne," she said, giving the boy a little push towards the old woman. "Dermot, you're to saddle Toby—saddle him yourself—and ride out through the shrubbery to Bally Ulick. Be speedy, child!"

Dermot grew crimson. "And leave you, Madame?" he cried. "Not I! Let me go—I'll tell the Meinherr we have no room for him."

He twitched his sleeve out of his mother's grasp as he spoke and made straight for the door. Ethna ran after him.

"Dermot, I forbid you!" she called. "Oh, Anne, catch him—catch him!"

It was her mistress whom Anne caught.

"They'll not hurt the child, my lady," she answered. "'T is yourself should get away. Come now, my lady—come till we get to come at the stable. Oh, God save us, I hear them in the hall! Oh, we're distrhoyed—we're distrhoyed! Maybe I could hide you in the linen cupboard, my lady, or——"

Ethna did not wait for the end of the sentence. She had freed herself from the old woman's fingers and was already out of the room and at the head of the stairs that ran down from gallery to hall.

The big door stood open, framing a chevron of darkness in which the curve of a horse's neck and the glitter of a stirrup showed dully. Inside, at the foot of the stone steps, stood Albrecht Van der Wynykt with two heavy looking men at his elbow —one of whom held the Lisronan steward, Antony Gilpatrick, by the collar of his coat.

Ethna paused on the top step of the flight. Dermot, half way down, was explaining politely enough, but with a note of defiance in his voice, that his mother could not this time offer Meinherr Van der Wynykt the shelter of her roof.

Van der Wynykt laughed.

"*Her* roof!" he said, with an accent on the pronoun, and an upward glance at the slim brocade-clad figure above him. "Her roof—and vy not, my lord?"

Lady Lisronan, meeting his eyes, shivered. She put out a hand as though to support herself against the wall, and slipped her fingers along the stonework until they met one of the suits of armour which hung there. There was a skene dangling in the shadow of the breastplate. It seemed to her that the moment might be near when she would need that knife.

"Because we lack room for so great a company," said Dermot stoutly, eyeing the huge figure before him with ill-concealed disgust.

Again Albrecht Van der Wynykt laughed.

"Lack room, do you?" he returned. "Well, 't is easily made. Throw that fellow out of doors,

you two," he added, in Dutch, to the pair who
held Antony Gilpatrick.

Antony, guessing the order, began at once to
struggle and protest, but there were half a dozen
dismounted men outside the door who swarmed
in at his first movement.

"Sir, I must really beg an explanation!" cried
Ethna, angrily, as the man, still writhing, was
dragged over the threshold. "If you seek lodging
for the night, we will do our best without this
violence. My son was over hasty in what he said."

Again Van der Wynykt grinned.

"The river will cure him o' that," he said.
"Explanation, my lady—vy certainly. This
house—it is mine now——"

He moved forward as he spoke, and Dermot
twisted round and sprang up three steps—keeping himself between the Dutchman and his
mother.

"Your house," said Ethna slowly. "Your
house!"

"My house. By favour of his Majesty."

Lady Lisronan put a hand against the wall
again—this time to support herself in good earnest.

"But I—I have taken the oath!" she cried
piteously. "I have done nothing to incur his
Majesty's displeasure—I—I cannot understand it."

"I care not a d— whether you understand or
not! The house is mine now, and your Papist
crew may run or burn—as they please! You hear
that?"

A sudden dull clamour of screams and shrieks rose from the kitchen regions, and then, loud above it, the bay of angry hound voices and the thud of blows.

Albrecht Van der Wynykt listened a second, grinning.

"Now, mayhap, you understand," he said. "Meinherr D'Arcy is not here to interfere this time, my lady. You'll have to shriek mighty loud before he hears you."

"Is he dead?" It was Dermot who asked the question—Dermot, still watching the Dutchman as a trapped rat might watch a terrier.

"Aye—dead and rotting. Come in, you d—d fools and shut that door! There's a wind would flay an eel."

Three of the six men who had dragged away Antony Gilpatrick made haste to obey. They flung the big door to with a clash and stood against it, their swords and breastplates gleaming dully in the half-light.

Ethna came down a step. "We can only go," she said dully, laying a hand on Dermot's shoulder.

"I'm not asking *you* to go, my lady," put in Van der Wynykt. "Not at all. You shall stay. This young cub can join the others."

He put out a hand as he spoke, caught the boy by his neck, as a man catches a kitten, and without an effort flung him down the stairs to the men below.

"Truss him up—we 'll drop him in the river as soon as 't is light," he called; adding, "No, no, my lady—you vill stay with me! There's no d—d Irishman to interfere this time."

He flung his arm round Ethna as he spoke, and lifted her off her feet.

"You shall show me the house, my lady," he said with a loud laugh. "Afterwards——"

Ethna's self-control snapped like a string. She could see over Van der Wynykt's shoulder a glimpse of Dermot being fastened with a belt to the bolt of the door, and the sight seemed to loose some devil of fury in her brain.

She wrenched her left hand, which still held the dagger, free and stabbed fiercely, blindly, at this red leering face above her.

Van der Wynykt, his foot on the top step, staggered.

"You devil!" he roared. "You Irish devil!"

He twisted round at the last word, swung her up above his head, and then hurled her—with all the tremendous strength that was his—down to the bottom step of the flight.

Ethna, as she shot through the air, was conscious of a sound of thudding paws flying over polished wood, and realised in a lightning flash of thought that Anne had fetched the three deerhounds. And then there came a crash, as though the whole world had fallen to pieces round her—and after it oblivion.

CHAPTER VI

BEYOND THE LAW

DERMOT LISRONAN could never in subsequent years recollect clearly what happened after the moment when his mother's body struck the bottom step of the flight. Fury so passionate that it blinded and deafened him to all else had taken possession of every fibre of his being. He saw only vaguely the huddled heap of striped brocade that shot across the flagged space between the last step and the wall and then collapsed in a dreadful limp heap.

He was only conscious of crying wildly to the hounds as they rushed through the open door of the gallery, and yet more wildly when that monstrous figure on the top step went down before their onslaught.

From that moment to the one, many seconds later, when the monstrous figure was carried away into the gallery by his three men, and Anne, weeping and signing herself, came creeping down to unstrap him, seemed a long delirious nightmare.

He would have picked up the skene and tried

to finish the work which the hounds had begun—
had indeed nearly completed—but for Anne.

"We must get her ladyship away, Master
Dermot," she whispered, while she wrestled with
the strap. "We must get her out into the darkness before they come back."

And then the strap gave and she at once turned
away to that crumpled heap of brocade under the
wall.

Dermot stood for a second by the bolt to which
he had been strapped, feeling all at once dazed and
sick and miserable. The frenzy of a moment
earlier was ebbing fast, leaving in its wake a
horrible consciousness of what had happened,
made poignant by all the ghastly details of the
scene before him—by the blood which dripped in
sluggish streams from step to step, staining all the
staircase; by the two dead hounds, and Cuconnacht, the third, whining in a corner; most of all
by that limp bundle of brocade at which he was
afraid to look.

"Oh, vo, vo!" wailed Anne under her breath,
as she knelt by it. "May their bodies have no
grave and their souls no rest that did it. They
have her destroyed. Murdered she is!"

She turned Lady Lisronan over very carefully
as she spoke, straightening out her limbs and peering at her face, which was caked with blood.

"Is she—dead?" whispered Dermot, in a terrible
and unchildlike voice.

Anne shook her head.

"Unbolt the door—an' be quick," she whispered
back.   "The rest of them's gone to the stables,
so we have the chance to slip out.   Quick now!"

"Can you lift her alone?"

The old woman nodded.   She was large and
strongly built, in spite of her stoutness, and
desperation gives strength.

By the time Dermot had got the bolt undone
she was on her feet, with the bundle clasped
grotesquely against her bosom.

"Draw the door to after ye—and call the dog.
He'd maybe track us," she whispered as she
staggered past Dermot.

The boy obeyed mechanically.   He was beginning to feel as if the whole thing was a terrible
evil dream—one so bad that it could not be true.
This sudden transition out of the blood-stained
hall into the black September night lent so much
colour to the idea that he began to try and wake
himself.

Anne stumbled a yard or two from the door and
then collapsed.

"Bet up I am, God help me!" she moaned.
"Oh, what'll I do—what'll I do at all?"

She began to cry quietly with the complete
abandon of the peasant.

"Where's Antony—or some of the others?"
asked Dermot, feeling as though the hell he had
been told of as the natural portion of bad little
boys had suddenly and causelessly become his.

"Heth, where would they be only dead?   Did n't

I run to the head of the kitchen stairs before
ever I loosed the dogs—and what did I see in it?
Hugh an' Martin an' old Michael—an' the three
of them stretched below me on the floor. Aye,
an' more than that, that I'd not be telling the
likes of ye!"

Dermot turned round and round, like a fly in a
spider's web. All he knew was that these brutes
must not come near his mother again.

"The boat, Anne—we must make shift to carry
her to the river," he said, struck by a sudden
inspiration.

Anne grunted. The river was nearly half a mile
away, down a steep hill.

"'T is hardly I'll battle it out," she muttered,
getting up. "Take the feet of her, Master Dermot," she added, "I'll lift her head. We can but
thry."

And try they did, with the pertinacity of utter
desperation—but it was a terrible progress, if
progress it could be called. A yard or two of
feeble staggering, a minute during which Ethna
lay on the ground between the panting old woman
and the exhausted child, and then another yard
of the vain heart-breaking struggle.

It was a black dark night, with a drizzle of fine
rain, and neither could judge of their direction
save by that instinctive knowledge which people
have for a familiar place.

At last, after an hour, Anne collapsed. "'T is
bet up I am," she said in a hoarse whistling voice,

and a second later Dermot heard a heavy thud on the ground.

He left his position at his mother's feet and felt along the ridge of damp brocade until he came to the head. Beyond it there was a space of wet rank grass, and a little farther on a heap of stuff.

He found Anne's face presently, and held his hand in front of her lips, where there seemed to be no breath.

"Anne! Anne!" he whispered frantically, his mouth close to her ear.

Then, as she still lay silent and inert, the boy, himself very near the limit of his endurance, dropped forward on the turf and burst into tears. The paroxysm did not last long, for he knew that they must be close to the house still, and fear of seeing his mother once more in the Dutchman's arms drove him like a goad.

He got up, with a glance back to where the building lay. Now and again a window would flash into being, a golden square against the darkness, as some one moved past it candle in hand. A glow hung in the air above the stable yard, bespeaking lanterns. Plainly their enemies had not yet settled down for the night, and until they did it would be useless to creep round to the kitchen regions in search of help. His child mind could not take in the fact that those of their men who had resisted were dead. It seemed to him that if he could only find Antony or Martin or

Hugh—or even old Michael—things might be righted.

After a moment's thought he slipped out of his coat and spread it over his mother, though the amount of her it covered felt distressingly small. Then furtively, like some little animal, he crept away into the night. His idea was to cut across the shrubbery—a dense mass of age-old holly and laurel—to the outhouse beyond the stable, where the grooms slept. It could not be that none of them were left.

As he ran stumbling over the tussocks, his mother's words in the withdrawing room flashed suddenly into his mind. "Take Toby and ride to Bally Ulick," she had said. Fool that he was, not to have remembered it before! Well, it was not too late yet, if he could find any one to go.

Sir Martin FitzUlick would help them. He might even, being a Justice of the Peace, put the Dutchman in prison—a thought as warming as a fire.

To reach the shrubbery was simple enough, but a short cut through a place so dense with undergrowth proved in the dark no easy matter. It seemed to the distracted boy that every bramble, every bush, even every tree, had a hundred hands. He was trying to kick himself clear of a mass of briars when the sound of muffled sobs caught his ear.

He stopped a minute to listen. Some one was crying very near him—crying hysterically, apparently under a cloth.   He heard, too, an agonised whisper:

"Whisht, Brigie—whisht, child! Whisht, for God's sake!"

Dermot's heart leapt so violently that for a second he could not speak.   He had recognised the voice.   Then: "Mary—Mary Gilpatrick!" he murmured, turning to where the sobs had come from.   "Mary—answer me!"

There was a second of petrified silence, and then a movement among the ferns almost at his feet.

"Master Dermot?" whispered Mary Gilpatrick, the steward's wife, fearfully.

A second later Dermot was crouching beside her, pouring out his tale in quick, low-toned incoherent gasps.   He could see nothing, for the place was dark as a mine, but a smell of wet frieze and a sound of sniffling told of the presence of another child beside the terrified Brigie, whose head was buried in her mother's blue cloak.

"Antony, is it?" said Antony's wife, with the curious fatalism of her race.   "Sure they 're after hanging him, the very way Cromwell's men hanged me poor father.   Whisht now, Brigie, astore! She 's after seeing it, and it has the life scared out of her.   God knows, we got terrible trouble this night!"   She paused a minute to sign herself, and then went on.   "There 's no one in it, only them that 's dead--unless it 'ud be Tim, the omadhaun. That one 'ud go hide in the hay whiniver he 'd

5

be scared, an' mayhap he 's in it yet. If we had him here now."   •

"Yes — he 'd carry her to the boat — he 's strong," agreed Dermot eagerly, and got to his feet again. The haystack was just outside the shrubbery. It seemed worth trying for Tim. "But please wait here, Mary," he whispered.

To go at all tested his courage to its utmost. The proximity of other human beings, however helpless and terror-stricken, was such a solace that nothing but the thought of that motionless figure lying in the long grass would have induced him to leave them.

A lucky flounder having landed him at last on the shrubbery path, he crept along it stealthily, as he had done many times before in play; crept along until a golden glow ahead made him pause. It came, he knew, through the gate of the outer yard where the haystack was—a steady dim fan of yellow light that illuminated one laurel bush, making the flat leaves glisten against the darkness like emeralds.

Dermot stood and peered through the branches. He could see the arched gateway, high and black, framing a slice of wet pavement aglimmer with broken golden reflections cast by a hooped lantern which stood in the middle of the yard. He could also see one of the stone legs that supported the haystack, and something dark lying near it—and his heart leaped.

Tim, the omadhaun, slept in most unlikely

places—slept moreover so soundly that no noise
ever woke him. Perhaps he had set the lantern
there; perhaps, since all was utterly still, it would
be safe to venture in and look. He dived out
under the laurel bush, a slim little shadow with
ghostly shirt sleeves, and stole, velvet-footed, to
the gate.

The yard, a small one fenced by high walls
and kept exclusively for the hay and straw stacks,
appeared quite empty—except, of course, for
Tim lying in the shadow of the rick.

Dermot, mindful of other futile efforts to wake
the omadhaun, made straight for the lantern, with
a heart thumping so loudly that it deafened him
to all else. There was no sound, no hint of the
enemy's presence, but one could not tell. Every
shadow seemed full of eyes, every dark corner a
menace.

He caught up the lantern and scuttled like a
frightened rabbit to the rick, in momentary expectation of being clutched by unseen hands. Tim's
clothes, he noticed, had spread out very widely
round him—widely and blackly—almost like a
pool of dark glittering water; or was it a pool, and
not clothes at all?

Dermot hesitated, wondering why even Tim the
omadhaun was silly enough to sleep in a pool of
water, and holding the lantern out before him to
make the more sure that it *was* Tim.

And then, quite suddenly, the light fell full on
the pool, and on the bundle, making clear all its

details—and the child's heart seemed to stop. For a breathing space he stood staring wide-eyed at the hideous mangled travesty of what an hour before had been a man, and then with a shrill agonised scream dashed down the lantern and fled.

He rushed blindly through the gate, blindly through the laurel bush beyond. Chance more than any thought brought him back to where Mary Gilpatrick crouched in the ferns. She heard his running feet and his sobs of horror, and sprang up to intercept him.

Dermot, conscious only of that ghastly sight— the culmination of all the terrors of that terrible night—clung desperately to her, burying his face in her breast as Brigie had done. But, unlike Brigie, he was silent. Spasms of horror shook him from head to foot like an ague. Mary could feel the clutch of his ice-cold trembling hands, could hear the frantic hammering of his heart as he pressed against her, but her whispered agonised questions elicited no answer. It was a long minute before he found power to speak.

"Tim!" he sobbed, "Tim!" and gasped convulsively.

Mary Gilpatrick guessed the rest.

"Sure I had no call to let ye go," she muttered, thinking dully of how Cromwell's men had served her father, and Mountjoy's her grandfather, and of a sight that she herself had seen when she was Dermot's age.

Her fortitude gave way at the thought; she

melted into sudden tears—an example promptly
followed by Brigie, and then by the ten-year-old
Dan. The sound of their distress roused Dermot
to a recollection of his mother's plight.

"Come, Mary," he whispered, and took her by
the cloak. Mary followed blindly, making no
effort now to check her own woe or suppress
Brigie's. But before they reached the place where
Ethna lay she spoke.

"'T will be making day in an hour, Master Dermot," she said between two sniffs, "an' then wid
the blessing of God we might get help."

A moment later Anne's voice came hoarsely to
them through the darkness.

"Mary Gilpatrick, is that yerself—and have ye
the young gentleman? Ye have. Oh, glory be
to God, and me thinkin' them that destroyed
us had him cot!"

Dermot began to feel about his mother's body.
"Oh, Anne! She has n't moved, Anne!" he cried
with a little wail of despair that threw the small
Gilpatricks into fresh paroxysms of woe. "She
has not moved since I went!"

Anne, who knew and shared the desolating fear
that filled his small mind, caught at him as he
bent over Lady Lisronan and drew him into her
lap.

"'T is better she should n't, avick," she whispered. "Maybe they 'd hear us so. Be aisy
yourself now till we 'd get light, an' then Dan can
be running down to the Black-Farm, to me brother

Shaun.   He 'll be up here mighty quick onct he
have the word.   Whisht now, Master Dermot, be
aisy!''

She clasped the boy to her as she had done when
he was a baby, adding, "I 'd be away to Shaun's
myself this minute, only I 'd think bad to leave
her ladyship—let alone that twenty men 'ud not
find yez all again in the dark, and yez in dread to
call out.   We can do nothing—nothing at all—
until we 'd get to see!''

.   .   .   .

Two hours later the first glimmer of dawn crept
greyly into the heavy east.   Dermot, sitting on
the grass by his mother's side, watched it
apathetically.   He had reached a stage of things
when nothing seemed to matter.   Mary Gilpatrick's
sniffs, the sobs of Brigie, the mutterings of Anne,
even the absence of movement in the figure under
his hand, appeared a matter of indifference to him.
He stared at the lightening line where earth and
sky met with eyes that hardly saw.   Somewhere
at the back of his mind there lurked a vague desire
to tell Father Moran that he had made a mistake in his conception of hell—but nothing more
personal.

The cold light as it strengthened brought out
details of a scene that he could never afterwards
forget, though at the time he hardly noticed them.
Mary Gilpatrick turned from a black shapeless
blur to a shivering figure wrapped in a blue cloak;

Ethna's brocade gown, soaked and stained out of recognition, detached itself from the green of the grass and became a separate thing; Anne appeared, rocking herself to and fro, haggard and grey with beading mist. Her stiff uprising, with many groans and calls on her God, was the last item of that ghastly night that he remembered clearly.

The departure of Dan Gilpatrick in the grey dawn on one furtive errand and his mother on another; the arrival of Anne's two brothers from their respective farms, solemn of face and intensely agitated; the carrying away of Ethna, and the subsequent appearance at Shaun Ronan's white-washed house, where she lay, first of Father Moran, and later of Sir Martin FitzUlick, with his peruke crooked, his cravat untied, and a countenance crimson from fury and knowledge of his own importance; these things passed him by. Child though he was, he had reached the edge of the world and looked over, and those who do that lose for a little space all hold on the things of life.

CHAPTER VII

THE SONG OF MAELDUNE

THE days that followed that night of terror made an indelible impression on Dermot's mind. There was much that he could in no wise understand; the curious resignation of the peasants, the helplessness of Sir Martin FitzUlick, the mystery and sense of stress about Father Moran's hurried visits—Father Moran, whose comings and goings had hitherto been as open as the birds'.

He was pondering on them this afternoon, as he knelt beside Sir Martin's eight-year-old daughter, Aideen, in the octagon "library" of Bally Ulick, whither Ethna had been moved from Shaun Ronan's farm. The problem weighed more on him than his elders imagined. He thought of little else.

"His honour, my father, does not allow us to play with these chessmen," said Aideen complacently, turning the white queen round and round in her fat paw. "Also we are forbade this room—Barry and me—but we come here often."

She glanced sideways at Dermot, anxious to impress this absent-minded guest, who had taken the prohibited chessmen too much as a matter of course.

"Happen we 'll be beaten and put in the dungeon an' we 're caught," she added.

"Your father cannot throw people into dungeons," returned Dermot. "I asked him—and he told me 'no.' What is it, Aideen?"

"I hear people on the stairs!" gasped Aideen. "His honour and others. Oh, wirra, wirra! Run and peep, Dermot!"

Dermot, alarmed, made haste to obey. There indeed was Sir Martin coming up the narrow ill-lit staircase, and behind him two brother Justices of the Peace, Major Sugrue and Colonel Conway.

Dermot looked back at Aideen, who stood by the window seat, a square quaint little figure with her curly yellow head and her stiff long-waisted pink frock, into the bodice of which she was stuffing the chessmen pell-mell.

"Hide!" she whispered, pointing to a piece of tapestry that hung loosely from ceiling to floor and was kept taut by the legs of a chair.

Dermot, his courage somewhat shaken by the sour looks of Sir Martin's two guests, was full ready to accept this suggestion, and a moment later he and Aideen were standing very close together and very flat against the wall, both hoping devoutly that the musty folds which dangled a bare half-inch from their noses would not make them sneeze.

Major Sugrue's was the first voice they heard.

"You brought Lady Lisronan here—and her son? You voluntarily thrust yourself into the matter!" it said lugubriously.

"Good God, Sugrue! would you have had me leave a lady and a child—any lady and any child— at that scoundrel's mercy?" demanded Sir Martin hotly.

"You have set yourself within reach of the new law. The penalty is a ruinous fine—ruinous— and mayhap a year in the Tholsel of Dublin. Have you thought of that?"

"Yes."

Through a small flaw in the tapestry Dermot saw Major Sugrue shrug his shoulders.

"I was credibly informed that you have called the Dutchman out?" he said.

"I did. But the fellow won't fight, d— him! I shall proclaim him as a coward—a thieving, white-livered coward—at the races next week!"

Colonel Conway raised his eyebrows. He had long before labelled FitzUlick weak and a fool, adducing in evidence thereof that he had allowed his Catholic wife to bring up both children in her own faith.

"Why, man, Wynykt is the King's favourite. You 'll ruin yourself!" he protested.

Sir Martin laughed bitterly.

"The King!" he said, "the King! The King

who won our swords to his side by the promise of religious toleration!" He paused a minute, and then added: "The English of all this is that you will not help—you two?"

"I help no Papist," said Sugrue sourly.

FitzUlick glanced at Conway. "Well, Dick?" he asked.

"What do you propose?" said the Colonel, with ill-concealed irritation. "An appeal to the law, forsooth?"

"Yes, that is what I had thought of. There must be some justice in the land."

Conway rubbed his peruke over his head.

"The law!" he said in a tone of derision. "The law invoked against a king's favourite! Faith, you 're a simple man, Fitz! This fellow Wynykt holds the Lisronan property by direct favour of his Majesty, I 'm told. There 's but one thing to be done. Let my lady betake herself speedily to France. I will do my best to aid you, Martin, out of the trouble you 've brewed for yourself; but I cannot help her ladyship—nor will I try. That is my last word on the matter. We 're of one mind, Sugrue and myself."

"Madame de Louysnes, her sister, is travelling into Ireland at this moment," said Sir Martin shortly. "I 'll waste no more breath on you two. To my thinking, there 's no choice for any man . calling himself a friend of my Lady Lisronan— and I 'll wager a hundred guineas Owen D'Arcy will say the same when he returns."

"*If* he returns," put in Major Sugrue gloomily. "His silence is suspicious. I will wish you good day, FitzUlick."

He moved towards the door. Sir Martin and Colonel Conway followed him.

"Queer talk they had!" commented Aideen after a long five minutes of silence. "We were better away, Dermot."

She whisked out from behind the tapestry, blinking and pulling at her bosom, which, like Eugene Aram's, was ill at ease, owing to the number and hardness of the chessmen.

Dermot came out more slowly. What he had overheard had added a tithe to the sudden burden of unhappiness and disillusionment thrown on him in the past week.

While he was standing thinking about it, and paying no attention to Aideen's chatter, her brother Barry burst headlong into the room.

"Morgan and Owen D'Arcy have been cast into prison, and Owen D'Arcy hath died there of gaol-fever!" he announced breathlessly. "Simon Farrelly, who was Owen's body-servant, is but just come from England with the news. Owen was imprisoned, an' it like you! for calling out some Dutch bodagh—so saith Simon—and Morgan as having aided him. A pretty country that, where a gentleman may not fight whom he pleases! Oh, and that reminds me, I've this very minute seen old Blind Tadgh, the minstrel, coming hither across the bog—so we'll e'en go down and catch him before he has eaten and drunk, and make him sing."

Barry advanced upon his sister as he spoke, seized her by the gathers of her gown, and took from her the chessmen which she was replacing in their box.

"Come on, Dermot," he said. "You told me yesterday you 'd not heard Tadgh sing."

Dermot obeyed mechanically. Horror succeeding horror had so dazed him that this latest catastrophe hardly counted.

"Tadgh will come to the guard-room," said Barry, commencing to bump down the steep worn staircase in a sitting position. "When he has sung we 'll make him tell us the tale of how Broghill's men put out his eyes with a hot knife and drove him over a cliff."

"They slew his father and mother and all his kinsfolk first," put in Aideen hastily, lest the tale should lose some of its lustre.

"They laid wagers on whether the fall would kill him or no. 'T was a mighty high cliff in the Galtee mountains," went on her brother in staccato jerks. "He was all broke up—you can see the twists of him under his coat. Aideen cried last time he was telling us."

"You lie!" retorted Miss FitzUlick, becoming a lively scarlet. "An' any one would cry—Brigie did. See, Dermot—there 's Tadgh—there, below us."

Dermot looked down the stairs in the direction

of her pointing finger, and saw a gaunt, bare-headed, bare-legged old man, whose body was so twisted and distorted that one hip stuck far out from under his tattered tail-coat. Silvery white hair straggled over his bowed shoulders, a patri-archal beard fell nearly to his hands, which were crossed on a stick. Slung about him like a plaid he carried a huge cow-hide cloak of incredible antiquity. His closed eyelids gave him a curiously aloof expression.

"God save you kindly, my little noble gentle-man," he said in sing-song Erse to Barry, "and the little lady—and the young strange chief that does be with you. Will I be making music for your honours the day?"

Without waiting for an answer he turned about and faced the open hall through which he had entered.

"They have the harp away," he said, pointing to the place where, in accordance with the medieval custom that prevailed still in all things at Bally Ulick, the harp should have hung ready for passing minstrels.

"'T is in the guard-room," answered Barry.

He put his hand in the old man's arm and impelled him gently across the dingy vaulted hall.

Lady Lisronan, anxious that her child's youth should not be tainted by premature knowledge of man's inhumanity to man, and that he should as much as possible escape that lust of hate which

even now defiles too many Irishmen, had forbidden
Tadgh to come to her house.   It was Dermot's
first near view of the old minstrel, his first chance
of hearing him.   He followed eagerly across the
threshold of the guard-room and stood watching
Tadgh with rapt attention while he tuned up the
battered ancient five-stringed harp.

A heavy gloom pervaded the guard-room of
Bally Ulick, even on a midsummer morning.   The
sunlight that did succeed in filtering through those
deep-set arrow-slit windows and lying in bars of
gold on those lead-grey walls, those dark flagstones worn by four centuries of soldiers' feet,
seemed an alien thing.   There were patches of it
to-day, yellow as fire, in the vault-like dimness,
and Tadgh, with that curious instinctive knowledge common to the blind, had stopped just where
a ray fell fullest.

His silvery old head was bent over the harp, his
long white beard swept the strings as he worked.
Dermot, horribly fascinated, could see an old scar
running from knee to ankle down one bare leg,
and the fantastic twist of the distorted hip.
Tadgh's injuries had a personal application now.
He wondered piteously if his mother would walk
like him when she was able to walk.   That Ethna
would never again set foot on the ground was a
fact he had not as yet realised.

"What shall I sing, my little noble gentleman?" asked Tadgh presently, in Erse, turning
to Barry.   He always seemed to know by some

sixth sense exactly where each member of his
audience was, and always looked in his or her
direction.

"The story of Maeldune first," said Barry.

The old man struck a chord on the harp. His
voice had a lingering remnant of sweetness, and
he chanted with a peculiar significance that suited
well the sixth-century tale of *Maeldune's Voyage
of Vengeance*. The saga drew word-pictures,
clearer to the children's eyes than any work of
brush or pencil, of each island visited in that
strange journey. The Island of Shouting; the
Island of Silence; the Isles of the Fruits, of the
Flowers, of the Sirens; the Flaming Island with its
peak of fire; the Bounteous Isle with its sun-bright
hand; the Misty Under-sea Isle, vague as a mirage;
the Island of the Two Combatant Towers, one
"of smooth-cut stone, one carved all over with
flowers"—which for ever "shock'd on each
other, and butted each other with clashing of
bells."

The allegory in it escaped them, but the primi-
tive human passion gripped all three. Dermot, to
whom the tale was new, waited with almost savage
impatience for the moment when Maeldune should
slay the slayer of his father.

"Oh, no—no!" he cried fiercely, when Tadgh
reached the verse which told how Maeldune
and his men came to the last isle, where
dwelt the holy man, "who had sailed with
Saint Brendan of yore," and how the holy

man taught the chief of a thing higher than any vengeance.

Tadgh took up the cry. "Deed aye! He had no call to be putting hindrance on Maeldune that way, for as holy as he was!" he exclaimed, smiting his hand across the harp-strings with a passion which matched the child's, "Maeldune had a right to kill the one that wronged him—so he had! Aye! Who but he?"

The words were, to Dermot, like a light flashed through the dark places of his mind. With a child's intense self-consciousness, he saw Maeldune as himself; the man who had slain Maeldune's father as Wynykt; the sainted hermit as Father Moran. A feeling which had been lying inchoate in him—the feeling which lies inchoate in every Celt—was stirred to life.

Standing there in the shadows of the guard-room, a little brown-faced figure, with sombre unchildlike eyes fixed on the blind minstrel, he vowed Maeldune's vow. He told himself that never should man turn him from his vengeance until Albrecht Van der Wynykt lay dead at his feet.

Aideen began to clamour for the *Lament of Fearflatha O'Gnive*, and Tadgh to pluck again at the chords. But Dermot turned. It seemed to him suddenly that he need not wait. Sir Martin had pistols. There was a pony in the stables. He would ride to Lisronan that very day and shoot the usurper dead in the house which he had desecrated.

6

He ran upstairs to his host's room where the pistol-case stood. Barry, who on principle meddled with everything prohibited, had shown him how it opened and where powder and ball were kept.

The door of the room in which Ethna lay was ajar, and she heard his footsteps and called to him as he clattered down the staircase. Dermot went in unwillingly, the pistol held tight against his right thigh.

Ethna from her day-bed near the window signed to him to come close.

A bandage across her head was the solitary sign now of Wynykt's brutality; but she herself knew very well that the numb paralysis which held all her body from the waist downwards would last as long as life lasted, and that for her there remained only a living death.

Simon Farrelly's letter had not yet been delivered to her—Simon's news having induced "a wakeness" in the serving-wench who should have borne it up the kitchen stairs—and she was still ignorant of its ill news.

"Well, avick! What have you been doing with yourself?" she asked, looking sharply at Dermot.

The boy fidgeted.

"Nought, Madame," he muttered. "Tadgh the minstrel is below. He sang to us."

Ethna frowned. She understood the shadow on her son's face.

"Poor man—he is somewhat crazed," she said

lightly. "One must not heed his words over-much. What is that in your hand, Dermot?"

"A—a pistol."

"Mercy, child! Not loaded, I hope? What do you with a pistol, my son?"

Dermot shifted from foot to foot. He would have moved away a pace from the day-bed but that his mother caught at his left hand.

"Dermot, I know what use you would make of that pistol," she said gravely. "Very well I know. You would go to Lisronan and—and shoot that terrible man. Tell me the truth."

Dermot lifted his eyes to hers sullenly.

"Yes—and I will yet, Madame, for all you may say," he cried with fierce defiant haste.

"You will break my heart if you do!" exclaimed Lady Lisronan. "Dermot, listen—no, don't turn away. Promise me you will not do this;—promise."

He shook his head.

"Oh, but you must—you must, Dermot!" Ethna cried frantically, gripped by a horrible fear. "I—I—forbid it—I am your mother!"

The boy's face hardened into a look of savage resolution. He made no response, but stood with one shoulder turned to her and his fingers tightening on the pistol-butt.

Ethna, clutching his left wrist in cold, tremulous fingers, poured out a torrent of incoherent, panic-stricken protestations.

"Promise! Promise!" she begged wildly—and

then, as Dermot still stood silent, burst into tears.

The sound of her sobs brought old Anne in from the passage.

"Whisht now, my lady—whisht now!" she said at intervals, while Ethna poured out her tale.

"Sure it's a wonder ye wouldn't know better than to be fretting her ladyship and she so sick!" she put in, in a furious aside to the boy, and then, having seized his hand and wrested the pistol from it, added, "Is it shoot that one, heth? Cromwell's curse on him! What would he be doing while yourself was shooting at him? Waiting for ye, I suppose? How simple ye are!"

Lady Lisronan, who had recovered herself a little, held out both hands to Dermot.

"Dear heart, promise," she whispered. "For while I live, at least."

"But, Madame——"

Anne's hand caught the boy's arm and pinched it viciously.

"Have done, Master Dermot," she muttered.

Ethna's words and Anne's action struck a new terror into Dermot's heart. "For while I live," his mother had said.

"I promise, Madame," he said hurriedly, looking down at the slight inert form with terror-stricken eyes. "At least until you give me permission—but it is not right this should go unavenged. It shames me."

Anne turned away. Ethna watched the door close behind her before she spoke.

Her words, when she did, were in substance the holy man's words to Maeldune, and Dermot listened to them as unwillingly as the sixth-century chief. He could see no reason in his mother's wish. He acquiesced only because of that desolating fear which she and Anne had conveyed to him.

"I will do nought, Madame, until you bid me," he said dully when Ethna had finished.

"But you understand, child—you take my meaning?"

Dermot shook his head.

"No—nor ever shall," he answered.

Ethna sighed.

"Go and put the pistol away," she said wearily.

The boy went—weighted by his new care. Anne, who was waiting for him on the staircase, sighed when she saw his face.

"Ye did right, alanna," she said in a low voice, "ye did right not to cross her ladyship. Sure she 'd lose her life fretting. She should n't get any trouble, so she should n't, no matter what contrariness it 'ud make for ourselves. Ye understand?" Anne paused for a second, and then added in a low and vehement undertone: "But your day will come, Master Dermot—your day will come an' when it does—heth! it 's not me will put hindrance on ye! Sorra night but I dream I have his black heart between me two hands—

sorra night but I dream I see his blood red on the
ground. Ten years is no long while, Master
Dermot. God knows there's many in Ireland
have waited three times ten years—aye an' six—
an' they wid a strong bitter hate scalding the
hearts of them every hour they'd live. Let you
be the same, your honour—not forgetting—but
able to wait."

The old woman's voice sank to a whisper.
"Aye—to wait," she repeated, and then walked
away.

The voices of the other children roused Dermot
from the reverie induced by Anne's words.

Tadgh, released at last, had gone to eat and
gossip in the kitchen.

"Come down to the bog gap, Dermot," called
Barry excitedly from the stair-foot, "Shevaun
hath brought word of travellers on the bog. 'T is
mayhap your aunt."

"Barry says she will have a black boy in her
train, and a gold coach, and an ape, and a green
bird with a red and blue tail!" screamed Aideen
as she scampered away after her brother, leaving
Dermot to replace Sir Martin's pistol and follow
as best he might.

There were indeed travellers on the bog; but not
a coach, not even a lady on horseback—merely an
overgrown boy riding a black pony a pace ahead
of two evil-faced well-mounted men.

"That's Toby! That's your garron, Dermot!"
cried Aideen shrilly, pointing at the pony. "Why

does that boy ride him? Order the creature to get down!"

"It's the son of that cut-throat Dutch thief," said Barry in a very loud voice. "Horse-stealing is his trade."

The rider of Toby grew crimson. He was about Dermot's age—a fair, fat child with a good-tempered face. He drew rein irresolutely, in evident desire to deny the accusation thus hurled at him.

"I—I—" he began.

"Ride on, Mynheer. No speak dese dam' Irische," commanded one of his attendants.

The other took a pistol from his holster. At sight of the weapon Aideen's courage gave way.

"Barry, oh, Barry! he's going to shoot us!" she screamed, clutching her brother.

The Dutchman, with a laugh, proceeded to prime and load, and take aim first at Dermot, and then at Barry, to whom Aideen was clinging.

"Hi, Jan, you fool, come away! Come away! Here is a large party almost upon us!" called his fellow-servant suddenly in Platt Dutch.

He jogged forward, caught Toby's rein and set off at a canter. Jan, after a single glance round, followed.

"This must be Madame de Louysnes," said Barry, eyeing an approaching body of horsemen which had appeared unexpectedly out of a hollow of the bog. "Hush, Aideen! Don't cry, you baby! He did n't shoot us, and if he had 't was

your part as an Irishwoman to laugh in his ugly
Dutch face.   Aye, and defy him, even though he
killed you!   The FitzUlicks are shamed through
you, you little coward."

The last words were spoken in a fierce undertone,
lest the newcomers, now very close, should hear.

They were a party of ten, headed by Ethna's
half-sister, Madame de Louysnes, and her husband.
There was no gold coach, no black page, nor ape,
nor bright-tailed parrot; but the six armed men
and the two grooms leading pack-horses, who
made up the retinue, wore an air of trim efficiency
almost equally imposing.   Their buff leather coats
were new, their weapons shone with a burnish
rare to Irish eyes.

At sight of the children Madame de Louysnes
drew rein and jumped lightly to the ground.

"Dermot, how fares your mother?" she asked
quickly, without any preliminary greeting, seizing
the boy by the shoulders.   "Make haste, child!"
she added, giving him a little shake.

Dermot saw the agony of suspense in her eyes,
and knew that some one had told her.

"No worse, Madame," he answered.

"No worse—well, that is something," said
Esmée de Louysnes, drawing a long breath.   She
glanced down at Dermot, and added: "How like
her you are!   'T is seven years since I saw you,
and the resemblance was not so noticeable then.
You see it, Raoul?"

Monsieur de Louysnes smiled.   He had dis-

mounted, and was standing between the two horses
desperately bored, but contriving nevertheless to
live up to his reputation of being at once the best-
tempered and the best-looking man in France.

"Celle-ci sera la petite demoiselle FitzUlick,
n'est ce pas?" he said, looking at Aideen.

His wife raised her eyes.

"But of course! And Barry—who does not
remember me!" she exclaimed. "I can think of
nothing but my poor Ethna. We chanced on your
good curé—Père—Père—ah yes, Moran, Père
Moran—and he told us. He shall hang—that
Dutchman!"

Raoul de Louysnes gave his shoulders the faintest shrug. He knew a little better than his wife
the difficulties of hanging a king's favourite.

Esmée turned again to her horse.

"I must e'en hurry on to Ethna—the poor
child," she said. "I shall see you later, Dermot."

Dermot moved forward a step. Esmée, settling
herself in the saddle, met his glance.

"Yes?" she said interrogatively.

The boy came to her stirrup.

"Madame, my mother will not let me have
vengeance on Wynykt," he said in a low voice as
she bent towards him. "Mayhap you could persuade her. She hath made me promise—but a
promise can be given back."

Their eyes met in a long look which laid the
foundation of a lifetime's friendship.

Raoul, courtier though he was, had some trouble

to suppress a smile, but his wife saw nothing but the tragedy of it.

"I will talk to your mother on the subject, Dermot," she said very gravely. "Now, do not keep me from her."

She nodded to him and rode on.

"No black boy—no ape!" murmured Aideen, who was secretly rather relieved by this omission.

"No one takes apes or black boys on a journey, you little omadhaun," said Barry very dictatorially, to prevent reference to his previous pronouncements on the subject. "Dermot will see those when he goes to live with Madame de Louysnes in France. I shall visit you there, Dermot. Doubtless there 'll be many horses to ride and much hawking. Eh?"

Dermot, staring after his aunt's *cortège*, made no reply.

CHAPTER VIII

"THE WILD WOLF—HATE"

TWELVE years later; a bitter, windless February night with frost in the air and a sprinkle of snow crisping under foot and lying white on the roofs of Paris.

Esmée de Louysnes, seated by the fire in her little upstairs boudoir, stared out gravely at those same whitened roofs and the crimson sunset sky behind them. Years had only served to deepen that love of beauty which she and her sister Ethna had had in common, and she thought of her now as she looked at the icicles fringing every eave and at the glory of rose colour above. Ethna would have appreciated the beauty of it—Ethna, who to her dying day had taken delight out of trifles: a handful of early roses, the curve of a wave, the painting on a fan.

Madame de Louysnes's face changed subtly as she thought of her sister's ruined life and premature death. Here, in the privacy of her own room, she could give rein to feelings ordinarily curbed lest they should augment the fury of Dermot

Lisronan's hate—could hope—nay pray—that some day, somewhere, the man who had made her suffer would pay to the uttermost farthing.

Ethna's last words to her had been a prayer that she, Esmée, would use her influence to keep the young man from taking vengeance, and Esmée had promised; but now, three months after, when the first sharpness of loss had settled down into that dull ache which is so much harder to endure, she found that her mind dwelt continually on the idea which she knew lay nearest her nephew's heart.

She too had Irish blood in her veins—enough to understand the Gaelic cry: "Revenge! revenge! To-day for revenge and to-morrow for mourning!" —enough to sympathise with Dermot's unspoken wish, suppressed because it had distressed his mother, but strong as a flame.

The opening of the door roused her from her reverie. She glanced round and saw her husband in riding clothes, and speckled with snow-flakes, which he was regarding disapprovingly.

"My compliments, Madame," he said. "Are you alone? Yes. Well, I but looked in on my way past to tell you a piece of good news. Dermot is in Paris. He hopes to wait on you almost at once." Monsieur de Louysnes crossed to the hearth as he spoke.

Though he was an *habitué* of "le Roi soleil's" Court, and a gentleman of many *amourettes*, he had a strong affection for his wife and a pleasure in pleasing her very little the mode. He smiled now at her little start of delight.

"Dermot? Oh, I am glad!" she exclaimed.

Raoul de Louysnes nodded. He too was glad to see Dermot. Esmée had given him no children — almost her only dereliction from wifely duty—and Ethna's son more or less filled a blank in both their lives.

Madame de Louysnes looked into the fire thoughtfully.

"Poor boy, 't was a bad home-coming last time!" she said, after a moment.

Her husband looked up at the ceiling with a grieved air. He was essentially designed "not for heart wounds but for scratches," and his sister-in-law's death three months before had been quite the most uncomfortable incident of all his placid existence. He who hated emotions had found himself unable to escape contact with them; had indeed to go to Versailles for a fortnight to recoup. Fortunately Versailles was quite as good a place as any other from which to pen beautiful sentiments to a wife vulgarly prostrated by grief, and that the Court happened to be there, and the heroine of the latest *amourette*, was of course merely a coincidence—one not to be mentioned to Esmée, of course. Women did not understand these things.

"*Tiens!* That is three months ago," he said, "youth forgets."

Esmée shook her head.

"Dermot will not—easily," she answered.

Monsieur, alarmed by the topic, pursed up his lips. Unhappily his only way out was by another gloomy topic, but he pursued it hastily as being the more impersonal.

"Morgan D' Arcy is dead," he said.

Esmée glanced up.

"Poor man! He suffered much," she said softly.

"He has bequeathed what he had—'t was not much—to Dermot."

"Oh? Ah, yes, I remember, 't was poor Owen's wish that if Morgan and his brother died without children Dermot should inherit. He mentioned it in the last letter he wrote me, twelve years ago— the night before he died." She paused a second, and then—as though struck by a sudden thought— cried: "Oh, Raoul! Does that mean that Dermot will return into Ireland?"

"I think I had better go and change," said Raoul de Louysnes hurriedly. Turn it as he might, the conversation bristled with tragedy.

Esmée smiled a small, slightly bitter smile. She knew the good-looking butterfly whom she, some fifteen years earlier, had endowed with all her worldly goods—a very comfortable supply—and with a special place in her heart, had, in fact, never entertained any illusions about him—a fact Monsieur de Louysnes would certainly not have believed had any one been tactless enough to inform him of it.

"Yes—go and change!" she said. "I should not have kept you talking when you are damp."

"Nay, I knew the news would interest you, Madame."

"It does—profoundly."

She sighed to herself as the door closed behind her husband, and then laughed a soft little laugh.

"Poor Raoul," she thought, "what a fright he was in! And how little he knows me after all these years. I wonder what he would think, could he guess that I married him simply because he was the handsomest man I 'd ever seen and it gave me pleasure to look at him! Though, indeed, that is a sentiment *he* ought to understand."

She laughed again and then grew grave and stared into the fire. It was nearly dark outside the window now. The rose-hue had faded into clear steel grey, shot with points of glittering light, and the eaves had a ghostly look.

Esmée leaned back in her straight chair and looked idly down at her black velvet gown and the diamonds on her long white fingers, which flashed back answering sparks of blue and scarlet fire to the golden wood flames.

Again the opening of the door roused her, but this time she sprang up—and there was a look in her eyes as she turned to greet her nephew, that Raoul de Louysnes had never seen.

The first words over, a silence fell between the two—the silence of a great grief stirred again into active life. She sat down once more in her chair, and Dermot stood by the corner of the hearth with his arm on the chimney-breast.

He had altered very little in essentials in the twelve years spent out of Ireland. The slim, brown-faced boy had grown into a lithe, active man, brown-faced still and small-featured, but with no particular claim to good looks, nor any especial virtue, mental or physical, to mark him out from dozens of other young Irishmen who came over to escape the utter degradation which awaited them at home.

He lacked altogether the sense of humour that had distinguished Ethna, lacked too that *joi-de-vivre* usually so strong in the young of his race. Laughter or lightness of heart were not in him. He took life seriously and soberly, seeing in it, not a game with a game's ups and downs, but a responsibility to be gravely accepted.

Esmée, studying him as a woman studies the character she loves and has in part moulded, marvelled sometimes at the uncertainties of atavism. Neither the Ronans nor his mother's people, the O'Malleys, could show for at least four generations a single Scotch or English strain, yet all this boy's attributes were those of some solemn northern people devoid of any fire save the steady flame of a set purpose. There was in him the makings of a bigot, and a slave to duty, but not of a fanatic or an enthusiast.

Madame de Louysnes wondered sometimes with a certain rather grim amusement whether any woman had ever before been called on to influence two such opposite characters as her husband and this nephew of hers. The same thought recurred to her now as she looked up and met Dermot's handsome, melancholy grey eyes. But she knew what was in his mind, and her voice had all the sympathy of a caress as she said softly:

"It is terrible, this first coming back here. I know what you feel."

Dermot looked round the room.

"It had to be—sooner or later," he said, and Esmée felt that the answer was utterly characteristic. Even as a child he had been reserved about his griefs, difficult of access, aloof. She made no reply, and a little silence fell between them.

Madame de Louysnes, like most impulsive people, was always at a loss with those who did not meet her half-way. There were a hundred things to say, of course, but words seemed lacking. She realised suddenly how Ethna had bridged the inevitable gulf which a complete divergence of character must make between even the best of friends.

Dermot spoke first. "Has Monsieur told you about Morgan D' Arcy, Madame?" he asked.

Esmée nodded. "Poor Morgan. It 's hard to conceive. He found existence such a rare jest always. So he has carried out Owen's wishes, Dermot?"

"Yes."

"The property and Pouldarrig come to you?"

Dermot's face darkened. "Not openly," he said. "You forget the penal law, Madame—I can hold no property. Nominally they belong to Sir Martin FitzUlick. You remember Sir Martin?"

"Well. His daughter stayed with me here not so long ago. It was when your regiment was in Dauphiné. She is a charming girl."

"Aideen? I forget her. I see her brother frequently. He's in Galmoy's regiment."

Madame de Louysnes glanced up. "Barry! How is he?" she asked. "I have not met him for some time and I delight in him. I have never— even among your country-men—chanced on a man so perpetually and happily in mischief. I hope he has n't lost the habit."

"Why?"

"Oh, because 't is youth's privilege—one has all middle age and old age to be wise, and, ah me, but it 's dull!"

Dermot Lisronan smiled. He had a brilliant melancholy smile, without a hint of either humour or happiness in it.

"Well, Barry FitzUlick is some way off middle age at that rate," he answered.

"Aideen told me he had worried his father vastly by declaring for King James," said Esmée. "Sir Martin, if I remember rightly, leant to the side of safety—wherever that lay—and then of course he is a Protestant."

"And one of the best men that ever lived!"

Madame de Louysnes nodded quickly. She

felt much nearer her nephew when he spoke with
that note of warmth in his voice.

"One of the best," she echoed. "Poor man, he
paid heavily, I fear, for his services to—us."

The brooding look in Dermot's eyes deepened
at her words.

"I have three months' leave, Madame—and I
am going into Ireland," he said slowly.

His aunt glanced at him with an air of apprehension.

"Into Ireland. Oh, Dermot! Why?" she
asked.

"To settle the score," he answered. There was
vehemence in his tone, but a curious submerged
vehemence not of youth.

"To—do you mean?"

Dermot nodded.

For a second two pairs of eyes, the middle-aged
woman's and the young man's, met in the firelight
with a deep and complete comprehension. Then
Esmée, remembering her promise to her sister,
looked away.

"Your mother—did not wish that," she murmured.

"That is why I have waited so long—the only
reason." The young man paused for a second and
then went on, still with the slow cold vehemence
that was so infinitely more convincing than any
loud fury: "I have had it in my mind ever since
that night twelve years ago. There are times
when I think of nothing else—nothing. I 'd give

my remaining years here and my hope of another life for the power to make him suffer all she suffered." His voice dropped to a fierce tense whisper.

Esmée, every fibre of her being in accord with his desire, tried hard to think of Ethna's last wish.

"You could never do that, Dermot," she said feebly, "and your mother would be so distressed if she knew—she made me promise——"

"I know what she made you promise, just as I know what you really feel about the matter," he interrupted. "Madame, believe me, you cannot understand my feeling—even she could not. I waited because she wished it—but she never knew what that waiting meant, she never guessed."

He broke off, biting his lip, and Esmée saw that he was shaking from head to foot. "God! It won't bear thinking about!" he ended, with a sudden note of passionate fury in his voice such as Madame de Louysnes had never heard before in all her fifty-five years of life.

"Vengeance is a difficult thing, Dermot," she said slowly. "'T is ever so impossible to reach the guilty save through the innocent. Revenge as the peasants know it is not for us."

"I shall find a way—at worst I 'll rid the earth of him. There must be a hell somewhere for such as he!"

Esmée shook her head despondently. She

would have spoken, but Dermot stopped her with a gesture.

"It will bear neither thinking about nor talking of, Madame," he said, with quick bitter finality. "I had to tell you—but I beg you to let the matter rest now."

There was a long silence after his words. Madame de Louysnes lay back in her chair, staring thoughtfully into the fire and facing a prospect which had been hers once or twice before, after the news of heavy fighting reached Paris and before the list of casualties—the prospect of life without Dermot.

"I suppose you 'll go," she said at last, with a sigh. "A man must 'dree his weird,' as the Scotch say. Shall you be glad to see Ireland again?"

"Glad? Yes, i' faith! To me no country will ever be quite the same as Ireland—no other!"

The warm note was back in his voice; he looked over her head into the shadows of the room like a man who sees visions. He did indeed in that moment; visions of grey peaks capped with clouds and themselves shadowy as clouds, beyond a waste of tumbling waters—Ireland's welcome to the returning exile. Visions of a far brown bog-land, swept by golden bursts of sunlight and purple cloud shadows; visions of a swift amber-hued river swirling through a glen of rowans, slender and scarlet-berried. His thought at the moment was the thought of an Irish poet long centuries before,

a thought which an Irish poet of a later day has
put into words:

> 'T is Ireland has my love,
> Fair be her fortunes! Oh, the fields my childhood
> knew,
> The flowers upon her fields, the fair skies over them!
>
> .   .   .   .
>
> Oh, for the thrush's note
> In her glad woods first heard—the blackbird's whistle
> there!
> The red stags of her glens, the eagles of her crags
> That first I climbed.
>
> .   .   .   .
>
> My heart, a bird above the waves,
> Flies to the glad green fields of Ireland that I love,
> I am a lonely man till I am home in Ulla.

Dermot, being particularly inarticulate in these
matters, could hardly have expressed the sentiment
in the most prosaic phrases, and would not if he
could; but he understood it.

Esmée's exclamation of half-disgust: "That
grey land! How can you even like it? I should
die there!" only evoked a smile from him.

"You are not Irish, Madame," he answered,
"or but half Irish at best. I would not die anywhere else—or live anywhere else, an' I had my
choice." He paused again, frowning, and then
after a second went on, "There's another reason
why I should go. A hundred years back, or may-

hap more, a D'Arcy brought much stolen gold out of Spain—ingots and bars to the value of many thousands. Fearing Carew's soldiery, he hid this treasure somewhere, either in Pouldarrig Tower or in the country round. 'T was said he feared also those from whom 't was taken, some Catalonians. He died suddenly, leaving no clue, and from that day to this none have ever found 'D'Arcy's hoard,' as the country people call it."

"And you are going to try your luck now, Dermot?"

"Yes."

Madame de Louysnes sighed. "I fear me a curse goes with gold so gained," she said. "I have seen strange things in my life—but never happiness following evil-doing."

Dermot was not listening. He occasionally built castles in Spain—not those wonderful shining domes, piled tower on tower and surrounded by a rainbow, in which youth generally delights, but lesser works with solid foundations and almost tangible walls—and from the thought of D'Arcy's hoard had risen the dearest of these.

"That gold, Madame, it must be of great value," he said suddenly. "And the King needs money just at present."

"Oh, so 't is for him you would seek it?"

"Yes. But I have said nought of it yet. So many have failed—and I may too."

Esmée de Louysnes laughed. "Oh, Dermot!" she cried. "You are n't Irish—you really are

not!   Nay, now I've hurt you, I didn't mean to—
but—"   She broke off, gave her shoulders a little
shrug, and then added, "I wish you all luck in
your venture.   But for pity's sake, dear, think of
the old couple who have no other interest save
you, and try not to leave your bones amongst those
weary bogs."

CHAPTER IX

THE HOUSE OF RIMMON

DERMOT LISRONAN indicated to the slip-shod, pink-cheeked serving-wench a small table set apart under the window. He had no inclination to eat his supper in company of the four dishevelled three-parts-drunk buckeens who were roystering on the hearth. It was enough to have to endure their jokes and their reek of stale tobacco and brandy across the width of a room.

He pushed at the casement, which hung awry upon one hinge, and succeeded presently in opening it enough to let in a little of the warm westerly wind that blew sweet with hill scents over Cork town.

Outside lay Finn's Quay, a sea of liquid mud churned into pools by the constant traffic. Though the old legitimate trades were dying fast under the iron injustice of the new law, signs of them still remained. Artificers still went to and fro, pig-tailed sailors paraded the street, an occasional foreigner might be seen.

Dermot sat down to his table, conscious of

rudely curious glances from the hearth. His well-groomed air, his burnished sword-hilt, and general trimness of attire were sufficiently out of keeping with the squalor of the surroundings to be conspicuous. Self-respect was dying fast in all classes, oppressors and oppressed alike, and the outward signs of it had almost vanished from the land.

The quartette of buckeens bore patent evidence of this. They were plainly well-to-do; but their clothes, expensive of their kind, had the air of having been worn for days at a stretch, and their faces suggested that those days began, continued, and ended in drink.

Dermot was eyeing them with contemptuous disgust when the door opened. He glanced at the man who entered, at first casually, and then, as the idea dawned on him that this was some one he ought to recognise, with puzzled interest.

The fellow looked a scarecrow—a mere collection of incongruous rags, hung anyhow on a lean, bent figure—but his air, his way of walking, the outline of a profile that had once been good-looking in a weak effeminate fashion, all betokened breeding. And they were, furthermore, familiar to Lisronan; they had some niche in the memories of his childhood.

The battered travesty of a gentleman had slouched in an aimless fashion right round the room before he noticed Dermot, but when he did, his start of astonishment was obvious. His mouth fell a little more ajar—he cast a furtive wary glance at the roysterers, and edged near the table.

"Your servant, my lord," he said just above his breath. "You are welcome home. But, mayhap, you have forgotten me?"

Dermot smiled and shook his head.

"I was puzzled for a moment," he said, hoping the fact that this moment had not yet passed did not betray itself in his face. "Twelve years is a long time."

"Begad it is. And so you 've not forgot poor Jimmy Taaffe—I would there were more like you!"

Dermot's eyebrows went up for a second. James Taaffe! Was this scarecrow Sir James Taaffe, of Castle Taaffe, whom he had last seen at a hawking party near Lisronan, well mounted, smartly dressed, greatly favoured of ladies if somewhat despised by men? Jimmy Taaffe, who danced so much better than he rode, who could n't hit a haystack at twenty yards, and had earned the undying contempt of one small boy by declining to follow his peregrine over the bog-drain!

"You 're thinking that times are changed, eh?" asked Taaffe bitterly, with a quick glance round the room. "God help us all now! But you—you have conformed, I see," he added, his eyes on Dermot's sword-hilt.

"Conformed! No, i' faith! What put that in your head?" retorted the young man, sharply for him.

Sir James's mouth twitched. "You carry a sword," he said in a half whisper.

"And shall—while I am on Irish soil."

There was no defiance in Dermot's tone. He spoke quietly, in the fashion of a man who has arrived at a decision from which he is not to be turned.

Taaffe shook his head. "You will lose your liberty—your very life, mayhap," he whispered.

The other looked at him in silence for a second, with frank contempt in his grave grey eyes. Why argue with a creature like poor Jimmy Taaffe?

Reluctantly, urged thereto by a wolfish glance at the food, he invited him to share his meal. It was not the poor devil's fault that he had been born a coward—the first Taaffe to bear that stigma—and he wore an air of semi-starvation.

"Dine with you, my lord? Aye, will I right gladly," exclaimed James, adding: "Had I not met you—but, there, we will not talk of it. What wind blew you to this God-forsaken country?"

He dragged a chair close to the table as he spoke, and looked critically into a jug of claret which the girl had just dumped among the dishes.

"Will it be drinkable, think you?" asked Dermot, anxious to change the subject.

"They have excellent wine here," said Taaffe. "Shall I see mine host? It is, after all, an important matter."

He rose hurriedly and shuffled off, determined that so rare an opportunity should not be wasted.

Lisronan shrugged his shoulders. Four hours on Irish soil had shown him that the main object in life was claret, and the second brandy. To a man brought up among people cultured, temperate, and intolerant of gross excesses, the thing was incomprehensible. Mentally also he shrugged his shoulders, as he sat waiting for the poor wastrel who typified what Irishmen were to be when the new law had done its work.

Jimmy Taaffe reappeared before long with a fresh supply of claret.

"I can vouch for this!" he said solemnly, filling a goblet. "Your good health, my lord. Success to the mission, whatever it be, that bore you to this cursed country—and a speedy departure from the same!"

"Is that the best you can wish a man—speedy departure from his native land?"

"Yes, i' faith. Damn Ireland, say I! Good wine this, eh?"

Taaffe dragged a dish towards him as he spoke and began to eat ravenously. There was a curious travesty of breeding about all his actions that made their very roughness the more painful to witness.

Dermot, watching him across the table, thought again and again of the elegant stripling who had once for a short season fluttered about Lisronan, a victim to Ethna's charm.

"You are not drinking," said Taaffe presently, pouring himself a fourth or fifth bumper of claret.

"Here, I 'll give you a toast—a curse rather—such fit our condition best!"

His face twitched. He lifted his glass and held it across the table towards Lisronan, with a sullen flame in his bloodshot eyes.

"May the curse of God fall on Albrecht Van der Wynykt!" he whispered fiercely. "May his bones find no grave and his soul no rest!"

Dermot's hand tightened so suddenly on his goblet that the wine splashed over the table.

"You too?" he said in a low tense voice. "Hath he served you evilly too?"

James Taaffe looked round the room. Neither wine nor the sense of his wrongs could efface his natural caution.

"Evilly? Yes, by God, that he has!" he answered very low. "He married my sister. Oh, 't is a pretty tale. Came to our house, Castle Taaffe, one night twenty-six years agone, seeking shelter. My father and I were abroad—Margaret and my mother alone, save for the maids. She was a pretty girl, Margaret. He—oh, well, you can guess that part! My father forced him to marry her at the sword-point—not that he was altogether unwilling. God, the life she had with him! Then came Dutch William and his laws. My father was dead then, and Castle Taaffe mine. When I saw how things were going I—I—I carried my sword to the Dutchman. There were many did it, you know, Lisronan."

"Two thousand—out of, I think, thirty-five,"
said Dermot in his quiet well-bred voice.

"It did n't serve me," Taaffe went on, ignoring
the interruption. "Van der Wynykt laid claim to
my property as Protestant next-of-kin—I was cast
forth to starve—I—I 'd have conformed had it
availed. 'T is a question of necessity—one may
say that there is a Scriptural warrant for it too,
since the prophet bowed himself in the house of
Rimmon; but Wynykt—curse him—had the ear of
those in power, and I should have gained nought.
That 's eleven years past now.   Eleven years I 've
been homeless—an outcast."

He paused to swallow what was left in his
glass.

"I 'll make the fellow suffer, though," he
continued after a second, banging his clenched
fist on the table. "Burn me, if I don't take
him unawares some dark night and show him
that James Taaffe is not lightly to be tram-
pled on. Burn me, if I don't make him
rue the day he thrust me forth from Castle
Taaffe!"

"You have waited somewhat long, have you
not," asked Dermot drily.   Thirst for vengeance,
prated of by this unhappy braggart, seemed suddenly a poor and rather discreditable thing.

"Waited?   Aye.   But I never had my chance,"
returned Taaffe craftily. "He—he goes armed."

"Do not you?"

"He rides with a guard, half a score strong—I

should lose my life in the attempt, and where then would the benefit lie, eh?"

Dermot gave his head a slight scornful upward jerk. What was to be said to such a man—especially as from host to guest?

"He drove my poor sister out of her senses," went on Taaffe. "For ten years before her death she was crazed, and faith 't was no wonder, seeing the usage she suffered! When the spirit took Wynykt, he would flog her before him stark naked up and down the long gallery at Lisronan—once, crouched outside the window, I saw her running hither and thither like a coursed rabbit under the whip—and once——"

"For God's sake, stop!" broke in Dermot, with a passionate gesture of dissent. "If you are minded to speak of such things I am not minded to listen to them! That you have let the fellow live is beyond my comprehension."

"I tell you 't would be too dangerous to molest him," returned James Taaffe peevishly. "Of late things were better for Margaret. Her son Willy, since he was come to years of discretion, sheltered her. No bad lad, Willy. Does not forget that he has a poor devil of an uncle outlawed through no fault of his own."

Dermot pushed his plate away. He found it almost impossible to sit at the same table with this creature, who at every word displayed fresh depths of degradation.

But James Taaffe, once started on his grievances

was hard to stop, especially when primed by claret.

"I make no doubt, were Castle Taaffe Willy's I 'd see some of my own again," he said smiling, "instead of living with the grey dragoons under the roof of heaven. I tell you, my lord, life in winter in the Lisronan woods is a bitter thing! And they 're coarse fellows for the most part, no deference for a gentleman. They would have me work like themselves."

Dermot's disgust found vent. "Well? Why not?" he asked scathingly.

James Taaffe looked across the table with eyes of outrage. "Work! A Taaffe work!" he said tragically. "Upon my soul, Lisronan, you 've learnt some vastly queer ideas in France!"

"You accept their—" The word "charity" hovered for a second on the young man's lips, but his natural reluctance to hit a man already down choked it back. "You—you share their bread," he said lamely.

Taaffe sniffed. That any one should fail to appreciate the prestige his society conferred on the grey dragoons—men who, evicted by the new law from their possessions, had preferred an outlaw's life on Ireland's wildest hillsides to service abroad—was incredible.

"I am of infinite service to them—infinite," he answered.

Dermot let the remark pass. He knew little of the grey dragoons, save that they were in most

8

cases wastrels—the leavings of better men fled
to where there was "room to pray and room to
dare"—a colony of human ravens preying on the
new settlers.

"If you are coming to Lisronan 't is more than
likely you too will 'share their bread,'" said Taaffe
with angry emphasis on the last words

Dermot winced.

"I—did think of going to Lisronan," he answered hastily. "At least——"

"You 'll find mighty few friends there," put
in James Taaffe, as the young man hesitated.
"Father Moran is dead."

"Father Moran! Since when?"

Taaffe glanced up, somewhat mollified by the
poignant distress in Dermot's tone.

"You had a regard for him, my lord—I 'm sorry
I spoke so bluntly," he said.

"I wondered he had not written lately. How
did he die, Taaffe?"

Sir James hesitated, his momentary annoyance
submerged in a very genuine regret.

"My sister held firm to her faith through all,"
he said slowly. "Outwardly she conformed, but
at heart. never! Her wits were clear enough on
that issue, poor soul. When she lay a-dying, she
prayed so hard for Father Moran that Willy, the
boy, defied his father and went to fetch the priest.

"'T was on a Sunday evening, and Mass just
over in the little black glen near the lough. There
were a dozen of us still lingering there when the

boy came, and not one but tried to stop Father
Moran, well knowing 't was certain death for him
to go. But he would not be said—not he."
Taaffe paused frowning.

"Willy brought him in by a lower window, and
so to her chamber," he went on after a second,
"and would have held the door against his father
and his fellows but that 't was not to be done.
They were a dozen to one. Wynykt thrust Father
Moran forth through the casement onto the
flagged walk thirty feet below—and—and the
sacrament after him." Taaffe's voice sank to a
whisper. He signed himself swiftly and furtively.
"'T will scarce bear speaking of," he muttered,
more appalled, it seemed, by the sacrilege than by
the thought of his sister's suffering or the murder
of the priest.

Dermot's face twisted like the face of a man in
intense bodily pain.

"Father Moran—did he die then or afterwards?" he asked, with strange grim quiet.

"Three days later, in Shaun Ronan's hut,"
answered Taaffe.

There was a silence after he had spoken.

Lisronan sat motionless, looking across the
dingy room, the flame of a hatred more bitter
than hell, more passionate than any love, alight
in his grey eyes.

He hardly heard when James Taaffe began to
tell of a strange fear which had come of late to
Albrecht Van der Wynykt.

He felt again, as he had often felt before, that no life was long enough, no death sufficiently harsh, to wipe off the score between him and this man.

CHAPTER X

"A LAND OF MEMORIES . . . AND GRAVES"

OF all the instincts of the human heart there is none more difficult of analysis than love of country. Who shall say why it stirs faintly in the men of the fat and profitable plains, and fiercely in those whose lot for generations has been cast among miles of barren bog and on untillable mountain slopes?

Altogether inscrutable, altogether beyond the power of description, is that silent voice which speaks to the Irishman and the Pole and other men who have suffered for the right to live on their native soil. Vague it may be, vague as the pale grey smoke of gorse-fires drifting on a March evening along the hillside, mysterious as the glint of level moon rays seen through bare wind-swayed branches, subtle as the sound of moving waters on a dark night; but he must be blind and deaf who would deny it the mighty strength of a passion woven from the fibres of the first heart that ever beat in the misty dawn of time.

The Irish know the sentiment better than any

other nation; so well indeed that they have almost succeeded in giving it expression both in their poetry and in their music. It is there always—a cry, a yearning—now woven into one of those wonderful age-old epics which, like Ireland herself, have youth eternal; now running passionately through a little simple melody and making it unlike any other music in the world; now embodied in a shadowy legend, almost laughable to modern ears.

Dermot Lisronan, nearing home after twelve years of exile, felt it; his heart was stirred by a note in the murmur of the westerly breeze across Monadarrig bog as it had not been stirred since his childhood.

Far, very far off, where the bog-land's farthest sapphire-dark rim melted into the silver horizon, a line of faint blue peaks rose, ghostly, ethereal, remote as the hills of Tirnanogue. Full-bosomed white clouds came from them, sailing slowly, slowly over a high pale sunlit sky, each with a trailing shadow in its wake, a shadow deeply, softly purple as the bloom on a ripe damson, a shadow that moved like a dim host across the madder-brown folds of the bog. The willows wore delicate feathers of the faintest brown, the stream a line of grey liquid light, the breeze a live thing, sweet and plaintive, that shook the tasselled rushes in its passing.

Dermot forgot the savage mission which had drawn him back to Ireland as he sat on his horse at the head of the sheep-track. There was no-

thing of human passion in the message of these
wide, wild spaces.   They whispered the doctrine
of the fatalist—the futility of life, the impotence
of man's endeavour.

Lisronan sighed, shortened rein, and rode on,
troubled for the first time by a doubt.

His way did not lie across Monadarrig bog to the
foot of the cloud-haunted mountain peaks, but
right-handed, down into a narrow fertile valley
that ran northward like some green oasis in a
brown desert.   From the curves of the sheep-track
one could see evidences of a civilisation arrested
many times in its progress and now apparently
killed; a little stone-roofed church where St.
Patrick had preached; a round tower, high and
slender, looped about by the silver shallows of the
river; an age-old cross with wealth of delicate
tracery and ringed arms.   The inevitable Norman
stronghold, aggressive even in decay, was there,
its cavernous windows wreathed by fluttering glittering ivy leaves, its grey broken battlements crying aloud of the time when, "From the heart of
Ireland came the call for fighting men."   There
too, was the ruined Franciscan Abbey, so familiar
to Irish eyes; and there too, at the foot of a hill,
the village.

Dermot looked last at the village.   That line
of mud hovels roofed with heather represented
eighteenth-century Ireland.   None had chimneys,
few even one window—very fitting habitation for
a people denied education, religion, and even the

fruits of industry should any have sufficient hardi-
hood to work.

Lisronan thought of some of the houses which
he had passed on his journey from Cork—square,
staring, whitewashed buildings, set generally in a
sea of mud and surrounded by squalid débris.
Few had shown any sign of care on the owner's
part.   All, or nearly all, bespoke that apathy and
recklessness which were the first-fruits of the new
law.   Why sow where you or your Catholic
children might not reap?   Or why—being newly
endowed with forfeited property—husband that
which at any Jacobite success might be reft from
you and returned to its original possessor?   It
was not a cheering land to traverse, and Dermot's
face was grim as he rode down from the bog to the
valley.

Crossing the ridge where heather and grass met,
he noticed a crowd of people on a green hillock
about two miles away.   He pulled up and stared
curiously at them.   The evening before, just at
sunset, he had come upon a group kneeling round
a little altar which was skilfully hidden among
the rocks of a pass; and the hasty uprising, the
sheep-like scurry to right and left, the scared faces
turned on him, had hurt him like a stab.

These people to-day were obviously not praying.
He wondered what common end had brought them
to the hill, and curiosity prompted him to turn
his horse's head in their direction.

As he drew nearer he realised that they were all

watching something in the piece of country between where they stood and where he rode. A second later his mount, a wiry little grey garron, snorted aloud and flung up his head. Dermot, looking about for the cause of this excitement, saw a handful of men on horses sweeping across the green incline below him. Most of them rode rather wildly, though it was obviously the first part of a race. Elbows and heels were working— a peruke had been left behind in a hedge—a loose horse dodged in and out.

The leading man seemed to Lisronan to have his hands full. His raw-boned chestnut mare, her head between her knees, was raking him out of the saddle at every stride, and though he clutched and hauled at her vehemently he was plainly not master of the situation.

Dermot shifted his glance to the fence which lay just before the riders. It was an ugly place enough —a low straight bank, narrow on top, with a drop and a wide gripe on the outside.

"That fellow's safe for a spill," thought Lisronan, adding, as he looked again at the out-of-hand mare, "he's mucabus, too."

The remark applied equally to the others—it was, in fact, the secret of their very erratic horsemanship—but either they were less drunk than the rider of the chestnut or better mounted, for there was a distinct slackening of pace amongst them as the bank grew close.

Only the mare charged on, lunging viciously at

her bridle, maddened by the jagging pull on the bit and the thunder of hoofs behind. Dermot saw her hurl herself at the bank as though it were a stone gap, clear it without laying an iron on its narrow top, and then, realising the gripe, try to kick back.

The result was a foregone conclusion. She landed on her chest and knees on the edge of the drain, turned over like a dog, and like a dog was up and away again in less than a second, dragging her rider, whose right foot had slipped through the stirrup in his fall. The dead-weight bumping along near her heels frightened her, and after a couple of furious plunges she swerved away, at right angles to the course and up the long sloping hill on which Dermot stood.

Lisronan got his little grey by the head and swung him round. He remembered all at once that the hill ended in a forty-foot drop down a sand cliff into the river. The chances of saving the mare's rider were slight, for she had a head of nearly a quarter of a mile—but there was a chance. The grey could gallop a bit, small though he was, the grass on the hillside was short, the slope gentle.

"Damn the brute—hanged if she has n't got her bridle off!" muttered Dermot, with a glance at the medley of broken straps that dangled from the mare's off-ear. The chase had been a stern one, and both horses—half a length apart still—were stretched like greyhounds.

Fifty yards ahead a green ragged lip of cliff

showed up with vivid clearness against the violet-grey distance beyond. Above the whistle of wind and the thunder of hoofs Dermot could hear the wash of fast flowing water. He looked at those sunlit grass tufts fluttering over a dark void, looked at the sweat-streaked, blown, bare-headed chestnut, and drove his little grey forward frantically with hands and heels.

To get the mare's girth undone was the only chance now. There was no time to try to head her off, no time for anything but a snatch under the flap of the saddle, and a prayer that the tongue of the buckle might be a loose one. He had just realised the jar of the strap running over the bar when the grey gave a swerve and a violent prop, and stopped dead within a yard of the edge.

Dermot, as he was whisked round like a tee-totum, had an impression of a chestnut body bunched for a slithering scrambling second on the very lip of the cliff and then shooting forth into space. He so fully expected to find that all his effort had been useless, that the sight of man and saddle asprawl on a torn-up roll of turf, which met him when he turned, was a relief. He jumped down and led the grey over to where they lay.

The rider of the mare—a largely-built young man with a tangle of chestnut hair—was by this time effectually sobered. A flint had cut his cheek open from eyebrow to chin, and the blood oozed sluggishly through the thick coating of mud that plastered his face. He sat up as Dermot came

near and began to try and work his ankle out of
the stirrup.

"Hurt?" asked Lisronan laconically.

"I think I'm all right," answered the young
man, "thanks to you. I suppose the mare's
killed? Damn this thing—I cannot loose it!"

His voice faintly stirred some chord in Dermot's
memory—a jarring chord at once illusive and
inexplicable, since to the best of his knowledge
the two were strangers.

He looked critically at the face of the man he
had saved. One side was comparatively clean,
and by it he judged that the unknown, freed of
mud, and without the marks of dissipation which
at present were written large on his mottled cheeks
and in his bloodshot eyes, would be a good-looking
young man.

True, he had the unkempt air common amongst
the Irish squirearchy—an appearance of having
slept in his clothes and neglected for days to
use either comb or razor—but in this he was no
exception to a lamentable general rule of which
Dermot, since his arrival in Ireland, had seen many
examples.

He could not identify the young man, or understand why his voice had been so vaguely and yet
unpleasantly familiar, and after a second of intent
scrutiny he turned away and went to the edge of
the cliff.

There, forty feet or more below, like a golden
rock in the steel-coloured sunlit water, lay the

mare, with the river sweeping round and over her, and lifting her long tail on its quick ripples. Her owner came limping along and looked down at her.

"She was always a jade," he said carelessly, and then turned to Dermot and thanked him for his most timely assistance. "I would n't have given much for my chances if I 'd gone down there under her," he added.

"Nor I," answered Dermot in his matter-of-fact way.

The other stretched out his arms. "Gad, I 'm damned stiff and sore!" he exclaimed with a grimace. "Was n't I the fool ever to run Fly-by-night at all, knowing that she 'd ask nothing better than to bolt? Oh, well, 't is little use troubling about it now. It might have been worse!" He paused, glanced curiously at the man who had saved his life, and then asked: "How did you know about this infernal place?"

"I have been here before," answered Dermot curtly.

"Have you indeed? Lud, now I took you for a stranger! Come out of England, mayhap?"

There was a query in the young man's tone and on his mud-stained features. Every line of his huge person expressed the frank curiosity of the peasant. He was plainly not a person accustomed to the usages of polite society.

Dermot smiled slightly. "I 'm sorry about the mare," he said, "but she got the bridle off before

I overhauled her, and I could do nothing with her. There was no time."

"Oh, damn the mare!" answered his companion. "There are a score more in the stables, and my father won't grudge me one. You are not of England, do you say—where then?"

He looked Lisronan up and down as he spoke, from his spurs to the crown of his hat.

"Ireland," said Dermot, with a lift of his eyebrows.

He turned to the grey and shortened rein, preparatory to pitching himself into the saddle again; but the owner of the mare caught his arm.

"Nay, sir, I hope you will come home with me and give my kinsfolk a chance of thanking you in person!" he exclaimed. "We live some seven miles from here, in the House of Lisronan."

"The House of Lisronan!" repeated Dermot in a curious breathless voice.

He shook the other's hand off his arm and turned and faced him.

"Is your name Van der Wynykt?" he asked slowly.

"Yes—William Van der Wynykt, son to Colonel Albrecht Van der Wynykt. Mayhap you 've met him?"

The colour went out of Dermot's face, leaving it grey and set.

"I have," he answered slowly. "I am Lisronan."

There was such a fury of cold implacable

hatred in his voice and eyes that William Van der Wynykt winced.

"Lisronan!" he cried, growing scarlet; "Lisronan—good God!"

For a second neither spoke. All the fury of hatred which had smouldered in Dermot Lisronan's heart since that black night twelve years before flamed up afresh, intensified by the knowledge that he had unwittingly done his enemy a signal service. His face was terrible in its unrelenting bitterness. Words could not have more plainly expressed the passion of regret that shook him.

Willy Van der Wynykt realised the thought with an acuteness strange in his father's son. All his life he had had moments when their acquisition of the Lisronan property weighed heavily on him. He had seen his mother weep in secret over it, had heard her lamentations at the curse which she felt must be entailed upon Albrecht Van der Wynykt's descendants by the act. A knowledge of his father's tyranny and of the hatred that surrounded them on all sides had tinged his childhood with a vague horror—and he had never entirely forgotten the incident at Bally Ulick gate.

"I suppose that—that—you could—could never —" he began, and then paused, and added lamely: "Oh, d—n it, I can't say what I want!"

Dermot turned his back on him and swung himself into the saddle, but before he could ride off Willy Van der Wynykt found words.

"Lord Lisronan—I personally regret—I mean
I 'm—   Well, when *I* have the power I 'll make
such reparation as—as is possible," he stammered,
adding, with lamentable absence of tact: "You
saved my life to-day."

Dermot gave him a glance which Willy Van der
Wynykt found it difficult afterwards to forget.

"Reparation!" he said, and laughed.

Willy, staring ruefully enough after the little
grey and his rider as they cantered away up the
slope, felt as if some one had struck him across the
face.

CHAPTER XI

THE MASTER OF LISRONAN

OLD Shaun Ronan and his wife lived in a thatched cottage on Monadarrig bog. Their sons, when Albrecht Van der Wynykt turned the whole family adrift, had followed the path chosen by Ireland's best men and were now in the ranks of the Brigade; but the old couple clung to the land they knew. Ethna, out of her own small possessions, had kept them from want; and Dermot meant, now that greater prosperity was his, to cajole them into France and there provide well for their comfort.

This prospect was the one pleasant thought in the tumult of bitter reflections which filled his mind as he rode up the black bog track to the little ring of wind-bent alders that surrounded Shaun's cabin. Every inch of the way, every hill and tree and little babbling stream, touched some agonising chord of memory. He could hardly bear to look over the brown folds of bog to a horizon that spoke as with tongues.

Shaun's cottage, like most bog-cottages, lay in

a slight hollow with a little garden round it, fenced by a wall, half brown flint and half fuchsia bushes. On this spring day, when moss bright as emerald green velvet hid the narrow flagged path from gate to door, and gleamed on the thatch; when the alders wore a veil of young honey-coloured leaves, and daffodils nodded golden heads in the quivering grass, it looked a bright little place enough, but Dermot pictured it on a winter night, swept by storm, flooded by the peat-stream, over-whelmed in a sudden movement of the bog.

He had slipped out of his saddle and was fumbling with the catch of the little wooden gate, when Shaun Ronan came stooping through the cabin door.

His first quick glance at Dermot was one of such unveiled apprehension that it stung the young man like a blow. Shaun had seemed to him in the days of his childhood a hero—a mighty being who drove the big white-faced bull before him with a switch and had power over the most riotous of the colts. Moreover, on the morning after that night of horror, it was to Shaun's house that Ethna had been carried, and by Shaun himself. No words could have brought Ireland's cowed state before Dermot as vividly as that one glance of fear from a man hitherto so courageous.

"Shaun! You have n't forgotten me?" he called out, holding his right hand over the gate.

Old Ronan started.

"Master Dermot?" he whispered, and then

shuffled into a run. "Oh, Master Dermot! Master Dermot! That the blessing of God may be on your honour, ever and always!" he cried, dropping on his knees and fervently kissing the outstretched hand.

"You did n't know me, Shaun?" said Dermot with his melancholy smile.

Old Shaun got up and unlatched the gate.

"Twelve black years, your honour," he answered. "Twelve black years! Give me the baste, Master Dermot, till I lead him widin. 'T is a crabbed place."

"Hitch him to the alder, Shaun. 'T will serve better than to bring him among your flowers. Where 's Nanoe?"

Shaun glanced all round before he answered.

"Away to Mass she is," he said in a half whisper as though the ducks might turn informer.

"Mass? On a Tuesday! 'T is not a holy day surely?"

"'T is not—but sure, Master Dermot, we—we—do—be in dhread always. 'T is the days ye 'd least be thinkin' it his riverence has to come—the way others would n't be thinkin' it either. Ze understand?"

Dermot understood.

"God!" he said fiercely, and then: "Shaun—why should you stay here? Come to France. You shall have a good farm, and you 'd be near Michael and Maeldune, and Shaun ogue—you never can see them while you bide in Ireland."

"Into France, is it?   Yerra.   No! No!" answered Shaun hurriedly, looking out over Monadarrig with a sudden hunger in his grey old eyes.

For two thousand years his ancestors had lived on or near the bog, and it held him with a chain infinitely stronger than any tie of blood.   Michael and Maeldune and young Shaun were dear to his heart, but they did not call him as Monadarrig did—nor ever would.

"Herself would n't go," he added.

"I 'll talk to Nanoe.   Mayhap she will change her mind," said Dermot.   "Were you going to Mass, Shaun?"

"I was so, your honour."

"I 'll come with you.   I—I heard about Father Moran."

A look of savage bitterness darkened Shaun Ronan's face.

"That God may serve the one that murdered him as that one served his riverence!" he muttered. "Sure, meself and young Mr. FitzUlick got the poor father lying under her window in the rain an' the dark like a dog!   'T was here we brought him, on the back of a little garron—and 't was widin in the room here he died, Master Dermot. There was no bad word out of him against that one, only praying for his black soul ever an' always. His riverence was the good man, God rest him!"

The last word was almost a sob.   "We have Father Talbot now—one ye 'd be hard set to scare, I 'm thinking," he ended.

"I can't conceive why you've stood Wynykt all these years!" said Dermot passionately. "You had hands! No weapons, say you? You had the weapons God gave you! Goes attended always, does he? Twelve armed men? Well, are n't there twelve men in Monadarrig? None could cavil at equal numbers and a fair fight!"

Shaun shook his head dubiously. His kind had been harried and persecuted for so many generations that they had come to regard persecution as part of their lives. The day of vengeance would arrive, of course—the vengeance itself was never for a moment forgotten—but it could be waited for through three, four, even five lives.

Dermot, remembering how he had chafed at the years of delay imposed on him by his mother's wish, marvelled at such infinite patience.

They talked of many things, he and Shaun, as they walked along the bog-track to the little glen where Mass was to be celebrated. Dermot learnt details of Albrecht Van der Wynykt's mistreatment of the late tenants, and of the hatred which he inspired among even his own descendants. That the Dutch settlers were good farmers his eyes had already shown him. They prospered in spite of the system of rack-renting inaugurated by their master; but, if Shaun were to be believed, they loathed Van der Wynykt—and remained loyal to him solely out of fear of the dispossessed Catholic population.

"Them that does be in the big woods has them

pairsecuted, ever an' always," said Shaun, with a glance across the bog to the far-stretching, tree-covered slopes of Slieveronan Mountain, ten miles away. "Grey dragoons is the name we have on them."

Lisronan nodded. "I met one in Cork," he said. "He told me of Father Moran's murder."

Shaun Ronan walked a few paces in silence. Then he took off his hat and signed himself solemnly.

"Was he telling your honour of the curse Siveen Dwane laid on Wynykt?" he asked in a lowered voice.

"No. I remember old Siveen Dwane though—she lived in the hut near Pouldarrig Rath. A big, fierce old body, was n't she—and one folks suspicioned of casting spells?"

"The very same, Master Dermot—Saint John between us and harm! Father Moran, God rest him, was after saving her grandchild—a little small slip of a colleen that fell in the river—and when Siveen got word of what was done on his riverence she was clean mad. Ye 'd not like to see her, let alone be listening to what she 'd say!

"She legged it away to Lisronan House, and it making dark—and when she got there she stood in agin the flowery bush fornint the door. Ye mind the bush, Master Dermot?"

Dermot nodded. Remember the white rose bush on which his mother had set special store? Why, he could see it as Shaun spoke!

"Siveen stood in agin the bush an' she waited. 'T was n't rightly dark, and 't was n't rightly light. She was there maybe half an hour whin she heard horses trampling, and there was that one—Cromwell's curse on him—an' he ridin' up to the house, an' twenty more wid him. Siveen stepped out then, the way he 'd see her. She stepped out and stood in front of the horse. Divil a bit would the baste go on. Whatever dhread was on him he 'd not stir, only stand and snort. Wynykt let a roar at Siveen, 'Curse you—stand aside!' sez him, and he shouting wid rage.

"'I 'll not stand aside for the likes of you,' sez she. 'You that murdered God's good man! You that 'll be dead yourself come four years!' She said that, standing up fornint him, and shaking her hands at him like as if she was throwing pishogues on him.

"'Cut her down, you d—d fools!' shouts Wynykt, and he striving to drive the horse near the way he 'd strike Siveen, and the baste raring and lepping with the dhread he had.

"'Aye. Cut me down!' sez she, letting a mad laugh out of her. 'The man who does it won't set eyes on the sun again. Dead he 'll be!' sez she. 'Dead the same as yourself when the four years is past. Faith, 't will be better for him nor for you!' sez she, laughing again. The sight 'ud leave your eyes to see her your honour, an' she standing up facing them all. Sure, she put fear on the whole of them. Were n't they sitting there

wid the reins loose in their hands and the eyes of
them staring.   They did n't heed Wynykt for all
he roared at them.   They did n't heed anything
only the woman.

"'Aye, 't will be better for any man in the ring
o' the world, no matter what way he 'd die, than
for you!' sez she to Wynykt.   'There 's blood on
your hands now, but again ye die 't is your own
blood will be on them.   There 'll be dhread on
ye ever an' always—black dhread! Ye 'll be in
dhread, for fear your own would poison you, and
in dhread to meet any strange man for fear he 'd
strike you down.   There 'll be days ye would n't
dare stir abroad, and days ye 'll be travelling
hither and over, thinking maybe 't is safer so nor
in your own house.   Aye, but ye 'll not escape,
for all your striving! Ye 'll not know the week,
nor yet the hour, when the life will be struck out
of ye—but it 's the black death ye 'll die, the black
bitter death, an' you prayin' on your knees to one
that 'll not listen!'"

Shaun paused.   His voice had risen to a trembling height of passion that brought the whole
scene home very forcibly to Lisronan, but now
he hesitated.

"She said more that I 'll not be telling your
honour," he went on after a second.   "She put
terror on them all.   Ye 'd hear the scabbards of
their swords clink-clinking agin the stirrups with
the dhread of her.   When she had it all said she
shook her two hands at Wynykt, and away wid

her into the dark an' no one axed to hinder her. But as to that one—that black-hearted murderer— faith, the face of him was like the face of a dead corpse. 'T was hardly he could walk in at the door. He have the fear on him still. He have a man to be ating bits of his food fornint him, the way he'd see is it poisoned; and there's weeks he'd be away entirely, and weeks he'd not set foot over the threshold, so there is. And in regard to any stranger, I'm telling ye, Master Dermot, he'd not get to come next or nigh him, if 't was the King of France himself."

Again Shaun hesitated. Then in a tentative voice he added:

"There's them of his own people would sell him—aye, an' right glad to!"

Dermot shook his head.

"I won't come at him by treachery, Shaun," he said. "I learnt to-day that he was not in Lis-ronan; but I've waited—I can wait until either he returns or I trace where he has gone."

CHAPTER XII

"YE 'LL remember Kylenoe, I 'm thinking, Master Dermot," said old Shaun at last, breaking off suddenly in an impassioned discourse on the hardships endured by Father Talbot and the few Catholic gentry who yet remained in Lisronan. The hardships of his own class seemed to pass him by. It was in his eyes right enough that "the likes of" his kinsmen should starve, but utterly wrong that his reverence should lack a roof-tree and Sir Turlough O'Clery a saddle-horse. "Ye 'll remember Kylenoe?"

Dermot nodded.

Half an hour's walking had brought them to the lip of a little shallow glen, which now lay before them filled by misty pale gold spring sunlight. At the bottom of it was the acre or so of ancient nut trees from which it took its name, and beyond these, on the brown open hillside, with their faces to the east, sat a large company. They formed two even squares, three or four yards apart—the men on the right-hand side, the women on the left.

Just above them a dry stone wall meandered through the heather. Dermot, as he drew near, noticed that it held two large slabs of granite, the smaller perched tablewise on top of the other which directly faced the waiting crowd. A step more showed him laborious carving upon the face of the larger stone—a cross, I.H.S., Gloria in Excelsis—and upon the smaller, the pyx.

He stood for a second watching each new arrival make reverent genuflexion to this poor altar—and then knelt himself, and followed old Shaun in among the men.

Some paces away to the right stood Father Talbot, apparently counting the stones in the wall. He was a tall, very gaunt man, with a long, thin, and severe face—a face full of courage and resolution. He dragged one leg when he walked, the result, so Shaun whispered, of a pistol-shot fired by Albrecht Van der Wynykt. Dermot guessed his age to be about thirty-five.

The counting of the stones ceased. Father Talbot made a sign to the half-grown boy who stood beside him, and a second later a box was raised from its hiding-place in the wall. Some chord seemed to stir in Dermot's heart, as he saw the silver taper holders, the bell, the jewelled crucifix, which he had last seen twelve years before on the High Altar of Lisronan Church, lifted forth into the spring sunshine—and after them a velvet altar-cloth which his mother had worked. The shimmer of gold and purple brought her back to his memory with greater vividness than anything he had seen since his return. He remembered so well the embroidering of that cloth—the gleam of gold thread between her white fingers, the sheen of the velvet as it lay on her knee—the fact that he was not allowed to touch it or to bring the dogs into the room where it was. He looked away while Father Talbot made ready the altar, for the thoughts aroused by that square of velvet burnt like a white-hot iron and he grew restive under the pain of them.

Shaun had chosen a place among the lower rows of the congregation, where the mere turn of his head showed Dermot the path from the nut trees. A girl was hurrying along it now, looking up at the congregation as she came. The young man glanced at her casually at first and then, as her singular prettiness became evident, with growing interest. She looked a child, at most seventeen, and her dress and bearing proclaimed her a lady, but fear was written large in every movement, in every line of her face, in every glance of her soft dark eyes. Dermot thought instinctively of an Italian greyhound. There was the same grace, the same air of appeal, the same suggestion of innate timidity.

The girl slipped off her glove, crossed herself, and then dropped on one knee and bent her head almost to the daisied grass, with a movement at once exquisitely graceful and exquisitely reverent.

A lively wonder as to who she could be began

to wake in Lisronan's mind. He had seen many
fair women in France, but never one with more
wonderful colouring than this unknown girl. Her
hair arranged after a by-gone fashion in wide
satin-smooth curls on either side of her forehead,
was as pale and pure a yellow as the primroses at
her breast. She had a complexion of infinite
delicacy—in colour and texture like the inner
petal of a white rose—appealing dark brown liquid
eyes, and a soft childish mouth of the type which
Greuze immortalised. To the man or woman
capable of looking beyond her exceeding prettiness,
such character as she possessed was an open book.
Neither intellect, strength, nor capacity lay in those
delicate features.

More than once during Mass Dermot found his
thoughts wandering to the girl. It seemed to him
that the women among whom she knelt eyed her
askance and drew away from her. She cast a
single rather piteous glance at them, and there-
after gave all her attention to the service with a
complete earnestness that gained her the young
man's approval. He found himself, when it was
over, watching for the genuflexion which had
bespoken such grace of both body and spirit.

Outside the place sanctified by its sacred usage,
the congregation made little groups and talked,
just as in past days they had talked outside Lisronan Church after Mass. A dozen of Dermot's
former tenants surrounded him, eager to kiss
"his honour's" glove and welcome him back.

They were all elderly men, for the young ones had
in almost every case gone abroad—to France, to
Austria, to Spain.

It was melancholy work enough greeting these
poor derelicts, and Dermot felt slightly relieved
when they parted, at the approach of a lady whose
presence he had not noticed before. He knew her at
once, though it was years since they had last met.

"Mistress Aideen!" he cried eagerly, and kissed
the hand she held out with a fervour unusual to
him.

"I never thought to see you here, Dermot,"
said Aideen FitzUlick. "Welcome! 'T will be
an immense pleasure to my father and Barry.
Are you long come into Ireland?"

"Three days, Madame."

The smile died out of her face.

"I pity you," she said in a low voice. "I pity
you—coming back to—to this."

He nodded, with a glance at Father Talbot,
who was replacing his vestments in the box.
Cloth and crucifix and bell had gone from the
little altar. The taper flames no longer glim-
mered against the hillside like pale flowers.

"Come and I will make you known to Father
Talbot," said Aideen FitzUlick, laying a hand on
the young man's arm.

All her gestures were light, quick, essentially
Irish. Dermot was reminded of Barry, though he
realised with regret that Providence had denied
to Aideen her brother's good looks.

Father Talbot proved to be in a hurry. He had had a sick call from the other side of Monadarrig bog just before Mass. He said a few words to Dermot, gripped his hand in iron fingers, and limped away.

His departure was the signal of release for two figures who had been doing sentinel on the high ground above the glen.

"We seem to be the last left," said Aideen. "My pony is down there." She pointed to the nut grove, adding, with a laugh, "As I 'm under charge of old Maura and Danny, I shall be well scolded an' I delay. Pray, Dermot—la! of course I should say 'my lord' now that we are both old people—but—somehow—somehow——"

"Somehow you are too kind to—now when there are so few to call me Dermot," he put in gently with his melancholy smile. "Forgive the interruption. You were going to say——"

"I was going to say that I hoped you 'd come home to Bally Ulick. 'T would vex us all sorely if you went elsewhere."

Lisronan appeared to consider the proposition. It was his most un-Irish attribute, this tendency to reflect before he spoke.

"I will ride home with you now—and right gladly too," he said. "But—as for staying—well——"

"Well, sir—as for staying—what? I think you might look on Bally Ulick as home."

Her tone had a tinge of vexation, and his answer came more quickly than usual.

"Nay, 't is because I do—because I look on your father as my truest friend, that I hesitate. We brought trouble enough on you once, God knows, and I would rather shoot myself than endanger any of you again."

Aideen laughed. "La! But Barry puts us in jeopardy every hour by his mad actions," she answered. "He is running his neck into a noose at this very moment. Also he and I are Catholics. *C'est tout dire, Monsieur.* You must talk French to me—I am forgetting all I learnt at the Convent de Notre Dame de Paris."

They were close to the nut grove by this time, where Aideen's two elderly servants waited beside an elderly horse and a shrewish cob. Both were looking along the edge of the wood with an unconcealed spiteful satisfaction, and the young man, following their glance, saw the fair-haired girl engaged in a vain struggle to free her pony's rein from a low branch round which it was twisted.

Once again a wonder as to who she could be crossed his mind. He went forward quickly.

"I will undo them for you, Madame—if I may?" he said.

The girl stepped back a pace, with a quick upward glance of pure fear. It almost seemed to him that she expected a blow.

"Oh! Dicky—my garron—has been turning round and round the tree," she said incoherently.

Dermot examined the reins. They were coiled

in knots across the lichened bough, and a few more twists on "Dicky's" part must have either hanged him or broken the bridle.

Lisronan, while he was unravelling the tangled leather, stole a furtive glance at Dicky's owner. Her hood had fallen back, leaving her primrose-coloured head bare to the pale sunshine, which emphasised the fairness of her skin, the darkness of her arched eyebrows and long straight lashes, the soft brilliance of her pathetic eyes.

Dermot, being a man, did not notice that her habit was of the fashion of twenty years before, and so threadbare that even the frequent patches hardly served to hold it together, or that the Point-de-Flandre cravat at her neck had been washed and rewashed out of all semblance of lace. He realised only that she was a lady and beautiful, and for some strange reason in disfavour among the peasantry.

She stood very silent while he righted the pony— and only answered his inquiry as to whether he might put her up by a halting affirmative.

"Have you no servant, Madame?" he asked, as he slipped the reins into fingers that trembled visibly.

Dicky's rider shook her head. "Oh, no—no!" she whispered, and clucked nervously to the pony, in obvious desire to be gone.

Dicky, however, showed no inclination to move —in fact he backed a pace towards the tree from which he had just been liberated. Instantly the

10

reins dropped on his withers and his rider clutched the horned off-side pommel.

"Oh!" she cried in an agonised undertone. "Oh!" Dermot took Dicky by the head.

"I will lead him onto the path for you," he said, glancing about for a straight and clean twig. "He wants a whip."

"Oh, I should not dare to whip Dicky," she answered, gathering up the reins again. "If you will but put him onto the path, sir, 't will be of infinite service to me. He will go on then. He always goes home. Thank you many times—I am vastly obliged!"

She gave Dermot a pretty timid little smile as he let Dicky's head go, and a second later was jogging away down the track—with a lamentably crooked seat and reins held as if they were something breakable.

"A shame to send that child out alone," thought the young man, turning again to Aideen and her servants.

All three were by this time mounted—old Maura behind Dan, Aideen on her cob—and all three looked preternaturally solemn.

"Who was that?" asked Dermot of Miss FitzUlick. "She's too pretty and too timid to ride the countryside unattended."

A wave of colour came into Aideen's face. She bent to straighten a curb rein already quite straight.

"Julia Van der Wynykt," she said in a suppressed voice.

"Van der Wynykt! His daughter?"

"Yes."

Dermot said nothing for a second. His face betrayed his thoughts with bitter clearness.

When he turned to Aideen he had an air of incredulous impatience.

"Surely you must be mistaken," he said. "Van der Wynykt's daughter a Catholic!"

Aideen glanced at him with a comprehension and a sympathy in advance of her years.

"Her mother was—and the girl is—secretly," she said; adding, "The poor creature has a terrible life, I believe—for no one—none of—of *us*—will speak to her. And as for the country people— well, if it were not for Father Talbot, they would have made opportunity to kill her ere this."

Dermot was not listening. His mind had gone back to the slender, shrinking figure with the pale gold hair and the appealing eyes.

"His daughter," he said to himself under his breath. "His daughter! Good God!"

CHAPTER XIII

BARRY

FOR the first mile or so after they left Kylenoe, neither Lisronan nor Aideen FitzUlick spoke. He was thinking curiously of the timid graceful girl who had turned out to be Wynykt's daughter; she weighing the advisability of a certain course of action.

At last, where two sheep-tracks met, she turned in her saddle and rather abruptly told the servants that they might go home—Lord Lisronan would escort her back. Then, as the old horse with his double burden went jogging away over the bog, she glanced at Dermot.

"I 'm going to take you straight to Barry," she said. "He 's at Drumglass village. 'T is a bare mile from here, down this track."

She pointed with her riding-whip as she spoke and turned her cob to the right.

"Doubtless old Shaun Ronan told you such news as there is to tell," she went on after a moment. "'T is a quiet life we lead here with but few distractions—except——"

Dermot looked up expectantly as she hesitated. "Except—?" he asked.

Aideen gave her shoulders a rueful little shrug.

"La, I did n't mean to begin upon our grievances," she answered rather awkwardly, remembering what the sum and substance of those grievances was. "But I *was* going to say, 'except unpleasant distractions.' Barry keeps me in a constant ferment. He is so indiscreet, and our enemies are so vigilant."

Dermot urged his horse nearer hers.

"Do not fear to hurt me," he said slowly. "By 'our enemies' you meant Van der Wynykt—Sir Martin can have none other, surely? How does the fellow dare to persecute a man loyal to Queen Anne and a Protestant? What are Major Sugrue and the other Protestants about to permit it?"

"Major Sugrue, poor man, was never overbold," returned Aideen with a laugh. "He told my father t' other day that were we his children and did we 'persist in our errors' he would turn Barry adrift and keep me in solitary confinement on bread and water. Nay, he strongly advised my father to do so—'so as to stand well with those in authority.'

"'Young woman,' quoth he to me but yesterday, 'it grieves me sorely to see one so young hardened in sin and given over to idolatry.'

"'Sir,' quoth I with my best reverence, 'it grieves me to hear one old enough to know better discourse upon what he understandeth not.'

"I fear me were it a question of help Major Sugrue would give none—lest we two heretics should profit thereby."

The smile which her imitation of Major Sugrue had brought to Dermot's face died away again.

"He has reason—after a fashion," he said slowly. "Under King James he was flung forth from his property, penniless."

"True," she retorted, "but by whom? The son of the man whom his father drove out when Cromwell scourged the land with fire and sword. The second and third generation are prone to forget the sins of the first. Mayhap 't is but natural Major Sugrue should overlook the fact that he holds O'Dynor land while an O'Dynor works like a hind at his gate. Oh, a truce to this talk! Doubtless my ancestors took and held by right of might also! Doubtless these new-comers, who are taking Ireland for their own, will in their time be driven out by others. Our history has been this for so many centuries. See, there's Drumglass."

She nodded at the high ridge of bog-land that rose before them, bare, wind-swept, crested with chimneyless, heather-roofed cabins, some whitewashed, some of mud, which stood up like little cairns against the sky line.

Here and there from a doorway smoke drifted out in thin blue spirals—almost the only sign of life the village showed. There were neither fowls nor animals to be seen. The winter had been severe—the previous potato crop worse than usual. Still no one had actually starved, and in rural Ireland in the eighteenth century this was of itself a matter for congratulation.

Dermot surveyed the cabins critically as he rode up towards them. Heather makes bad roofing in a windy place, and most of the houses had that leaden look that comes of being continually soaked within and without.

One threshold was occupied by a very old woman, who sat grinding oats in a quern—and the extreme care with which she from time to time collected off the surrounding mud occasional grains that had jumped out over the stone lip of the quern, was in itself eloquent.

In a hollow immediately below the village lay a holy well, with a huge thorn tree on either side of it.

Aideen pulled up beside this well, slipped out of her saddle, and silently pointed to where, forty yards or so away, a tall man, whom Dermot recognised at a glance as Barry FitzUlick, was addressing a little crowd.

He stood amongst them, his right hand holding his chestnut mare carelessly by a lock of her mane, his left on his sword-hilt. His voice had the note that belongs only to utter and sincere conviction, his whole manner betokened an earnestness almost savage in its intensity. No one hearing him could have doubted that he spoke from his heart.

Partly for this reason, partly because Irishmen

are the readiest and the most sympathetic listeners
on earth, he held his audience literally spellbound.
Not one head turned in the direction of the new-
comers, not one pair of eyes strayed from his
honour's handsome, serious face.

Dermot, who knew Barry FitzUlick as the most
light-hearted, reckless, and happy-go-lucky of his
sex, watched and listened in a maze of astonishment. Among all the strange things bred of a
strange unhappy land this seemed to him the
strangest.

There was a short silence when Captain Fitz-
Ulick finished, a silence broken only by the
whispering breeze and the dull harsh noise of the
quern.

Then Barry spoke again. "The choice is yours,
boys," he said shortly, taking the mare's rein.

He turned and led her away from the little
group without another word. He had told them
of the countries where they might live men's
lives and do men's work—the rest lay with them.

He began to whistle as he walked down towards
the holy well and finally broke into a snatch of
song—three lines sung in tones sweet and mellow
as a blackbird's.

"You see how it is," said Aideen, with the air
of one displaying a miracle. "He rides about on
Kate, openly carrying a sword, openly advocating
'heresy and sedition,' as Major Sugrue calls it—
assuredly he will turn my hair grey! Barry!"

Barry stopped and glanced about him.

"Oho, Madame—is this the way you go home from Mass?" he said. "Hullo, Dermot! What good wind blew you here? Hang me, if I knew you were coming! Where did you chance on the fellow, Aideen?"

"In Kylenoe. But, Barry astòr, your carelessness passes conception! We might have been the Dutchman!"

"Dogs might fly," returned Barry with a light-hearted laugh. He clucked to the mare, led her over to where they stood, and slapped Lisronan on the shoulder. "It 's good to see you, Dermot," he said warmly. "Why did n't you tell me you were journeying into Ireland? We might have taken the road together. I came in Walsh's brigantine, and hang me if a Dutch man-o'-war did n't give chase to us. 'T was as good as a hunt."

"You forget to mention either that you 'd got leave or were thinking of the voyage," said Dermot smiling.

Barry laughed. He laughed at most things in life—with one or two notable exceptions—made the rest the subject of wagers, and even in the case of the exceptions hid his vehement earnestness under a cloak of flippancy.

He was a tall and largely built young man, with a handsome well-bred, resolute face of that fair Danish type so rare in Ireland. Essentially a fine animal, essentially Irish in almost all his attributes, he presented as great a contrast, both mentally

and physically, to Dermot Lisronan as is possible
between two men bred and educated on much the
same lines.

Aideen looked curiously from one to the other,
weighing her brother's air of intense vitality, his
vivid changes of expression, the gestures which
emphasised all he said, against his friend's studied
quietness. Dermot, three years the junior, gave
an impression of being older by at least a decade.

Barry's delight of life was pagan in its thorough-
ness; a delight akin to that glorious joy that glad-
dens the sunlit world on a golden morning of early
May. Looking at him it was easy to see, under
the traits developed by later centuries, a Loughlan
warrior running his swan-shaped galley on the
low Irish shore, with a laugh for the chances of
being swamped where the surf ran white over the
sand, and a laugh for the chances of the coming
fight, and a happy certainty of Valhalla behind it
all. He was the one type that Ireland always has
produced and always will produce—a symbol of the
eternal youth of her, which is at once her salvation
and her ruin.

"Can't think how I failed to see you," he went
on. "Hast been here long, Aideen?"

It was Lisronan who answered. "Twenty
minutes, mayhap," he said. "I did not guess
you—had the people's interests so much at heart,
Barry."

Barry shrugged his shoulders and made a
grimace.

"'T is precious little I do," he said, with the slightly shamefaced air common to the young of either sex when detected in a virtue. "Remind a few who might otherwise forget it that King James still exists—and that, an' they so choose, they may still live as men instead of as rats. Rather a thankless task, but at worst it gives Wynykt's 'hell-hounds,' as the peasantry call them, some other quarry than Father Talbot."

"While if they catch you?" put in Aideen.

Barry indicated by gesture a man being hanged.

"They have n't caught me yet, my dear," he added, "and I 've a wager of five guineas with Ailill O'Conor that I keep my head out of their hands a while longer. Look—what 's that? A stag, as I live!"

He pointed excitedly down to a hollow about a mile away, across which a stag was lopping in the nonchalant fashion of his kind. His gait, and the faint long-drawn music of hound voices, growing momentarily nearer, proclaimed a hunt.

Barry thrust his mare's bridle into Lisronan's hand.

"Here, Aideen—let me put you up," he cried, catching his sister by the waist and lifting her into her saddle without further preamble.

His late audience at the same moment burst forth in twos and threes from the doorless apertures in their huts, and charged down hill *en masse* in the wake of their mentor, giving tongue as vociferously as the hounds.

"Come on! Oh, come on!" shrieked Aideen over her shoulder to Dermot.

She pointed to where the stag flitted like a brown shadow up a long grey ridge, got her cob short by the head, and shot away in pursuit of Barry, whose whole heart and soul were now set on getting a good start. Dermot saw nothing for it but to follow—though this sudden transition from the serious to the trivial both puzzled and displeased him.

Hounds came streaming through the hollow before the trio reached it, heads and sterns level, each one stretched to his utmost. They were a mixed lot—half the black-coated, tan-faced, Kerry beagle, who looks as heavy as a dray-horse and has the speed of a hare; and half the long-legged, grey and white Irish deerhound—as uneven and strange a pack as their followers.

Dermot, glancing back, saw men in fluttering rags on saddleless horses, men in slovenly but costly dress, men who even in the excitement of the gallop eyed each other with enmity.

"Oh, joy! He's heading for Bally Ulick right across Mona Seskin!" panted Aideen gleefully, as they galloped up the opposite lip of the hollow.

She nodded at a long strip of flat ash-coloured country that stretched away to the dark line of the Bally Ulick woods—bog from which the water had gone, and which, once cultivated, was now going back to nature.

Scent never lay well on Mona Seskin, but the

white rank grass which had saved many a fox's
life, showed the stag the more clearly to his pur-
suers. He had increased his pace a little, and his
point was obviously Bally Ulick wood, six miles
away—a prospect intensely delightful to the
FitzUlicks, however the riders of horses already
blown might feel.

.   .   .   .

That gallop remained in Dermot Lisronan's
memory for many a day as the most intensely
typical incident of his return home—a sudden
proof that the most deeply-rooted instinct of
Irish nature, the one national sentiment which
had power to heal for the time all feuds and
make all men kin, existed yet.

Barry, pushing ahead on Kate, his whole heart
and soul in the racing pack, scarcely seemed the
same man who half an hour earlier had addressed
that spell-stricken crowd on the hillside.

Spring sunlight lay palely on the dry bog, striking a glint from its wide rush-fringed gripes, over
which the stag sailed with such deceptive ease,
lighting the cob's patchy black coat and Aideen's
plum-coloured habit, gleaming in Kate's golden
quarters and red-tagged tail.

A man would have lacked all the elements of
youth who could have failed to enjoy that gallop—
the swing of an eager horse's best pace, his shortened stride, pricked ears, and snatch at the rein,
when a drain loomed in front—the soul-stirring
chorus borne backwards on a light wind—the

indescribable elation of it all. Dermot, hard to rouse though he was, responded for once, and put everything behind him except the delight of that glorious thirty-five minutes.

Half an hour at "view" pace is enough for most horses, however light the country may ride, and by the time the stag reached the bank under Bally Ulick wood the tail hounds were a field to the rear of the leaders, and Barry—the nearest man—a field behind the tail hounds. Dermot, when he reached the bank over which the muddy pack had straggled in twos and threes, rendered frantic by the sudden disappearance of their quarry among the brown shadows of the wood, found Aideen and her cob, both thoroughly blown, lying among the rushes at the bottom of the gripe.

"Hurt?—No. Wet?—Yes," laughed Miss Fitz-Ulick in response to Lisronan's anxious query. She dragged several yards of soaked habit-skirt up into the field, adding: "La! What a gallop! I 'd wager a louis the stag has gone across the glen. Oh, here 's Barry turning back. Well, Barry?"

"Not well at all—vastly ill," returned her brother from the wood. "Kate 's pulled off both foreshoes. Devil a yard farther can I go! You look wet, Aideen."

"Nabuclish! We 're only a stone's throw from home. Pray, Barry, and you too, Dermot, make yourselves scarce—I see a white horse coming across Mona Seskin, and it will be Mr. Lavelin—'Burnpriest Lavelin,' as the people call him." There was sudden fear in Miss FitzUlick's tone. "His animosity towards all 'Papists' is past imagining," she added, flinging herself with surprising agility right on to the back of the cob, which Dermot had by this time extricated from the gripe.

She faced him again at the bank, and then as he landed with a grunt in the wood, made an imperious signal to the others and trotted away down a green tunnel of over-arching hollies.

Barry and Dermot followed more slowly, leading their horses, the former excitedly describing in detail various by-gone runs in which stag or fox had elected to cross Bally Ulick glen.

At the back door of Bally Ulick they found Aideen waiting.

"Persuade Dermot to stay with us, Barry," she said. "I must e'en go and change."

"Of course he 'll stay here. Where else should he stay?" answered her brother. "I 'll aid him in his search for the D'Arcy hoard—and share it with him when it 's found."

Dermot, opening the door for Aideen, made no reply. When it had shut again behind her he turned and spoke.

"I 've a score to settle before I find the D' Arcy hoard," he said quietly.

Barry's air of levity dropped from him like a cloak. His eyes, which in colour were a curious shade between green and blue, like sea-water on a wild bright day, became suddenly hard as steel. He, too, understood the saying, "To-day for revenge," and would indeed have been infinitely more remorseless than Lisronan had he stood in Lisronan's shoes.

"I' faith, you have all our good wishes in that matter," he said. "There are those who 'd have settled the score for you, had it been possible to come at Wynykt by any fair means."

"Are there? Saving yourself, Barry, it appears to me the people take his presence easily."

Captain FitzUlick shrugged his shoulders.

"The peasantry are cowed beyond conception," he said. "When men for five or six generations have been ranked as vermin they come at last to seem no more in their own eyes. You remember how Spencer wrote of them?"

Dermot nodded, recalling a certain sentence of the poet's:

"They were brought to such wretchedness that any stony heart would rue the same. Out of every corner of the woods and glens they came creeping forth upon their hands, for their legs could not bear them. They looked like anatomies of death, they spoke like ghosts crying out of their graves. They did eat the dead carrions where they did find them, yea, and one another soon after, inasmuch as the very carcasses they spared not to scrape out of their graves; and if they found a plot of watercresses or shamrocks, there they thronged as to a feast."

"That was a hundred and thirty years ago," said Barry, as though he had been following his companion's train of thought. "Their bodily circumstances have been a little better—not much —since. They are now like to be as bad again whenever the season is severe. As to learning, and the right to live as human beings, they are in no better case now than then. What will another century of such usage make them? There's the question."

Lisronan shook his head dolefully.

"I understand, indeed, why you work to get them out of the country," he said in a mournful voice. "What puzzles me is that any, gentle or simple, stay in it."

"Well, precious few of the old stock of the gentry have remained," returned Barry, "and those who did are almost without exception a pack of hopeless sots. The new-comers seem no better— scarce a man amongst them, be he gentleman, half-sir, or out-and-out buckeen, but is mucabus by noon as regularly as the day comes round. But to go back to what we were saying about that d—d Dutchman. Have you any plan to your end—any scheme devised?"

"None—save to go to his house and challenge the brute. He can hardly refuse to fight."

"Egad then, it's he that will! He lets no strangers cross his threshold lest they should be come to murder him. He sleeps with a plate of iron under the bedclothes. Neither you nor any other man will come into his presence alive, Dermot. You can go to Lisronan, an' you will.

11

You 'll be shot like a stag for your pains and never win within speaking distance of the Dutchman. For myself, I hold you serve your purpose of vengeance better alive—a perpetual menace to Wynykt—than by dying under the skenes of his men. If nought else will serve you, why we 'll take half a score of grey dragoons from the woods of Lisronan and force the house. I ask nothing better."

Dermot shook his head.

"If we did that we 'd have every Protestant from here to Dublin up in arms at once," he answered. " 'T would be made a religious matter. No—I 'll not have half a hundred wretched peasants slaughtered or turned out of their cabins for my concern. This matter lies solely between Wynykt and myself—and I 'll find an issue if I seek for it another twelve years. Nor shall you be dragged in, Barry. You and yours have suffered enough for me as it is."

Barry made a quick gesture of repudiation.

"Not we!" he returned. "Never think that. We suffered because Aideen and I would not conform and because, having no nature for scum, we declined the Dutchman's acquaintance. There were a dozen in like case. Old Mr. De Lacy, the Protestant clergyman—you remember him? He would not countenance Wynykt or his harlots, and the Dutchman saw to it that he paid the penalty—two years in the Tholsel of Dublin, on the plea of a leaning to Popery, and a fine that left

him bare as any church mouse—poor old fellow.
He died two months back, mainly of want. My
own belief, Dermot, is that could we but wipe out
the Dutchman and his infernal crew, we 'd have
the goodwill of every Protestant for a hundred
miles, so greatly are they detested."

Again Lisronan shook his head. With three
years less of life, he had mastered one fact, as
incomprehensible to such a nature as FitzUlick's
as it is to the broader and saner English mind even
now—the bitter fact that only one Irishman in
two thousand wishes to see both sides of a question,
and that that one becomes by the very desire a
pariah.

"Well, you need not heed the matter for a day or
two, for the scoundrel 's gone hence—whither or
why no man knows," said Barry after a second's
silence. "When he returns 't will be time enough
to plan. If one could take one's vengeance as the
peasants do, all would be simple."

CHAPTER XIV

AN CRAOIBHIN DHUN

BARTLEY SULLIVAN, the hedge-schoolmaster, sat under a gorse-crowned bank, composing a poem. Before him a circle of flattened moss bore testimony to his departed pupils. School had broken up earlier than usual to-day, scattered by a rumour that Van der Wynykt's band was about—but any fears Bartley felt on the subject were not for himself. The ragged, ill-fed little man had a true poet's soul. To him the starlit river, the first flush of dawn above the crest of a hill, a spray of young honey-coloured oak leaves swaying in May sunshine, were of more account than any danger.

Love of country burned in his heart like a flame. Ireland to him, as to Hugh O'Donnell, was a "flower of flowers." He wrote her reams of passionate verse; bewailing her cruel past, prophesying a mighty future, pouring out his boundless desire to serve her, in Latin and in the old Erse tongue— which lends itself so readily to poem and malediction and prayer.

His devotion to his native land had indeed only one rival, pride of office. The task of teaching men who must otherwise live and die in ignorance was to him a high privilege, a sacred trust.

In this he represented a type by no means uncommon in those times of stress, when the most diabolical of the Penal Laws, the enactment which denied to a whole nation that right to learn which alone raises man above the beast, was beginning to make itself felt. They fought bitterly against it, those descendants of a race that seven centuries before had given Europe her learning; they fought against it as they fought against the effort to thrust on them a creed unfitted in every essential to the soul of the Irish Celt—but whereas in the one case they succeeded, in the other they failed. The ignorance they so feared overthrew them in the end. The crime is taking "its proper change out still in crime"—and that strange brutal justice, which holds humanity in the balance, has ordained that the innocent descendants of men who sinned wilfully through a hundred and thirty black years should now be among the worst of the sufferers.

Bartley's pupils paid him in kind—when they paid him at all—a griddle cake, a couple of potatoes, a night's lodging. For the most part he lived like Father Talbot, in some crevice of the bog-land or in the far-stretching woods beyond Lough Gulban, holding his classes in glens, under banks, anywhere where Nature gave shelter and covert. To be caught meant death; but all the

hedge-school master prayed, all he sought to compass, was a postponement of that fate until he
had educated a man to be his successor.

He sat now, goose-quill in hand, ink-horn by his
side, looking out west over the dark brown sweep
of the bog. He loved every inch of it—every
rush-fringed pool that mirrored the sky; every
dark green gorse bush, tipped with gold, ashimmer
with the fairy lace of wet cobwebs; the scraghs
vivid as emerald velvet, the little streams that
held pools of sunlight in their amber depths and
laughed to themselves as they ran. From where
he sat he could see right away to an ever-changing
far-off horizon, now pearl grey, now blue as the
heart of the butterwort flower—a matter of more
miles than a horseman would have travelled
comfortably in two days.

This wideness of prospect stirred a chord in
his breast which nothing else could reach. He
wrote here as he wrote nowhere else, touched by
that fire—surely the breath of some old pagan
god—that inspires the outpourings of the Irish
Celt.

He dropped his quill at last, and began to read
the lines aloud to those invisible watchers whose
gaze may be felt in Ireland's loneliest places;
who, unseen and unheard, observe the traveller
with an intentness which must in the end, unless
he be the veriest clod, penetrate his material
senses and touch his soul with a sense of strange
companionship.

Just as Bartley reached the last line, a sound brought him back to earth. He jerked up his head, listening intently.

Somewhere, not far away, a man was singing. The notes came down wind to Sullivan, low-pitched and sweet. He listened a second entranced, and then, in the silent alert fashion of one whose life for ten years has known no security, got to his feet and looked all about.

Some two hundred yards away, a man rode in leisurely fashion through the heather, the reins about his mount's neck, his feet dangling below the stirrups. Bartley noted the admirable cut of his long leather coat, the silver gleam of a sword-hilt, the fact that he wore no peruke under his wide-leaved Spanish hat, and rode a chestnut mare hardly up to his weight, all in a single glance. The next showed him who the newcomer was, and instinctively, mindful of the rumour which had broken up school, he looked all round the bog. He also made haste to drop down again under the shelter of the bank, conscious that "his honour" would certainly, if he saw him, hail him with loud-voiced cheerfulness.

Precautions were not for Barry. Witness the fact that he rode alone through an enemy's country, flaunting the weapon prohibited to Papists and singing as he went!

"God save ye kindly, your honour," murmured Bartley presently, rising like a snipe from under the mare's feet, and speaking in a tone which implied that Barry was putting an undue tax on the Divine Power.

"That you, an craoibhin dhun?" said Captain FitzUlick. He pulled up and smiled at the ragged little man, adding, "Gad, you lay as close as a hare! Where are the lads?"

Bartley dropped his voice to a whisper. "We got 'the word,' Master Barry," he said.

Barry whistled. "Hawks abroad! Eh?"

" 'Deed aye, your honour."

There was a second's silence. The mare rang tunes on her bit and switched an imaginary fly off her quarters, and her rider sat apparently in a reverie.

"I wanted a word with your lads, Bartley," he said after a moment. "I've a message to them. You know it?"

"I know it, sir—I do be keeping it in their thoughts ever and always. But it isn't me they mind—no, nor even his riverence—the way they 'll mind yourself—and that's the truth."

Barry was looking down at the flattened moss where Bartley's pupils had sat.

"A fine land where men must learn and pray by stealth!" he said bitterly, his face hardening into the intense, almost fierce, expression it wore on the rare occasions he was serious.

"Heth! 't is not the land but them that have the ruling of it!" retorted the hedge-schoolmaster.

Barry nodded.

"I 've brought you a book from Paris, craoibhin," he said, slipping a hand into one of his wide flapped pockets and producing a thin brown volume.

Bartley's wizened little face lit with a sudden delight good to see.

"Ah, your honour!" he said, and his outstretched hands were eager as a child's. To him a book was alpha and omega—a treasure to be carried inside his tattered coat, a friend to be cherished above any mere human kinsman.

"You will have read this yourself, Master Barry?" he asked, turning the leaves reverently.

Barry laughed.

"Not I! Never read anything I can help!" he returned. "And as for poetry! I say, Bartley, is there ought moving down there on our right near the Devil's Shoe?"

The hedge-schoolmaster's head, bent in loving survey of the printed pages, came up with a jerk. He glanced anxiously down to where the long ridge of stone known as the Devil's Shoe showed grey against the bog-land.

"Horses!" he said in a frozen whisper, "and men on them! Oh, God save us, Master Barry!"

Barry was looking sharply from side to side.

"A regular circle," he answered grimly. "Look —west, north, and south of us, and closing in at that. Well, I only wish to God I had pistols with me, so that more of these fellows should suffer!"

Bartley, signing himself with his right hand,

deposited his book in some inner receptacle of his coat.

"Light down off the horse, Master Barry," he whispered. "Light down and creep in under the gorse here. Meself 'll take the baste and entice them away. Quick now!"

He laid imperative fingers on Barry's knee as he spoke.

The young man glanced down at him with a smile.

"I believe you would, Bartley," he said, shortening rein and feeling for his stirrups, "and without a question. I must clear out. Get on, Kate!" He drove his heels into the chestnut's sides and she plunged forward snorting. Bartley ran a pace beside her.

"Master Barry! Ah, Master Barry!" he protested.

"They 've seen me," said Barry shortly. "Lie low, Bartley, you fool! They 'll get me yet, and what the devil's the use of their getting you too, man? Slip into the gripe!"

He nodded over his shoulder at a bramble-covered ditch on their right and urged the mare ahead with hands and heels.

Bartley dropped into a walk. A second later he was down under a tangle of leafless briars and last year's bracken, invisible as any water-hen, and praying passionately to his Saint that "his honour" might escape.

Barry was not mistaken in thinking he had been

seen. The glint of his sword-hilt, the gleam of the mare's orange-bright coat were noticeable from a long way off against the bog-land's brown undulations. He had been marked down some time before he reached Bartley's "school," marked and stalked like a stag. Now that the chestnut had begun to gallop the enemy began to gallop too.

Barry saw their intention at once. They were closing in in a semicircle, so as to drive him eastwards down a slope of wet, treacherous heather which led to a precipice. He knew every inch of the place—the heather-fringed cliff, the sheer drop into a gorge, deep, narrow, filled with rowan trees and boulders. To hunt him over like a fox, or pull him down on the edge—either would be good enough sport for these human hounds. He had no illusion about his chances. Press the mare as he might, escape was impossible. Two hundred yards away on either side were the enemy, riding for all they were worth, and drawing together as they came.

"A nut and a nut-cracker," thought the young man with an irrepressible grin at the absurdity of his simile. Existence for him had narrowed suddenly to a question of minutes—a short flight, a flight against overwhelming odds, and—if the gods were good—a chance of selling his life dearly.

The whole place rang with the rattle of hoofs, and the Dutchmen's guttural cries. Some one fired a shot which sent an endless echo reverberating along the ravine and startled a herd of red

deer on the opposite side.   Barry, as he bucketted
Kate recklessly through hock-deep mud and colo-
nies of stones and dry heather-tussocks, glanced
across at them with a fleeting recollection of his
hunt two days before.   Of fear as an emotion he
knew little.   It was represented for him by a
feeling of intense excitement, a fierce quickening
of all his senses.

He became extraordinarily conscious of minor
details of the scene—golden and emerald hues in
the patches of wet moss that stained the slope's
brown surface, a white streak down a horse's nose,
the colours of the coats worn by Van der Wynykt's
men, the blinding glitter of their sunlit steel—
extraordinarily conscious too of that submerged
fibre of his mind which insisted that he saw all
these things for the last time.

The enemy was very near now, almost as near
as the heather-fringed lip of the cliff which cut
across the ever-steepening slope a bare stone's
throw from Kate's nose.   Barry could see through
the tufts the gleam of running water two hundred
feet below.

After a single downward glance, he wrenched
the mare's head round with his left hand.   His
right went to his sword-hilt.   He was not going
over the precipice like a driven stag—not he!

Kate, lunging and slithering, got her hocks under
her and once more broke into a gallop along the
edge of the glen, nose in air, eyes fixed on the
approaching line of horses.

Barry looked at the line too, laughed angrily and pulled her into a walk. Now that they had caught him, further haste became a thing of no avail. These Dutch scoundrels should not say afterwards that he had refused to face them.

His attitude as he jogged along, looking up at them, the reins loose between his fingers, his bared sword agleam in the sunlight, was the epitome of insolent contempt.

A voice cried an order in Dutch. There was a flash of raised pistol barrels, four spurts of pale flame, a crackle of shots.

Barry felt Kate quiver and twist convulsively between his knees—saw the heather flying at him—was conscious of a mad plunge forward, of a crash like a world falling into ruins, and then of complete and overwhelming blackness!

CHAPTER XV

D ERMOT LISRONAN pulled up and looked across the ford to the twisted chimney-stacks of his home and the clustered trees which hid the house.

Here, on this very spot, he had first seen Albrecht Van der Wynykt twelve years before, had shown him where to cross the river, had proffered that hospitality that to the Celt is an instinct. There existed in the young man none of the instinctive avoidance of what is painful so common to youth. He had gone out of his way to see Lisronan House, and he now gave himself up whole-heartedly to bitter melancholy as he sat gazing through the smoke-grey dusk at the trees planted by his father and grandfather.

Twilight was falling on the wide bog, bringing with it that curiously blurred effect peculiar to bog-land after sunset. Though the light seemed strong, still the long chocolate-dark folds, the bent willows, even the little cabins close at hand, had all merged into one dim shadow streaked here and there by a wisp of mist.   An army might have passed an army and been no wiser.

Lisronan, immersed in torturing recollection, did not notice a figure that came hastily across the stepping-stones, vague as a shade against the silvery gleam of fretted water, did not realise another human being was near until a woman's voice whispered to him out of the darkness.

"Your honour," it gasped tremulously; "oh, your honour!"

Dermot looked about him.   "Who is it?" he asked.

A figure wrapped in the familiar dark blue cloak came panting up the slope from the ford.   Lisronan, bent low over his horse's shoulder, saw the face of Aideen FitzUlick's foster-mother, Brigit O'Fallon, who was also sister to Bartley Sullivan.

"Mistress Aideen, your honour!   Mistress Aideen!" she sobbed breathlessly.   "They have her cot!   'T is murdering her they are above on the green walk.   Oh, wirra—wirra!   She would n't mind me—she would n't be said or bid by me when Bartley brought the word that the young master was taken by them.   I 'm after running until I 'm bet up!   I 'm——"

Dermot did not wait for the end of the sentence. The "green walk" was what the country folks called that shrubbery path where he had found Mary Gilpatrick on that terrible night when Wynykt had taken possession of Lisronan.   That

Aideen FitzUlick should be there seemed inconceivable, inexplicable, but since it was so he must get to her with all possible speed.

He rattled his tired horse recklessly across the ford and up the slope beyond, guided by the angry barking of a dog—a sound which changed to frenzied shrieks of agony before he reached the edge of the shrubbery.

As he emerged on the moss-grown path along which he had run, blind with terror, twelve years earlier, he saw a trio of figures—Miss FitzUlick and two stout lubberly boys of about eighteen.

Aideen, hatless and dishevelled, her hair untied, her gown torn and twisted, was fast in the arms of the bigger youth, fighting like a wild cat against his efforts to embrace her, and beating at his red, silly face with impotent hands. The other had just succeeded in pinning her spaniel to the ground with a skene.

Neither noticed Dermot when he burst out from the undergrowth bent low over his garron's neck. Aideen herself hardly realised his advent until her assailant's arms fell suddenly from about her and he crashed down in a quivering heap at her feet. Her anxieties were all for the dog. She ran to it without a glance at Dermot, or a thought for the second youth, who had turned to run.

Lisronan had eventually to touch her on the shoulder to gain attention.

"Hurt? I myself? Oh, no!" she panted.

"But look at poor Sheelagh. Look how her leg is bleeding. Oh, the brutes!"

"I 'll tie up that cut if you 'll hold Lugach," said Dermot, thrusting the rein into her hand.

Aideen, breathless and shaken, obeyed him mechanically. The boy who had tried to embrace her was still lying where he had fallen—an inert senseless mass.

"Have you killed him?" she whispered. "Oh, Dermot, you have not killed him?"

"What brought you here?" he asked shortly, still absorbed in his half-spent fury.

Instead of answering, Aideen pointed suddenly to a clump of laurel a yard away. There, pale, trembling, wild-eyed, stood Julia Van der Wynykt, staring from the body to the agitated couple on the path.

She too whispered Aideen's question, "Have you—have you killed him?" in a voice barely audible.

Dermot, without answering, lifted Sheelagh in his arms and walked back to where the youth lay.

"Is he a kinsman?" he demanded.

"My half-brother—the son of my father's kept woman," said Julia almost inaudibly. "Oh, go—go away, both of you, before our men come!" she went on, creeping a little nearer. "They will kill you! My father is away—but if Minna sees Albrecht like this she will have you both shot. And Jan—you caught Jan and beat him sorely. He screamed."

Dermot, to whom she addressed the last words, glanced at his hunting crop. He had used it with such vigour that it was in splinters.

Aideen FitzUlick shivered violently.

"My brother! Oh, Mistress Van der Wynykt, do you know aught of my brother?" she asked, putting a quivering hand on the other girl's sleeve. "Your step-brothers would tell me nothing! nothing!"

Julia shook her head. She was obviously frightened out of her senses.

"Go—go—I hear them coming!" she repeated, with her eyes still fixed on Dermot.

"I hear nothing," said Lisronan impatiently. "What ails Barry, Aideen? And how came you here, in God's name?"

Miss FitzUlick looked dubiously at Julia.

"I 'll explain anon," she answered. "Take Lugach and give me Sheelagh. My cob has made off—doubtless he 's half-way home by now."

She turned her back on Miss Van der Wynykt as she spoke and cuddled the whining spaniel in her arms.

Dermot glanced at Julia. "He is only stunned, Madame," he said, mistaking the cause of her agitation. She made a quick gesture of repudiation. "Save for the danger to you, my lord, I would be glad if he were dead—dead!" she whispered fiercely. "No one shall know 't was you— I will tell them nought—only pray, pray go hence. Jan has run off, he may return at any moment!"

"Yes—do come," said Aideen, who meant willy-nilly to get Lisronan away. "I'm afraid to go home alone."

Dermot bit his lip. Flight was the very last finish to the affair which he would have chosen, but he could not abandon Aideen—and to keep her on the scene until Wynykt's men arrived was the act of an idiot.

He turned to Lugach, pulled the offside stirrup over, and shortened the near side leather.

"I'll carry Sheelagh," he said curtly, offering Aideen his hand to mount.

Julia watched wistfully while he settled her in the saddle.

"I—I—will not tell them," she muttered as he lifted the spaniel.

He looked at her with surprise in his eyes.

"But of course you'll tell them, Madame. Why not?" he said.

The colour flamed suddenly in the girl's white cheeks, her lips quivered.

"Pray come, Dermot," said Aideen.

She turned Lugach in among the undergrowth and rode off, sitting with as much ease and confidence as if she had been in side-saddle. Dermot, after a slightly perplexed glance at Julia, followed.

"Now, Aideen—the answer you would not give me five minutes back?" he demanded in rather a peremptory manner when he overtook the horse. "What brought you in this *galère?*"

"Barry!" answered Aideen, her voice growing all at once husky and piteous. "They have taken him prisoner. They hold him fast in Lisronan House—and we can do nothing—nothing—and they 'll kill him!" The last word was a sob.

"Oh, Dermot, help me—help me to get him out of their hands!" she whispered suddenly, in a tone of passionate appeal.

"Nay, I hardly think you need ask that!" he returned. "Tell me first how he was taken and what Sir Martin has done. We are safe enough here. 'T is all but dark, and I know every inch of this land."

Aideen repeated word for word the story Bartley Sullivan had told them when he reached Bally Ulick two hours after Barry's capture.

"My father took horse and rode straight away to Lisronan," she said. "A vain effort, seeing that Albrecht Van der Wynykt has no bitterer enemy in all Ireland. Yes—you spoke?"

"I said, 'he has one,' but go on. Van der Wynykt is away—I suppose Sir Martin saw the—er—the woman who I 'm told keeps his house! the mother of those clods?"

Aideen nodded.

"He did. She laughed, sneered, insulted him! You may imagine how such a creature would meet an appeal from an avowed enemy. She swore to my father that Barry should be brought home at daybreak to-morrow morning and hanged on the beech near the house—that tree we used to

climb when we were children. She is as brutal
as Wynykt himself!"

The girl paused to choke back a sob. Dermot,
hearing the desolate little sound, glanced up at her.
His face in the half-light looked aged and set and
bitter, but his melancholy eyes softened as they
met hers.

"You have courage, Mademoiselle," he said
gently.

"Courage!" she repeated. "Mayhap. I' faith,
I think when Ireland was created first the gods
knew how sorely the Irish race would need courage,
and gave us of that one gift unstintingly. But,
to return to Barry. I thought perchance Frau
Viebert would hearken to a woman when she
was deaf to a man—so I set out straightway for
Lisronan."

"Without your father's consent, I assume?"

"I did not tell him. But indeed, Dermot, he
hardly knows what is going on round him. He's
like a demented man. As a last resource, he has
gone to Dick Conway and Major Sugrue of Sugres-
town to beg their assistance—but neither will
interfere."

"No Justice of the Peace dare," said Dermot.
" 'T would be more than his life was worth under
these new laws. The suspicion of being disaffected
is enough. Did you see the Viebert woman,
Aideen?"

Miss FitzUlick shivered. "I saw her—I had
speech with her. 'T was she called those two

dreadful youths and bade them—Oh, don't let us talk of it! I was well-nigh mad when I set out for Lisronan—I knew 't would be of no avail, but I would leave no chance untried. To think of Barry in their hands——!"

"Do not!" said Dermot quickly. "We shall find a way to save him yet—you and I!"

For a few minutes after his words there was silence, broken only by the soft thud of hoofs on the turf and the creak of the saddle.

"I am for appealing to the outlaws—the grey dragoons," said Aideen suddenly. "A big band of them live in the woods beyond Monadarrig bog—the settlers hold them in great awe. Our difficulty would be to get word to them in time. Bartley knows where they lie mostly, but even he cannot tell for sure. What think you of that?"

Dermot shook his head. "As a last resource, mayhap," he said. " 'T would spell absolute ruin to your father—nay more, it might cost his life and Barry's unless they were very prompt in escaping from the country. No, an idea has struck me—I 'll tell it you when we are over the ford."

He pointed down at the river, which gleamed before them in the dusk like a dull silver ribbon, and taking Lugach's rein waded across beside him through the swift, waist-high water.

"Now listen, Aideen," he went on in French just above his breath, as they climbed the bank on the opposite side. "I know a way into Lis-

ronan.   The ivy still grows over the southern side,
I take it, as it used to do?"

"Yes."

"Good.   Do you remember the little window of
the still-room that was so masked with ivy-sprays
on the outside that none could see it, and that had
for shutter on the inside a sliding panel in the wall
—the invisible window we used to call it as children?   Unless some one has shown them the secret
of it, it 's twenty chances to one they 've never
realised a window is there at all.   If so, I 'll go
in by it."

"Certainly every other window in the house has
iron gratings set before it these two years past,"
said Aideen dubiously.   "I cannot speak for this
one.   And when you are in, Dermot?"

Dermot was silent for a second.

"I must leave that to chance," he said, with
a frown of reluctance.   That favourite action
of his countrymen never had commended—never
could commend—itself to him, but in this case
there appeared to be no other course.

"The girl might help you, perchance," said
Aideen in a slow reflective tone.   "She has the
will to."

"The daughter, do you mean?   *Dieu*, what an
idea!"

"Do not despise it, if you find yourself in difficulties," she retorted drily.   "A friend within the
citadel is worth having."

"A friend—that man's daughter a friend!"

Aideen smiled a grim little smile.

"She is a girl—and you are a man, and likely enough the first of gentle birth she has ever seen," she said. "A woman's judgment is worth something sometimes, my lord."

Before Dermot could answer, Aideen's foster-mother rose up out of the heather like a spectre.

"Are you hurted, alanna—are you hurted at all?" she whispered, coming close to Lugach and beginning to feel her whilom nursling all over with anxious hands.

Lisronan realised, as he had never realised before, the strength of that tie of fosterage which all through Ireland had bound class to class, and clansmen to chief, ever since Conchobar reigned over Connacht. He had no personal experience of it, for his mother had declined to put him out to nurse.

Aideen, bent over Lugach's shoulder, was whispering in rapid Erse in Mrs. O'Fallon's ear.

"Brigit says she can get you three men if you want them for to-night, Dermot," she said presently, turning to him. "Bartley Sullivan, old Shaun Ronan, and her own son Denis, Barry's foster-brother. You can trust all three to the death."

CHAPTER XVI

JULIA

JULIA VAN DER WYNYKT stopped on her way upstairs and peered timidly through the hinge of the dining-room door, which stood ajar. An hour earlier, hidden behind a curtain in the long gallery, she had heard details of what was to be done with Barry FitzUlick—details too sickening to recall.

She would have given a year of life for courage to steal the cellar key and release the young man— but courage of any sort had been denied her. From her mother she inherited timidity of so exaggerated a type that it verged on a mental warp. Her days were spent in avoiding her father, her step-brothers, and the woman who at present ruled Lisronan, Minna Viebert—a handsome Dutch virago, with a temper that matched her morals.

Looking through the crack, Julia could see two of the quartet of whom she was so terrified— Minna, decked out in tawdry spoils of war, with pearl drops that had once been Ethna Lisronan's in her large red ears; Jan, more than half drunk, his silly face flushed crimson, his eyes glazed. Willy, her one friend and protector, had gone off three days before, where, no one knew.

Julia shivered from head to foot and crept away up the shallow stairs. Her room was hardly more than a closet—a little oak-lined place isolated from the main body of the house by a flight of narrow steps, and almost unfurnished. Minna Viebert, with a spite not altogether common in women of her type, lost no chance of humiliating the daughter of her paramour. Everything of mental vexation and physical discomfort that feminine ingenuity could devise was Julia's lot. The girl's very meekness had been twisted into a rope to scourge her.

She crept into her room now with nervous, furtive haste, and, having bolted the door, spent a second in intent listening. Then, reassured by the silence, she dropped on one knee and began to feel along the surface. Dark though it was, a very little groping found her the spring she sought. A minute space of the panelling slipped back, and she drew forth from the tiny cupboard behind, rushlight and tinder-box.

Candles to go to bed by were among the many things forbidden by Minna Viebert. Julia had to arrange an old cloak carefully along the bottom of the door lest any thread of gold should betray her, before she dared to strike flint. Her worst nightmare was always that Minna would discover

this "cache," the most treasured secret of her
life. It held a store of rushlights—Willy's gift—
an old silver rosary which had belonged to Julia's
mother, and something even dearer—a small flat
parcel wrapped in a bit of brocade.

The girl drew this out now with stealthy noiseless movements, unfolding the stuff reverently.
Within it, set in diamonds that shot tongues of
blue and green and scarlet fire at the candle, was
a miniature of Ethna Lisronan. Years and years
before, Julia had found it in a bureau and had
venerated it because of its beauty. Lately, since
the Mass in Kylenoe, it had possessed a fresh
interest for her.

A single glance had told her who Dermot Lisronan was. His eyes were the eyes of her cherished
miniature. He had spoken to her, had treated
her as no man had ever spoken to or treated her
before. Such friends as Albrecht Van der Wynykt
could boast, were not of a chivalrous type. Coarse
compliments, suggestions that made her hot to
remember, unveiled insults, had been her portion
at their hands. Indeed, only the presence of
Willy Van der Wynykt had saved his sister from
the worst ignominy that can befall a woman. And
now Willy was gone! The thought sent a shiver
through her as she once more looked down at
the miniature.

It was a beautiful likeness, and beautifully
executed. The painter had caught the smile in
Ethna's soft eyes, the dawn of it on her sensitive

mouth, the pure tints of her skin.   Julia, though
she was not blessed with imagination, unless it
were in the conception of garments, was able to
picture Lady Lisronan as clearly as if she had
seen her.

And she became a person of infinite interest
now, this mother of the first man except Willy
who had inspired Julia with any sentiment other
than panic-stricken disgust. Unimaginative, un-
educated, and wholly unawakened to the possibility of happiness though she was, the girl had
all the makings of a sentimentalist. She would
have gladly worshipped a hero had she realised
the existence of such a thing. At present Willy
and Father Talbot filled her horizon, but her
reverence in both cases was tinged by fear, and
she dreaded inexpressibly lest one day some mention of the priest should slip from her by accident.

Dermot stood quite apart. The thought of how
he had looked at and spoken to her was like the
sight of an unexpected fire to a half-frozen traveller. Her mind went back and back to it. Half
a dozen times each evening since the memorable
day, she had stolen to her hiding-place, drawn
out Ethna's miniature, and looked long at the only
point of resemblance between mother and son—
the eyes, which were so like in colour and shape,
and so unlike in expression. An imaginative
woman might have woven a romance for herself
out of the affair; but Julia had no imagination.
She scarcely thought of any future meeting. All

her fancies were centred in that three minutes
on the hillside above Kylenoe.

Even his action in saving Willy's life—a fact
unwillingly related by Willy, who was very sore
on the subject—counted for less in her eyes than
his trivial courtesy to herself. Any man would
of course wish to save Willy, any of her father's
terrible, sottish, brutalised friends might—nay
would—have done the same; but to be polite to
Willy's sister—that was indeed a miracle!

It was fear for Dermot which had made her
interpose between him and her half-brother—an
action so foreign to her nature that she wondered
at it herself. Fierce determination to shield
Dermot at any cost had further prompted her to
lie flagrantly when appealed to for a description
of Jan's assailant. Woman-like, she cared nothing
that a Dutch tenant, already in disgrace for having
displayed resentment at Van der Wynykt's rela-
tions with his wife, should pay the penalty. As
long as Lisronan escaped the rest of Ireland might
perish. She had not meant to describe the man—
or any man—but his name was suggested to her,
and the suggestion helped an imagination never
strong and just then further weakened by fear.

The remembrance was unpleasant. She put it
from her and let her thoughts revert to the tall
grey-eyed figure who had helped her on the hillside above Kylenoe. Once more she slowly
recalled every item of his dress, every line of his
face. It gave her a curious pleasure to think even

of the buttons on his coat. There had been, as she remembered with vague surprise, no gaps amongst them; neither tear nor stain in the coat itself. Plainly, he differed greatly from the dishevelled gentlemen who now and then spent twenty-four stupefied hours under her father's table, or even from Willy.

Mechanically, still thinking of him, she replaced the miniature and began at last to unfasten her threadbare gown. She had just got it off when a sudden low tap at the door made her jump.

"Who—who's there?" she asked in a trembling voice, with an agonised glance at the panel that hid the cache.

The only answer was another and more imperative tap.

"Minna!" thought the girl, beginning to shake in every limb. She lost her head completely, as was her wont under the influence of fear, forgot the prohibited rushlight, forgot to put on her gown, forgot everything but the blow which would fall on her if she kept Minna Viebert waiting.

Directly she drew the bolt, an impatient hand pushed the door open, and Julia, white to the lips, backed away before it.

"Oh, Madame—" she began in a whimper, and then: "Oh, mercy, 't is—'t is not Madame!"

Dermot Lisronan, who had stopped on the threshold to glance back over his shoulder down the dark staircase, looked at her.

"I fear I frightened you, Madame," he said in

a low voice. "I have come to take away Barry FitzUlick—and I need your help."

Julia clasped her hands convulsively.

"Oh—you will be killed!" she whispered. "My father's men will kill you. How—how did you get in?"

"By a window. Never heed your father's men, Mistress Van der Wynykt. Is Barry in the low cellar—the one that floods?"

The girl nodded. Standing there against the light, with her white arms and neck bare, and her hair curling about her shoulders in pale gold waves, she looked like some old picture of the Blessed Virgin.

"Is the key in the Viebert woman's keeping?"

"Yes."

Dermot frowned. Already he had peered into the dining-room and seen Minna asleep among a round dozen of guardians. To venture in was to ensure immediate death—and immediate death meant not only that Barry would die too, but that Van der Wynykt would go scathless.

"I must have that key, Madame. Will you get it for me?" he said, as coolly as if he had been asking Julia to hand him something.

"I! Oh, no, no!" she answered in a frozen whisper. A spasm of terror puckered her face for a second. "Oh, I never would dare!" she moaned.

"I hate to ask such a thing of you; but the door being of iron one can't break it. It must be unlocked," he said, in his matter-of-fact fashion.

"There are two men on guard in the passage!"

"I know that."

Julia twisted her hands together.

"Oh, go! Go away while you may. You can-not save him. You will only die too!" she said, beginning to cry.

"I shall not go without Barry. If you won't help me, I must e'en try to get the key for myself. Listen. If I get the key and can do no more, could you—would you—have courage to——"

She interrupted him with a gesture of horror.

"Minna Viebert has a dozen to guard her!" she gasped.

"Do you think I should have troubled you otherwise, Madame? 'T is solely because—should they kill me—Barry's last chance is gone."

"You will—will go in amongst those men, those brutes?"

He nodded impatiently and turned, but before he had descended a step Julia's hand plucked at his sleeve.

"Lord Lisronan—I should suffer terribly if I did this thing. Minna would—nay, I know not what she might not do to me," she said.

Dermot glanced round.

"Could I save you—spare you—Madame?" he asked. "I mean—would you be willing I should? Would you permit it?"

"Oh—willing!" she exclaimed. "But would you protect me from *them?*"

"Of course. To the uttermost extent of my power."

They looked at one another in silence for a second—he gravely preoccupied, but sincere beyond question; she fluttering with a sudden mad hope of escape—eternal escape—from the brutal tyranny of her life.

"You promise to stand between me and their anger? To save me harmless? You promise it most truly?" she faltered, shaken by fear and yet willing to adventure, after the fashion of the sex.

"I swear it on the rood!" he answered.

Julia glanced back at the bed. "I will but slip into my gown and then come," she said, pushing him to the door.

Dermot, left outside in the darkness, stood perfecting his plans when he should have the key. It went desperately against the grain, this appeal to a woman—and that woman the enemy's daughter—but there had been no other way out. And though he would have given his life for Barry's gladly had it been feasible, would have gone in his calm self-contained fashion to destruction if his destruction had furthered matters, he was too practical a man to sacrifice his friend's one chance to a sentiment. But it said much for the dominance of what Ethna had called "the English side of him"; for this furtive re-entry into his own house, and the sight of what the usurper had made of that house, hurt horribly. In his country's expressive phrase, he was "spoiling for the fight"

13

which common-sense and his debt to Sir Martin prohibited.

"I regret this, Madame, more than I can say," he said rather abruptly, as Julia stole out of her room.

"I only hope I shall succeed," she sighed. "If I fail, what then?"

She looked up at him miserably, her long straight lashes damp with unshed tears. The thought of what her father's men would do to him came near to unnerve her utterly.

Barry FitzUlick in the same position would have assured her that she could not fail, or else laughed and shrugged his shoulders. Dermot frowned.

"You are naturally somewhat fearful, I take it," he said. "Yes? Well, in that case, your present agitation will be less noticed. I am nearly certain that the keys are lying on the table close to Viebert, and beside a big pasty. I saw something there that looked like the worked handle of the cellar key."

"Close to Minna?" repeated Julia blankly. "Oh—I—I—don't think I dare face it. If she were to wake!"

"You fear her so much?"

The girl nodded. "I—I—I—cannot!" she whispered.

A shadow of bitter disappointment clouded Lisronan's already grave face.

"To your room then—at once, Madame," he

said. " 'T is useless that you should be implicated
if you cannot help."

"You—you are angry with me, my lord?"

He shook his head, touched by the pathetic
despair in her tone.

"Angry—no, no! The mistake was mine. Go
back to your room—and bolt your door."

Julia hesitated a second longer, her inherent
cowardice struggling with certain instincts inherited from men who had been James Taaffe's
forefathers, but who had not resembled him in
any way.

"No—I will do it!" she said suddenly, gathering
up her gown. "You will wait, I suppose, at the
foot of the stairs?"

"No. I 'll come to the threshold."·

"Oh, but—but——"

"The gallery is unlit."

Julia made no response to this last remark.
With every step she descended her heart beat
harder and her knees shook more.

When at last they reached the dark gallery, and
saw the narrow streak of light from the half-open
dining-room door lying like a gold bar on the
shadowy floor, she could hardly stand.

Dermot felt her clutch at his wrist with ice-cold
trembling fingers, and took her hand in his as
though she were a frightened child. The warm
steady clasp did something to help her, but when
they came to the threshold and stood in the light,
he saw that she was the colour of chalk.

She clung to him a second, quivering in every limb, and then signed herself on forehead and breast and crept into the room.

Dermot, from where he stood, could only see the head of the table and the chairs in which Van der Wynykt's sons and their mother lounged in a drunken stupor. He averted his eyes from Minna Viebert. The sight of the creature at his mother's table, and wearing on her breast a pearl cross that had been his mother's, was almost beyond endurance. The Celt in him craved for power to thrust her, female though she was, into a fire and hold her there.

Neither the youths nor Minna Viebert stirred at Julia's entrance, but Dermot heard one of the armed serving-men, who flanked the table six a side, challenge her.

"How now, Mistress?" he said insolently in foreign English. "Der vorships did not summon you?"

Julia's voice, soft and trembling, came to Lisronan's ear. He noticed in the curious detached fashion of a man whose mind is at the uttermost pitch of tension, that it was a pretty voice, and not in the least like her father's.

"I—I—had no supper—I am hungry," she said. "I knew there was food here."

She spoke in little breathless terrified gasps, but the fact did not seem to surprise Van der Wynykt's body-guard—and Dermot drew his own inferences as to her usual treatment.

She stole into his line of vision, creeping along on tiptoe towards the place where the big pasty stood among a muddle of dirty plates. Dermot saw her pull it towards her, spoon some on to a dish, and then stretch her arm over the dish towards a pile of small cakes beyond. The lawn frills of her sleeves trailed upon the food, hiding what she had chosen.

She left the pasty awry and turned to the door, carrying her dish with its strangely-assorted contents.

The men watched her departure apathetically. Most of them were well disposed towards her in a mild way, and the two or three who possessed Albrecht Van der Wynykt's temperament and would have tormented her for sheer lust of cruelty, were the exception.

She staggered a little as she walked out, and forgot that Dermot had given particular instructions about shutting the door until he reminded her of it by a quick gesture.

When she had pulled it to, and while he was working with careful fingers at the bolt, which might so easily betray them, she stood by whimpering under her breath like a child.

Mechanically she turned when he turned, mechanically crept beside him back to the staircase; but on the first step collapse seemed to seize her.

"They will kill me to-morrow!" she said in a ghastly whisper, sinking into a heap at the young man's feet.

He heard the clink of pewter on wood, as her dish fell against the banisters.

"They have not moved. Their suspicions are not roused yet," he murmured after a moment of intent listening.

Julia's only answer was a sob. In the faint owl-light from the uncurtained stair-head window, Dermot could just see her, a vague blur on the white stairs.

"They will kill me," she said again inaudibly.

The young man paused a second longer to extricate the cellar key from cakes and piecrust. Then he bent, took the girl in his arms, and carried her upstairs to her own room.

She made no effort to resist, but lay inert, her head against his shoulder, her slender body shaken by sobs.

"I know they will kill me!" she repeated, as he laid her down on her bed.

Lisronan pulled a bent French coin out of his pocket.

"See here, Mademoiselle," he said gently. "If you need me, send this to Pouldarrig. Doubtless you 've some messenger you can trust? I will be here within an hour of receiving it."

Julia raised herself, glanced at the coin, looked up at him eagerly.

"You would come here? You would face the risk?" she asked in a tone curiously blended of bewilderment and joy. "To—to save me?"

"It would be a small return, Madame, for what you have done for me to-night," he answered.

Her eyes dilated nervously.

"I will send your token if—if they suspect me," she muttered. "I fear they will—nay, I know it. You are going straight to the cellar, my lord?"

"At once."

The ordinary usages of society were a sealed book to Julia. She put out a tentative hand in a hesitating fashion and blushed a vivid rose-pink when Lisronan kissed it with the grave courtesy of his adopted land.

"I am more grateful to you than I can ever express," he said, looking down into her bright, wet eyes. "I trust you will let me show it by summoning me if the need arises."

He slipped his hand from under hers, turned, and was gone.

Julia, as she watched the door close behind him, laid her cheek against the fingers which his lips had touched.

The bent coin lay still in her lap where he had placed it, a little shining spot against her thread-bare gown. She took it up with reverent touch, held it in her palm for a second, and then kissed it passionately. It was his gift—a link between him and her. Whatever need might arise, she would not part with it while life lasted.

But it was characteristic of her, that though anxiety tore her heart, and a terrible fear for Dermot overrode even her fear for herself, she lacked courage to steal downstairs, or even to listen in the passage outside her room.

Huddled under the bedclothes, with the door bolted, she lay through the interminable night hours, shivering, weeping, praying—alternately pressing both hands over her ears and over her eyes, and shaken by such a violence of terror that it bordered on mania.

CHAPTER XVII

THE HOUSE OF LISRONAN

A SHORT flight of stairs led down into that passage outside the low cellar, where the two men mentioned by Julia Van der Wynykt were on guard. Dermot from the darkness of the top step scrutinised these closely.

They sat together, with their backs against the cellar door, a burly pair of Dutch vagabonds, unshaved, unkempt, clothed in motley rags, and armed to excess. Two rushlights, stuck awry on a wooden holder, illumined their feet—one pair in burst boots, the other wrapped in strips of cloth—a square of the stone floor, a dirty pewter plate, and a single noggin. The rest was vague, dim, a mere blur of shadow on shadow.

Lisronan, from where he stood, could not even tell if the pair were asleep. The single noggin suggested that Minna Viebert had taken precautions. He had no time for speculation. Any moment, those in the dining-room might discover the locked door and guess that the enemy was

within their gates. All depended on quickness
of thought, quickness of action.

In his passage through the long gallery he had
unhooked from its place on the wall, the ancient
short-handled, smooth-headed iron mace which
he now held in his right hand. To fire a shot was
out of the question, but this weapon might well
prove of infinite service.

His youthful knowledge of the ground stood
him in good stead as he began very stealthily to
creep down the five uneven steps under cover of
the darkness. From the bottom to where the
Dutchmen sat, was a bare horse's length—a single
stride for an active man. He came along it
delicately as ever Agag walked in the court of
Samuel, the mace poised for a blow which would
stun his man outright.

Just as he got within striking distance, the
farther off of the two guards looked up,
stared for the fraction of a second incredulously, and then made a snatch at the rushlight
holder.

Before he could reach it or get to his knees,
a dull thud reverberated through the passage.
He saw his companion's body topple grotesquely
forward on to its outstretched legs, and found a
pistol barrel within an inch of his own face.

"A word and I shoot!" said Lisronan in Platt
Dutch. "Hands up!"

He brought the mace sharply down on the
man's right hand, which had gone instinctively

to his belt. The Dutchman with a sharp yelp of
pain backed against the wall.

"Ze grey dragoon—ze damn Irische!" he gasped,
seeing in his unknown assailant the spectre which
more or less haunted all the settlers.

"Unlock that door," said Dermot, dropping the
cellar key on the flags. "Quick—unless you want
a bullet in you!"

Van der Wynykt's fellow wanted nothing less.
He was convinced that the rapparees had seized
Lisronan and that his one chance of safety lay
in compliance.

"Mercy, Mynheer! 'Ave pity on von poor
man," he whined, as he lifted the key into its hole,
more than ever convinced by the sight of it that
enemies held the house. "I vill aid you, Mynheer
—I vill tell all I know."

Dermot pointed to the rushlight.

"Pick it up and go before me!" he commanded
curtly, remembering of old that this lower cellar,
hollowed out of the rock, flooded in a mysterious
manner whenever the river was high. It dated
from some far older building than the present
house, and was a veritable dungeon, low-roofed,
unlit, haunted by rats.

The door, swinging back through the ink black
pool which lapped at the threshold, made a swish
like the prow of a boat. Twin spots of green fire,
that had glowed by the dozen together on ledges
of the damp walls, vanished before the sound.

For a second Dermot could see nothing but the

rushlight's broken reflections, spreading in golden circles about the water. Then with the moving forward of the light he became aware of a dark bulk, chest-deep in water.

Barry FitzUlick, trussed like a fowl in coil upon coil of narrow rope, knelt against the wall, or rather hung forward from it on a chain that passed under his armpits and fastened to a ring behind him. Twenty-four hours of intense cold, joined to the torment of the ropes, had made him look scarcely human. His blood-smeared, contorted face was the colour of lead and set in a snarl of agony. He blinked at the light, but showed no other sign of life.

"We hold the house, Barry," said Dermot, for the benefit of the light-bearer, as he waded through the ice-cold water that rippled against the knees of his boots.

"Set the light on that ledge, fellow, and cut these infernal ropes!" he added curtly, his pistol still in his hand and his ears strained for any sound from above.

It seemed to him an eternity before the last spiral strand of taut hemp splashed down into the water, and let the captive topple over, numb and helpless as a corpse. Lisronan realised his condition with something akin to despair. This incapacity to move was a contingency on which he had not counted. It increased the danger forty-fold. It precluded any chance of going back to reassure Julia—as he had thought of doing.

His whole energy would be needed, firstly to get his friend out of the house, and secondly to support him on the horse which Shaun Ronan was to have ready outside the still-room window.

He watched in a frenzy of impatience a writhing attack of cramp that preceded the re-circulation of blood through FitzUlick's dead limbs. It seemed to Lisronan that that contorted figure would never cease to twist and writhe, and jerk out broken disjointed oaths in a harsh whistle of agony.

The Dutchman, who had again laid hold of the rushlight, was shaking visibly. His shadow danced in a grotesque manner over the rock wall, and the gleam on the pool ran to and fro like a live thing.

"It 's time we got you forth from this wet place, Barry," said Dermot, as the spasm at last showed signs of abating. "Come!"

He put an arm round FitzUlick, and half carried, half impelled him forward—a process assiduously aided by Wynykt's man, who saw only one hope of escape.

"You vill not forget me, Mynheer—an honest poor fellow alvays villing to aid your honour," he whined. "You vill not let dem Irische kill me. Nein?"

Dermot made no response to this request until Barry was propped against the passage wall. Then he turned.

"Back with you!" he said shortly, pointing to the cellar doorway; "and for your own sake keep a silent tongue in your head should any seek to break down this door. Quick!"

He twitched the rushlight holder out of the Dutchman's hand as he spoke, pushed him down the cellar steps, and turned the key in the lock.

"Do we indeed hold the house?" whispered Barry, staring perplexedly at the huddled body on the flags.

Dermot shook his head.

"I came by the window of the still-room—we must go that way," he muttered. "Give me what help you can, Barry. The need's pressing."

No more was said on either side. FitzUlick, propped by the wall on one hand and by Dermot on the other, made what progress he could up the stairs and along the passage to the disused still-room; but it was an agonising business, and a very slow one.

Just as they at last stumbled over the threshold, a thud and a muffled shout came dully to their ears.

"They 've found the dining-room door locked against them," said Dermot between his teeth. "We must hasten in our going. Our way is by the casement."

He let Barry go, and made a dart at the still-room window, blowing out both rushlights as he did so. A second later a square of faint grey appeared in the black wall.

FitzUlick remembered his passage through that aperture for many years—the pain, the acute and

ignominious helplessness that possessed him, the
element of absurdity which haunted it as it haunts
all Irish happenings, even when they are to the
last degree tragic. He was conscious of Dermot
pushing vehemently at his head, of hands tugging
no less vehemently at his right ankle, of strenuous
breathing, and the clink of a horse's bit—and then
of falling heavily astride a saddle and being saved
from a further fall by the clutch of a second pair
of hands upon his left knee.

Dermot paused a second on the window-sill,
torn by a fierce temptation to go back—to lurk
in the house until Van der Wynykt returned, and
force a fight on him. He had waited so long. It
was more than flesh and blood could bear, this
slipping into his old home by stealth, and slipping
forth again leaving his vengeance unaccomplished.
Sooner or later Wynykt would come back—if he
were not lying hidden in the building now, which
Dermot half suspected.

The voice of Bartley broke in on his
thoughts.

"We're needing you, sir," it whispered imperatively up the wall. "We're needing you to
lead the garron, an' he with rags on his feet an'
all!"

Dermot swore under his breath. Sir Martin's
claim, he knew, came first of all the claims that
could be made on him—Sir Martin, who at infinite
risk, and to his own great detriment, had succoured
Ethna Lisronan.

He slipped forth into the grey March night, which, fortunately for him, was very dark, and without a word took the pony's bridle and led him away towards the shrubbery.

CHAPTER XVIII

THE PRICE

DUSK was falling over Pouldarrig Tower. A cold spring storm—its fury nearly spent—hurled itself in shrill gusts against the old building, filling the small upper room in which Barry Fitz-Ulick sat with as many strange sounds as a straining ship.

The young man cursed the continued creak and clatter. It interrupted his slumbers. Irritably he flung a sod of turf on the fire. Though a day had elapsed since his release, the chill of those twelve hours waist deep in ice-cold water seemed to have got into his very bones. He turned painfully, and yet with eagerness, as Dermot came in.

"Well, Barry, how do you find yourself?" asked Lisronan in his unemotional fashion. "Fit to ride to-night?"

"I could—but I'd rather not. Why?"

"Well, a despatch has just come for me from Paris—sent forward by a courier. All leave is cancelled from this day week."

Barry whistled. "By gad, that touches me

too," he said. "Shall we win into France inside seven days, think you, Dermot?"

"We may—an' we start to-night—no later than two o'clock I would counsel."

"D—n it!" said FitzUlick, stretching himself as best he could. "I 'll be ready. This means leaving the score unsettled, I take it?" he added, with a tentative glance at Lisronan, who nodded.

"He is still away—I could not come by him—but I shall return," he said grimly.

Barry slipped lower in his chair.

"He had news of your coming," he remarked.

"He shall not—next time."

Dermot turned towards the door as he spoke.

"Devil sweep these Frenchmen!" grumbled Barry. "Three years without furlough, and then to be recalled at once! Anything 's good enough for the 'mere Irishry!' Wonder what sort of night we shall have?"

He got up stiffly as Dermot crossed the threshold, and dragged himself to the window—a narrow unglazed slit protected by a leather curtain. The cold evening breeze whined petulantly through the aperture, ruffling his hair.

He leant on the breast-high, fan-shaped inner sill and reviewed some of the thoughts which had forced themselves on his unwilling mind the previous night, when he lay twisted by pain and in hourly expectation of death. He rather wished that Dermot had not returned dungeonwards to his probings and rootings after the D' Arcy hoard.

It was curiously lonely and depressing up here in
the swift-footed silent dusk, even to a man who
rarely, very rarely indulged in introspection and
had never analysed an emotion in his life.

He was almost relieved when something climb-
ing towards the tower door with strange, hasty,
uncertain steps attracted his attention. It looked
black against the white bridle path and it staggered
from side to side as it came—now walking a few
steps, now breaking into a weak run.

"Some one hunted," thought Barry, with a
glance down into the glen, over the lip of which
this twilight creature had appeared.

There was no noise of pursuit, no clink of bit
or clatter of hoof—no sign of anything moving
among the sparse, starved oak stems. He had
drawn back, with some intention of going downstairs to Pouldarrig's one door, when the breeze
bore in a strange sound from outside—a little
whimper unmistakably feminine.

Fear, sharp as a knife-thrust, stabbed Barry.
What woman would come to Pouldarrig except
Aideen—and what should bring Aideen who, with
Sir Martin, had that forenoon set out for Galway
town, save disaster? Some mishap to his father—
some devilry of Van der Wynykt's probably.

As he once more pushed his head out of the
casement, the whimper came again.

"Aideen? Is that you? What is amiss?" he
called impatiently, peering down into the darkness
which lay below the window-sill.

A sob answered him. Some one was crying passionately—some one who lay in a huddled heap on the doorstep of Pouldarrig.

Barry snatched up a rushlight and dragged himself to the staircase, with his mind filled by instances he had seen and heard of the Dutch settlers' brutality.

"Aideen! For God's sake, what is amiss?" he cried desperately as he pulled open the heavy door.

A faint after-glow of sunset lingered still on this side of the tower, and a single glance showed him that the weeping woman was not his sister. She lay limp and inert, with her face pressed against the shale step, making no effort to move even when he lowered the light. He stared perplexedly at the dishevelled head between his feet. The figure as far as he could see was shabbily dressed, mud splashed, torn.

"What has befallen you?" he asked, putting a hand on the woman's shoulder. "Did you slip? Are you hurt?"

Again a sob was his only answer—but the head turned slightly, showing him a line of cheek white from the pressure of the stone.

"Who the deuce—?" he muttered, and then without more ado slipped his wrist under the woman's armpit and turned her half over. She gave a little scream as he moved the rushlight close to her face, and put both hands over her eyes, but he had seen enough.

"Mistress Van der Wynykt!" he cried blankly, "Mistress Van der Wynykt!"

Julia shivered at the words. "They—they—are—tracking me!" she gasped in the breathless whistle of exhaustion, making an effort to get up.

Almost mechanically he stooped, lifted her over the threshold, rebolted the door, and then propped her on the bottom step of the narrow shale staircase, that wound from dungeon to battlements through the thickness of the wall.

"I ran—all the time—I thought they were close behind me. I fell—coming up the glen," she whispered between long-drawn breaths, pushing the hair out of her eyes with mud-caked hands.

Barry looked her over critically. "Nay, I fear that was not your first fall," he said, eyeing the mud on her skirt and breast.

Julia nodded in a dazed fashion.

"Lord Lisronan will save me from them," she muttered. "He promised to." Her voice broke on the last word. She got up, steadying herself against the wall.

"I—I—am frightened to stay near the door!" she wailed, and then gave way suddenly to unbridled tears.

Barry, his hand under her elbow, impelled her gently up the steps. He thought it probable she might fall into a swoon, for which the mediæval staircase, worn of tread and steep as a ladder, was eminently unfitted. Julia, crying in a passionless, furtive fashion, let him lead her up to his room and across it to the hearth.

By the steady glow of the turf, Barry saw that she was wet as well as mud-stained, and that her shabby cloak, which hung about her in ribbons, was a mass of burrs. He pushed her down on to a settle, and went to fetch burnt Strasbourg brandy from a cupboard in the corner of the room.

By the time he returned Julia had ceased to cry, and was groping vaguely among her rags for a handkerchief. Afterwards it struck Barry as a comic element in the affair, that he should have handed her his as though she were a child; but at the moment his action seemed quite natural.

She made no demur over taking either kerchief or brandy, and for a moment after she had put down the empty goblet on the settle beside her there was silence.

Barry broke it. "Better?" he asked laconically.

Julia made another spasmodic effort to push her hair back.

"I want Lord Lisronan—I would have speech with Lord Lisronan!" she muttered, looking vaguely round the room.

"I 'll seek him. But first—are you come here on any special errand—to warn us, for instance?"

"Warn you?" she repeated. "Warn you? Oh —no—no—I come—because Lord Lisronan said— because they beat me—because—" She broke off and plucked at her skirt, like a woman whose wits are temporarily deranged. "If I could only

see my lord—" she finished with a little wailing
cry.

"You shall see him, Madame. But if what you
have to say concerns my father or sister, pray tell
me straightway—now—now!"

The apprehension of his tone made her look up
at him with puzzled dismay in her wet eyes.

"Your father—your sister?" she repeated,
stupefied by terror and the numbness of physical
exhaustion. "Your sister? Nay, sir, how should
I be concerned with your sister? 'T is not her
affair—nor yours—'t is my lord's."

Barry was by no means sure of this fact. He
had a conviction that this visit was connected with
his escape, and Dermot's expression when he
presently found him and imparted his news,
strengthened the idea.

Lisronan, who had been probing the cellar wall,
stood silent for a second looking down at his
tools.

"Wants me—Julia Van der Wynykt!" he
muttered with a frown.

"On an especial errand," said Barry drily.

Dermot passed a dust-grimed hand over his
perukeless head. "Plague take it!" he said, and
frowned again.

"She will tell me nothing."

"You? Oh, no, you would n't do. Leave the
things as they are—I 'll go to her."

He spoke absently, but with considerable
irritation.

"Look here, Dermot—" began Barry. But
Dermot was gone.

Julia heard his steps slowly mounting the shale
stair as she sat by the fire. She had employed
the moments since Barry's departure in cleaning
her face and hands, and was now trying furtively
to tidy her hair.

She got up when Dermot came in and turned to
face him, holding nervously to the back of the
settle. Almost the first thing he saw was, that
her hands were scored across by long red weals
and that her wrists carried innumerable newly
made scars.

"You wanted to see me, Madame," he said
slowly, coming across the room.

Julia's knees began to shake, she opened her
lips to speak, but no words came. Except her
brother, no human being had ever spoken as kindly
to her as this young man. It was not the fear that
he might decline his help that made her dumb, but
the recollection of what had happened.

"Sit down, Madame—pray," said Dermot
hurriedly, seeing how white she was and how she
trembled. "I fear your people——"

"They beat me!" she whispered shuddering.
"They beat me until the whip broke—" She
finished the sentence by an expressive glance at
her hands, adding, "My father will do worse—
if he gets me back! You will not let him! You
promised if he was angry—to—save me from his
anger!"

Dermot looked at the hands, which had evidently been raised to protect her face.

"The scoundrels!" he cried furiously, swept away for once by the impulse of the moment, "the inhuman scoundrels! Neither he nor they shall ever touch you again, Madame!"

"Do you mean I shall not be beaten any more—ever?" she asked, with the quick, credulous joy of a child. "Ever—while I live?"

She looked up at him eagerly and he, finding no adequate words, nodded.

"Not by Minna?" she asked. "Minna always beats me—when Willy is away—and she chances to be angry."

"Not by any one," he answered. "Good God, beaten!"

"There are worse things than beatings," she went on. "To-night they were—oh, I could not tell you what they were going to do to me to-night. They said they would——"

"Don't, Madame!" he interposed sharply. "'T was I brought this upon you—I thought a man would spare his own flesh and blood, however infernal a brute he might be."

Julia shook her head. "Ah, you do not know my father," she said, with a lack of tact which made Dermot wince. "He spares no one."

A silence followed this unhappy remark. Lisronan, wondering what on earth to do, looked perplexedly at Julia, who had turned to the fire and was warming herself. She seemed to have no more sense of the situation than a child.

Dermot remembered what James Taaffe had told him of the mother's imbecility, and reflected that Father Moran could have had little chance of instilling any principles into the girl's mind. Julia had come to Pouldarrig with no more thought as to consequences than an ill-treated dog. Blind confidence in Dermot, blind acceptance of his hastily-spoken words the previous night, and no consideration for—apparently no appreciation of—the real position.

Now what, in Heaven's name, was he to do with this human burden cast so suddenly upon him? To send her back to Albrecht Van der Wynykt, to pay the price of Barry's rescue, was out of the question. The marks on her arms settled that point beyond dispute. To take her to France when he and Barry started, as they meant to do, in two or three hours' time, was possible—but——

Dermot considered that "but" as he stood in the firelight looking down at Julia's lemon-coloured head. It was an age of universal immorality and iron convention. Julia, travelling unchaperoned with two men, was a woman undone—in the eyes of the world at least. The benefit of the doubt would never afterwards be hers, though there were men, no doubt, who would marry her—for a consideration.

He moved a pace into the window and glanced away to where, far across the dark folds of Mona-

darrig, a long band of faint pure green marked out
the west. She was a beautiful, ignorant child—
she trusted him implicitly, and she was daughter
to the man whom he hated with all the strength
of his soul. The first fact weighed less with him
than it would have done with most of his sex—but
it weighed.

He turned, saw the firelight on her fair, soft
face and in her pathetic eyes—and realised its
weight very fully.

"Your brother, Madame—where is he?" he
asked so suddenly that Julia started.

"Nay, I cannot tell you," she answered. "He—
he had a quarrel with Minna Viebert and went
away. 'T is four days ago now and I have had
no word. He told me he would never come
back."

"Why did not you go with him—if you 'll forgive
the question?"

"I spoke of it—but he would not take me. He
said I would hinder him and that by me he might
be traced—and that reminds me, he told me what
you did—how you saved his life. I have never
thank——"

Dermot's gesture cut the sentence short.

"Never thank me," he said impatiently; "the
word is unbearable—in some circumstances. Whom
else have you beside your brother that will befriend
you?"

"No one."

"No one? No relation? No friend?"

"None. Excepting indeed my uncle, James Taaffe—but him I have not seen for years."

"Oh, James Taaffe is out of the question," exclaimed Lisronan, with a momentary thought of the tippling scarecrow whom he had fed in the Cork inn. "Have you no other relatives on your mother's side?"

"None at all."

Dermot did not think it necessary to invent a question about Van der Wynykt's connections. The world knew the fellow for the son of an Amsterdam courtesan. What concerned him was to find out if Julia had any kin to whom he could with safety confide her. If not—well, he must ask Father Talbot.

"Is there absolutely no one—no one anywhere—who would protect you from your father?" he asked, after an uncomfortable pause.

"No one—save you," she answered very simply, and without a trace of *gêne*.

"I!" he repeated, red from embarrassment. "I, Madame, have no right—I mean——"

He paused, dumfounded by her simplicity, and by the sudden horror in her face.

"No right!" she gasped. "Oh, sir, you promised—you promised! I will work for you as a servant—a scullion, what you will. For God's sake, do not send me back to—to them!"

She flung out both hands and caught his coat.

"I would sooner you killed me quickly with your own hand," she ended with such terrible tearless

earnestness that it robbed the words of all suspicion
of exaggeration. "I would serve you faithfully
without wage—I can sew and make preserves.
Oh, have mercy on me, my lord. 'T was to aid
you I—I stole the key."

She dropped on her knees, as he stood silent
and confused before her, and kissed his hand
passionately, like a child asking forgiveness. He
was conscious of a curious thrill as her soft lips
touched his fingers.

"Please, Madame! You make me feel like a
brute," he exclaimed, lifting her to her feet. "Of
course you shall not be sent back. What puzzles
me is to know how—er—where you would be
best. Mr. FitzUlick and I travel into France this
very night."

"Might I not accompany you, my lord?"

She asked the question with an innocence that
was unmistakable. Lisronan, looking at her fair,
pure face, pictured to himself its expression when
she learnt that this man, whom she so trusted,
had allowed her in her ignorance to take a step
which would besmirch her for life.

"I must see Father Talbot, if he can be come
at," he said, after a moment's hesitation. "Eoin
will know his whereabouts. Should it be possible,
I 'll bring him here, that you may have speech
with him yourself."

CHAPTER XIX

FATHER TALBOT

THAT sudden and complete calm which so often
follows a spring storm, had fallen on the bog
when Dermot rode out into the dusk from Pouldarrig.   There was no sound except the stream's roar
as it leaped away down hill, no light but one long
pale green line in the west.   He hustled his mare
along, avoiding thought.   Father Talbot would
know what must be done—if he could only find
him.

The priest, hunted relentlessly by Van der
Wynykt and his men, had as many hiding-places
as a fox—caves on the hillside, deep and lonely
ravines, crevices in ruined walls, secret closets in
the whitewashed farmhouses where he went by
night to say Mass and to carry the sacraments to
the dying.

On this occasion Dermot, on old Eoin's advice,
took a line across Monadarrig bog to the ruin of
a Franciscan Abbey which stood among neglected
graves on a bare green hill five miles away.

It was quite dark when he reached the place,

and so utterly silent that the clink of his mare's shoe against a stone sounded preternaturally loud. Eoin had told him of the signal used by Father Talbot's flock—two shrill whistled notes like the call of a startled snipe; had explained that failing response, his honour must ride away without more specific inquiry.

Dermot knew what to expect when, having whistled, he presently heard the hoot of an owl, twice repeated. A minute later a snort from the mare told him that some one was near, though he could detect no sound of footsteps.

"Lisronan," he said in a low voice.

For a second the word went unanswered. He was conscious of being under close survey of unseen eyes.

"What call has your honour's lordship here?" asked a voice suddenly from the twilight gloom. It spoke in strange muffled tones impossible to identify, but Dermot guessed who the speaker was.

"An craoibhin dhun?" he queried very low.

A figure, dim as a shadow, detached itself from the darkness and came to his mare's head.

"Why d' ye want an craoibhin dhun, sir?" whispered the little schoolmaster timidly.

"I don't want you. I have need of—You understand without naming of names. Eh?"

"Deed aye, your honour! Well sure, he 's easy found—to-night I 'll take the horse below on the bog until your lordship is wanting him."

"Good. I shan't be long."

Dermot swung himself to earth as he spoke, put the reins into Sullivan's outstretched hand, and then walked up towards the abbey. The grass was ridged with graves over which he stumbled at every other step, unmarked graves sunk under a covering of moss. Ivy, two centuries old, smothered the ruin from end to end. The rustle of it in the wind was like a never-ceasing whisper.

Dermot had to grope to find the doorway, but, once inside, Eoin's instructions and the memories of childhood helped him. In spite of the thick darkness he remembered and found the exact spot where a curtain of ivy, trailing down from roof to floor, hid the narrow entrance to a little corkscrew staircase set in the thickness of the wall.

A vivid recollection of his last progress up these steep broken steps haunted him as he climbed. It had been connected with jackdaw eggs some fourteen years before.

He emerged at last into a passage hollowed, like the staircase, through the very heart of the mediæval wall. Part of it was open to the night sky, part roofed in—and in the covered piece Father Talbot had made for himself a resting-place.

There was a certain angle of stone behind which a candle could be lit without danger of detection from outside, a certain niche into which no rain ever beat—heaven itself to a man whose life counted for less than the life of rat or fox.

Dermot, with a dispassionate calmness very

rare among Irishmen, wondered why the God who had created so infinitely fine a thing as faith, had permitted humanity to deface and distort the greatest of His works. Protestants persecuting Catholics in Ireland, Catholics persecuting Huguenots in France—each side convinced that it did only what was acceptable in the sight of Him who said, "I command you that ye love one another"—a state of things at once so childish and so devilish that a sane man must laugh and weep over it in the same breath.

The priest had his lantern lit to-night. From its little cave of masonry it illuminated the white veins in the black surrounding slabs of flint and cast a circle of faint light on Father Talbot's lean figure, as he sat with his back against the wall and his head bent over a book, warming first one hand and then the other on a large roast potato which Bartley Sullivan had brought him for supper.

Dermot formed an opinion of the man's courage from his air as he looked up. The chances were a hundred to one on this sudden dim apparition being an armed enemy, but Father Talbot did not start, did not even rise.

"Who comes—and on what errand?" he asked, closing his breviary quietly.

"Lisronan, Father—to seek your advice," answered Dermot.

The priest got up.

"Lisronan? Ah, yes! I remember. You were

15

at Kylenoe," he said, coming forward. "Father Moran spoke to me of you on the one occasion that I met him. I will move the light. This place is rough for strangers."

Dermot glanced at the stone-strewed moss-covered floor, at the boulder on which Father Talbot had been sitting, at a pile of crushed bracken that had obviously served as a bed.

"Would it be dangerous for you to use Pouldarrig?" he asked abruptly.

"Yes. To you, to Sir Martin FitzUlick—and doubtless to myself. Our enemies—but 't was not on this matter you desired my advice, was it?"

"No. But I—I hate to see this. 'T is unfitted to a dog!"

Father Talbot smiled faintly and gave his shoulders a little shrug. "I am obliged for your thought," he said, in a tone which suggested some slight surprise that any human being should condescend to notice such trifles in a world of big things.

Dermot saw that he had to do with a different type of man to that gentle old humanitarian, Father Moran. Here would be no grieved sympathy for the backslider, no comprehension for the man who flinched from his duty. Neither himself nor his charges would Father Talbot spare. His stern soul, rigidly just, rigidly honest though it was, knew no relenting. He was the stuff of which martyrs are made, and, less tempered by intelligence, fanatics.

He sat down on the boulder again when Dermot had found an angle of stone to serve him as a seat, turned the lantern so that its light fell on his guest—and waited. To waste breath had never been his way. Men and women who came to make confession, to ask advice, to tell a story, must find the words unaided.

Dermot, who seldom spoke at random, sought his with that deliberation which was the most un-Irish of his many un-Irish attributes—and when he had found them he told his story in a few curt sentences.

There was silence after he finished. The ivy whispered, and from somewhere on the bog came a heron's harsh, screaming cry; but Father Talbot did not speak.

He opened the lantern, snuffed the candle neatly with two twigs, snapped to the little door again, and then turned to Dermot.

Lisronan was leaning forward, his elbow on his crossed knees, his grave eyes watching the priest's movements.

"Julia Van der Wynykt said nothing to you of Sir Hendrik Steen?" asked Father Talbot suddenly.

"I heard her mutter his name, but when I pressed her on the matter she cried, so I let it rest. Hendrik Steen! What should the child have to do with that scoundrel?"

"Her father will give her to him in marriage. She told me some days ago that Steen desired this."

"Steen! The brute's unfit to live! Steen

marry the girl! I' faith a bullet would be a better fate for her."

Dermot spoke more warmly than he knew, for he was stirred by a recollection of the latent appeal in Julia's soft eyes—and by the thought of what Hendrik Steen was. The story of the man's excesses had gone all over Europe; he was universally admitted to have passed even the wide bounds of that licentious age.

"Steen!" said Dermot again, and then rather sharply. "Well, Father?"

"You must marry her," answered Father Talbot, in the tone of one who has weighed a matter well and arrived at the only possible conclusion.

It was characteristic of Lisronan that he did not exclaim, did not protest, did not even answer the priest's quietly spoken words.

After a second Father Talbot went on: "If she marries Hendrik Steen she will lose her faith—her children will be brought up in error and outside the Church." He spoke in a tone of absolute finality. For him the matter began and ended there.

"You assume that she would be agreeable to— to this plan," said Dermot slowly. "But she may, nay, I should almost swear she *would*, decline it— we have met but twice, she and I."

"You know little of her home life, evidently. The unhappy child—" Father Talbot broke off, adding, after a second's pause: "She will not decline."

Dermot sat absolutely still. The Irishman's

trick of quick gesture was not his. His perturbation showed itself only in the grave grey eyes
that looked so unhappily at Father Talbot.

"Do you know how her father, Van der Wynykt,
treated my mother?" he asked at last in a low
repressed tone.

"Yes."

"And you tell me to marry her!"

"Yes."

"I came back to Ireland vowed to take vengeance on him. I shall have my chance yet—
and when it comes I shall take it. Does that alter
your opinion, Father?"

"No."

There was a silence after the quietly spoken
monosyllable. Father Talbot knew humanity too
well to speak that much advocated word, "in
season and out of season," which has hastened
so many hesitating sinners on the downward path.
Later he might remind Dermot who it was that
said, "Vengeance is mine—I will repay"—later,
when the fire had burned low and Time had taught
the young man his one inevitable lesson—the
vanity of all desire.

"I can't do it!" said Lisronan suddenly and
passionately, "I can't and won't give his daughter
my mother's name! His daughter!"

His face twisted in a spasm of bitter fury that
was as poignant as physical pain. Father Talbot,
knowing the average Irishman's capacity for
elaborate reviling of the stone wall against which

he is at the moment battering his head, awaited further protest, but none came.

"It is your duty, my son," he said at last, gravely. "Nay, more, it is an opportunity to serve the Church such as befalls few. Mere personal considerations should have no weight in the scale against the saving of a soul."

"The saving of a soul! Nay, 't would be the ruin of two!" retorted Lisronan, with fierce haste.

The priest raised his eyebrows contemptuously.

"That lies in your hands," he said. "You can make or mar according to your courage."

" 'T is not a question of courage—this."

"Yes—it is. There are few things in life but turn on that—our courage or lack of courage."

Dermot looked down at the floor. The word had called up a vision of Julia trembling in the doorway of her room. Life for her with Hendrik Steen would be a veritable hell, about that he had no delusions; and he had promised to save her— he who never gave his word lightly and without the fullest intention of holding to it.

The problem, as he sat staring at the broken flagstones grown through by tiny ferns, presented itself to him in the light of a game. When one played a game and lost, one paid the score as cheerfully as one might. He had played and lost, and the price was—not marriage with Van der Wynykt's daughter, *that* he vowed passionately it should never be—but the sharing with her of his name and his home.

"It seems to me, Father, that we have no further need of words," he said, rising. "My mare is outside—can you come back with me to Pouldarrig now?"

CHAPTER XX

FOI D'UN GENTILHOMME

"I WILL try to be a good wife to you, my lord," said Julia Van der Wynykt very meekly, with a timid glance at the figure by the window. "I will try always to please you in every way."

There were tears in her eyes and voice, but Dermot did not turn from the casement. He had hoped against hope that Julia would refuse to bind her life to that of a man whom she had seen only three times, had prayed fervently that any other way out of the *impasse* might be found than this one. Julia's acquiescence—tremulous with incredulity and delight, eager as the snatch of a starving dog at a bone—had sounded like a death-sentence in his ears.

"There are one or two matters I would have you weigh carefully," he said, after a moment's silence. "I came into Ireland vowing to take vengeance upon your father—I shall keep my vow. There is that between him and myself which nothing can ever wipe out. Have you considered this?"

Julia had not. She had considered nothing but

the fact that a life in which as far as she could see
there would be neither terror nor hardship had
been offered to her.

"I—I—do not like my father—I go in daily
dread of him," she said, twisting her slender hands
together nervously. "Father Talbot said——"

"Yes?"

Julia hesitated.

"Father Talbot said you—you would not beat
me," she muttered at last.

Dermot swung round.

"Beat you!   Good God, child, what do you take
me for?" he exclaimed, coming across the room to
where she sat.

"They used to beat me," she answered, with a
glance at the scarred backs of her hands.   Then,
as if his silence gave her courage, she added:
"Father Talbot told me I should be happy with
you."

"I wish I were as sure of that as he is!" said
Dermot impatiently.   "You, Julia, ought to be
a better judge on that point than Father Talbot."

Julia opened wide eyes of dismay at the mere
idea that she could be a better judge on any point
than the priest.

"No—oh, no," she protested.

Her self-effacement had a rather irritating effect
on Dermot.

"Yes—most certainly!" he retorted.   "Surely
you have some opinion on a matter which concerns
your whole life?"

He paused; but Julia made no response. She
was looking up at him with a distinctly puzzled
expression.

"*Dieu*, Madame, have you really no conception
as to whether I could—well, could make you happy
or not?" asked Dermot curtly. It seemed to him
that his future wife had the attributes rather of a
sheep than a woman.

Julia winced a little under the sharpness of his
tone.

"Never to be beaten—to go unhindered to Mass,
as Father Talbot promised. Nay, of course I shall
be happy," she murmured at last.

"You desire nothing more of life?"

The girl shook her head vaguely. Dermot
looked down at her with a slight frown.

"Julia, for pity's sake, think well of the matter,"
he urged. "Remember that if you make a mistake
now you must abide by it for the next fifty years.
There will be no going back."

"I' faith, I shall not desire to go back—my stars,
no! Never, never!" She emphasised the words
by a shudder.

"She can see nothing but the physical side!"
thought Dermot despairingly, with a feeling that
a trap had closed on him from which, struggle as
he might, there could be no escape. His intention
had been to tell her that their marriage would be
a marriage in name only, but the task—difficult
enough with a woman of quick comprehension—
seemed impossible with this unawakened and

stupid child. Marriage was too evidently a mere
word to her—"husband" of no more significance
than "brother."

He took what consolation was possible from the
reflection that a fan, a new gown, a handful of
sugar-plums, would be sufficient at all times to
keep her contented, and that to the eye at least
she was eminently satisfactory.

"I suppose we ought not to keep Father Talbot
waiting," he said awkwardly after a silence.

The colour mounted in Julia's cheeks, the ever-
ready tears to her eyes.

"Must I—must I be wed in this?" she asked
plaintively, holding out a fold of mud-stained rag.

"Would it matter—just for the ceremony?
There are, I think, some gowns in a *garde-robe*
in what was Mrs. D'Arcy's room, and you could
mayhap find one to suit you afterwards."

Her eyes, and indeed her whole face, lit up.

"No, no—now—now at once!" she cried eagerly,
springing to her feet. "Which is Mrs. D'Arcy's
room?"

"I will show you. But pray do not be long.
Father Talbot is impatient to be away—and he
runs risks here. Do you honour me with your
attention, Madame?"

"Yes—yes! May I choose any I like of the
gowns, my lord?"

Dermot shrugged his shoulders—a gesture he
rarely indulged in.

"*Grand Dieu*, Madame!" he began impatiently,

and then paused and added, "Yes, any you like. Can you find your way down to the living-room when you are ready?"

"Easily."

"And you will not delay?"

"I will be very quick."

They reached the door into Mrs. D'Arcy's room as she spoke, and she snatched the candle he proffered and whisked over the threshold with more animation than Lisronan had yet seen. He heard the squeak of the cupboard door as he walked on down the stairs.

"Marriage counts for less in her eyes than a new gown," he thought bitterly, wondering for the first time what Esmée de Louysnes would say. To have set out to kill a man and instead to bring back his daughter as bride! It seemed the act of a madman.

The chief living-room at Pouldarrig was, like the rest of the house, strongly reminiscent of medieval days, but this evening a turf fire gave it a more human air than usual. Shafts of red light lay warm on the dark beamed ceiling, and woke little answering flames in the heads of axe and spear and ancient sword hung haphazard on the grey wall.

Owen D'Arcy's old servant, Eoin, very bent now, shuffled about, lighting a candle here and a candle there, pushing the scattered wolf-skins into place on the floor, tweaking a faded square of tapestry that hung before the wide and deep-set window. His face worked angrily as he made preparation for this detested marriage. He would very gladly have turned Julia Van der Wynykt out of doors.

Father Talbot, a straight black figure well in keeping with that austere and faded room, stood under the great hood of the chimney, drawing warmth into his starved bones and a smell of scorching from his soutane. A fire was to him a rare luxury.

Barry, with a look of unusual perturbation on his fine features, sat frowning opposite the priest. Dermot had little doubt that Eoin's entrance a few seconds before his own had interrupted a discussion.

"You can go," he said rather impatiently to the old serving-man, pausing just inside the threshold to give the order.

As Eoin shuffled out Barry jumped up.

"Dermot! A moment!" he began in his headlong fashion. "Father Talbot tells me he is here to—to——"

"Marry me to Mistress Van der Wynykt?"

"Yes. Is it true? Your pardon, Father, but I—I simply cannot believe it."

Dermot's face hardened perceptibly.

"It is true," he said very curtly. "And being true, Barry, I see no use in saying more on the subject."

Barry's eyebrows went up a little.

"His daughter!" he said in a low voice.

Father Talbot raised his hand in a gesture of prohibition, but FitzUlick, after a single defiant glance at him, went on.

"I have every right to speak, and speak I will!" he exclaimed. "The riddle's easily read—she helped you to get the keys, and this is her repayment. Dermot, for God's sake don't be such a fool!"

Again Father Talbot lifted a hand, and this time Barry swung round on him.

"You've had your say, Father, I'll have mine!" he cried. "If one of us had to pay this score it should be me. But there's a way out—I'll swear there's a way out! Dermot, a word apart with you!"

Dermot, walking slowly over to the hearth, shook his head. Barry looked sharply at him.

"I've heard Father Talbot's side of the matter —now for yours," he said. "You have a side— if you'll only admit the fact. Doubtless you promised the girl to save her harmless—you did? Yes. But—but—to marry her! God in heaven!"

"The matter's settled," said Lisronan in a tone of hard finality. "My wish was that you should know nothing, but I suppose Father Talbot told you?"

"Yes."

"Let it rest there, like a good fellow. I—I'd rather not discuss it."

Barry FitzUlick laughed angrily.

"Aye! You'd rather keep your eyes shut—

until afterwards," he retorted. "Dermot, look here——"

He took Lisronan by the arm and drew him towards the window. Father Talbot heard nothing of the finish of the sentence save a low-toned eager murmur, but he knew what Barry was saying, knew the path which he was suggesting to his friend —the broad path, where the man treads scathless and the woman alone meets thorn and flint.

Barry's argument was the argument of commonsense—if one of two human beings must suffer let it be the least valuable. Decency prevented him suggesting openly before the priest the (to his mind) obvious fact that Van der Wynykt's daughter was fair game. Her fate, but for Dermot's advent, would have been easy to predict—or so Barry declared.

Under covert of the window, with an occasional quick glance back at Father Talbot, he put the matter very plainly to his friend. He pointed out in a few trenchant sentences how really superfluous Dermot's quixotism was—adding the outline of another means of saving Julia from her father that would doubtless satisfy the girl just as well, since she knew no better.

"There's the matter in a sentence," put in Dermot quietly as he paused. "She knows no better. Do you think I want it on my conscience that I sent an absolutely ignorant child—she's no more—to the devil? Let it be, Barry. My mind's made up."

"She 'd have gone to the devil in any case," retorted Barry. "Safe to—she 'll go there in spite of you. What else should Van der Wynykt's daughter do? Take her to Paris, man. Fifty guineas as a dower will find her a husband there. So shall you save yourself and your conscience. God, Dermot! How can you hesitate? Father Talbot! What should Father Talbot know of marriage? To him 't is a question of ethics— whereas——"

The door opening cut short the impatient sentence and instinctively all three men turned towards it.

Julia paused a second on the threshold, dazzled by the flare of light after the darkness of the staircase.

She had on a white satin gown, made when Charles II. reigned, with wide flowing sleeves, and a skirt that stood away stiffly from her slender waist. Her neck rose, round and very white, out of a broad collar of old lace, her hair gleamed like a halo against the dark doorway.

Barry, who had only seen her mud-spattered and in rags, was so much overcome by astonishment that he exclaimed aloud.

Even Dermot stared blankly for a second before he went forward to where she stood, her cheeks rose-pink from shy dismay, shimmering pearl-coloured ripples in each satin fold of her gown, and the vivid contrast between her bright hair and soft dark eyes emphasised by the golden glow of light.

"Egad! Dermot is n't such a fool after all," thought Barry the practical, watching Julia critically as she took her prospective husband's hand and moved forward beside him, a radiant vision in that dark old room. Of the three men, he was the only one who saw her as a woman. To Dermot she represented a duty, to Father Talbot a responsibility—a member of his flock to be kept at any cost from an alien fold. Barry alone realised her possibilities. Barry alone said to himself: "There will be trouble out of this."

CHAPTER XXI

"LITTLE BOY LOVE DREW HIS BOW AT A CHANCE"

"YOUR servant, Madame," said Barry Fitz-Ulick with his best bow. "But you are busy? I interrupt?"

Esmée de Louysnes turned in her chair, pen upheld.

"Yes—I am writing letters for Raoul. He permits me to conduct all his correspondence," she answered, and her smile suggested that to herself she added, "except his love letters." "Come in, nevertheless, Barry," she went on. "I have hardly seen you to speak to this sennight past. When the messenger who awaits these wearisome epistles has betaken himself off you shall tell me your news."

Her eyes dwelt appreciatively on the young man as she spoke. All her life Esmée had worshipped beauty in any form—man or woman, horse or landscape, flower or fabric.

"Dermot is out, I suppose, Madame," said Barry, stooping to pat Esmée's poodle, who lay curled luxuriously on a sweeping fold of her gown.

"Yes."

"And milady?"

A shadow crossed Esmée's face. "In the green room," she answered; and then, after a second's silence, added with suppressed passion: "Barry— I—I cannot get over this marriage. I cannot conceive how such a thing ever happened! Dermot —and that man's daughter!"

"Has Dermot not told——?"

"Oh, yes. He and she have both 'told' me— or think they have. Besides, what do mere words go for now when the thing is done? 'Nothing else to do,' forsooth! Dermot had but to ship the child off to me in charge of poor Owen's old serving-man, and I would have seen to it that she did not lack food or clothes—or a suitable husband. Instead of which, the boy wrecks his life for a scruple. Oh, 't would madden a saint! What were you about, Barry? Had you no say in the matter?"

Barry reddened a little, wincing from the quick contempt of Esmée's steel-grey eyes. Every additional hour spent in Julia Lisronan's company made him more loath to recall his original intentions towards her—and the hours had been many since their arrival in Paris a month ago. In fact— though this he hardly realised yet—the days on which he did not see her were surprisingly blank.

"A woman need not of necessity take after her father," he said rather brusquely. "And I 'll wager Dermot would not have found a prettier girl in all Europe."

Madame de Louysnes laughed sarcastically.

"There speaks man, the logical!" she sneered. "Lo! this woman is beautiful—she is also ignorant, inherently vicious, stupid as an imbecile—but since she is beautiful, give her to me! *Là!* Barry, and I used to credit you with some sense!"

She made a little despairing gesture with her hands and looked up at him curiously.

"I never dreamed you were susceptible," she added.

"Nor am I," he answered smiling. "I merely said that Julia was pretty beyond the ordinary. It counts for much, Madame—with some of us."

His glance at her was full of impish significance. Long ago, as quite a small boy, he had fathomed her maternal satisfaction in Raoul's good looks.

"Julia is beautiful," agreed Esmée. "But—eh, *mon Dieu!* a child—a baby! Silly—untaught—characterless—ignorant of the merest rudiments of an idea. Dermot might as well have married a kitten—save that the kitten could hardly develop the traits which are this girl's by right of inheritance. Bah! If I think of it I shall be unable to finish my letters. Go into the green room for a little half-hour, my dear boy, and play with the kitten. And, oh, by the way, if she *should* speak sensibly on any topic you might——"

Esmée paused, looking reflectively at her pen.

"Yes, Madame—I might—what?"

"Well, she has chosen, of all people, to admit to the intimacy of friendship Gustave de l'Afrie—the little empty-headed braggart son of Ninon de l'Afrie. A man about whom one hears—well, you know the type of story! I have hinted that he is undesirable; but I am of the older generation, therefore what I say must be weighted with prejudice. You, being her contemporary, will be listened to."

Again a wave of colour came into Barry's sunburnt face. His expression changed subtly.

"Gustave de l'Afrie!" he exclaimed, "that wastrel! What is Dermot about? Why does n't he help the child? He knows the life she led in Ireland, and that she had scarce spoken twice with her own kind when she came to Paris. 'T is he who 's to blame if she—knowing no better—is persuaded into a friendship with De l'Afrie!"

Esmée turned back to her correspondence.

"Dermot sees very little of Julia," she answered. "He has more important things to consider than the follies of such a little imbecile. He leaves those to me—and I am not listened to."

"I think Julia is mayhap less of an 'imbecile' than you guess, Madame," returned Barry, unaccountably nettled.

During the past few days a word against Lady Lisronan had somehow—why, he could not quite tell—assumed in his mind the aspect of a personal insult. She dwelt of late very persistently in his thoughts, this little "imbecile," with her soft fawn's eyes and her air of appeal.

Esmée shrugged her shoulders.

"Your sex is seldom a good judge of mine," she said, dipping her quill in the ink. "I can only hope that in this case you may be right."

"I am convinced of it!" he answered dogmatically.

He turned as he spoke and walked across to the door of the green room; but Madame de Louysnes's gentle laugh pursued him over the threshold and stung his vanity somewhat sharply.

The subject of their discussion was sitting in a high-backed chair by the window, crying. Her gown of lavender blue brocade harmonised to perfection with the delicate grey-green casement curtain; a lavender blue ribbon was twisted through her primrose-coloured curls, on which the sunlight lay lovingly, brightening their pure pale gold and the whiteness of the forehead underneath. Pieces of quilted purple silk and old lace, destined some day to be a hood, lay in her lap.

She glanced up at Barry, but her tears did not cease. She was that rarest thing in life—a woman who could cry becomingly. To her it was no nerve-racking feature-twisting emotion, but an hourly occurrence which might be indulged in without any danger of red eyes or a swollen nose. Even her sobs were gentle and well regulated.

"Weeping again, my lady," said Barry with a smile curiously blent of humour and more tenderness than a man has any right to feel for his friend's wife. "What is amiss this time? Yesterday 't was that some miscreant had spilt your needle-case, and the day before that the spaniel had put a muddy paw on your new slipper. What is it now?"

He stooped as he spoke, retrieved a wisp of cambric from the carpet and laid it on her lap.

"D–Dermot has been cruel to me!" whimpered Julia, with a little pathetic quiver of her chin. Her long straight lashes looked the darker for being wet, and her eyes held a world of grief in their liquid depths.

"Dermot cruel! Come, I cannot credit that," protested Barry, pausing opposite her. "What has he done—eh? Declined to take you to Madame de l'Afrie's route?"

"Worse than that."

"Worse? My stars! You 're making a pretty mess of that purple silk on your lap—I shall take it away until you cease to weep. I protest you should be clad in an oiled sheep-skin."

He plucked the embryo hood off Julia's lap and held it up. "In the name of all the saints, what garment is this?" he demanded tragically

Julia laughed, but in a rather tremulous fashion.

"'T is headgear—and 't will come to pieces an' you handle it so," she said, holding out her hands with one of her childlike gestures, which from their spontaneity were curiously fascinating.

She had in a marked degree that strange power of attraction that is so entirely beyond definition; that power of winning affection denied sometimes to the most beautiful, possessed sometimes by the plain and ungainly—and in itself so potent that the memory of it will cling to a mere written name.

"Put it on, my lady," said Barry, dropping the muddle of satin and lace into her outstretched fingers.

"I have no mirror," she objected.

"Any excuse to look at yourself, of course!" he retorted, glancing round for a silver hand-glass which he had noticed lying on a table near.

Julia drew the hood over her head with the solemnity of a baby. She gave no special thought to her audience, being wholly concerned for the ultimate success of her new headgear. It is doubtful if she even realised how infinitely the purple satin with its inner frill of lace set off her fair beauty.

The fact was not lost on her companion. His expression as he watched her interested survey of her own reflection would have made clear to a more experienced woman, a certain fact of which Barry himself was as yet hardly aware.

"Methinks 't will be quite nice," said Julia with a little satisfied sigh, laying down the glass and lifting off the hood. "Do not you?"

"Quite," he answered. "You must wear it to Saint Germain on Friday."

Her face clouded suddenly.

"I do not know that I can go to Saint Germain on Friday," she said in a plaintive voice. "Neither Madame nor Monsieur de Louysnes are going—and Dermot will not. He told me so this morning."

"So that was what you were crying about?"

"N—no."

"What then?"

She looked down and stroked the hood shyly.

"It was perhaps silly of me to cry," she murmured.

"It was most undoubtedly silly of you to cry, my lady," he answered, wondering why he had never noticed before how perfect a crescent her straight dark lashes made when she looked down. "What reason did you conceive to justify it?"

She raised her eyes and smiled at him with greater confidence than she either felt or showed to any other human being.

"How you quiz, Barry," she said. "Listen. Dermot has a trinket which I covet vastly. 'T is in the shape of a scallop shell and all set with rows and rows of tiny pearls. The chain it hangs by is set with pearls too. I saw it to-day in his room by chance and desired it—but—he—he would not give it to me. He said, 'My God, no—never!' in a most fierce voice, and snatched it from me and put it in an inner pocket of his coat. When I would have asked why, he left the room. 'T was as though some thief, some person whose very touch was contamination, had laid hands on what he valued. And I—am his wife."

Her voice broke on the last word. The eyes

she raised to Barry grew moist, the eyebrows above them took a pathetic curve.

Captain FitzUlick looked decidedly uncomfortable. That pearl scallop shell had been on Ethna's neck the night Van der Wynykt came to take Lisronan. It and a few rings were all that remained to her, and she had worn them continually in the last years of her life. Barry understood so well why Dermot would not give his mother's favourite ornament to "that man's daughter" that the knowledge held him tongue-tied. He wondered Julia did not guess.

After a moment's silence her soft little voice continued its complaint.

"'T is purely churlish of him—is it not?" she asked.

"She ought n't to admit a word against Dermot," thought Barry, who would not himself have uttered any complaint of those bound to him by ties of kinship if his life had depended on it.

"Egad, Paris is teaching you, my lady!" he said aloud rather drily. "A sennight back 'churlish' and 'Dermot' would not have been connected even in your thoughts. Doubtless he had good reasons—Dermot always has!"

Julia's face assumed that mulish expression not uncommon on the countenances of the inherently meek.

"There can be no reason in this case—save a desire to annoy," she muttered, beginning once more to set small neat stitches in the purple hood.

Barry laughed at her tone.

"Think, Madame—if you can," he said in a voice which robbed the words of all sting. "You will see a reason, believe me."

Julia thought. She even laid down her needle in order to give the process her undivided attention, but she came no nearer seeing a reason for her husband's action.

"You don't?" asked Barry gravely, as she shook her head. "Well, 't was his mother's—she wore it every day of her life. She has been a bare six months dead. Cannot you understand that 't would hurt Dermot to see the trinket on any one? To me it seems as obvious as the day."

The girl frowned and shook her head again.

"A stranger perhaps—but I am his wife," she said, "I have the right."

His glance at her was curiously blent of impatience and perplexity. He had all the Irishman's quick intuitive sympathy, all the Irishman's surprise at that lack of imagination which engenders inability to enter into the feelings of others.

"Right!" he retorted. "My dear child, an' you can talk of 'right' when affections are concerned, you 've a vast deal to learn! Here 's something coming into the street—a procession. His most Christian Majesty, as I live! Look out."

No need to tell Julia to look. The difficulty as a rule was to get her from the window. She sprang up, dropping her hood, and leaned eagerly out of the open window.

The King's passage down the Place Royale was quite unexpected and due merely to a sudden subsidence in the prescribed route. Heads popped forth from every casement as the procession turned the corner; there was an opening of doors, a running of feet, a dropping fire of cheers. Julia gazed wide-eyed at the train of gilt coaches with their slow, elaborately caparisoned, heavy-maned horses.

"Which is he—pray which is he?" she whispered eagerly to Barry, in the awed accents of a child.

Captain FitzUlick indicated a *calèche* in which there sat two people—one an exceedingly pretty young woman, pink-cheeked, bright-eyed, smiling, with two huge feathers, a white and a rose-coloured, on her powdered head, and a wrap of rose-coloured satin fastened with jewelled clasps about her shoulders; the other a man, in a silver-laced grey velvet cloak, and a hat so wide-leaved that Julia looking down could see only the ends of a heavy peruke.

"That was the Duchesse de Bourgogne, was it not?" she said, half-turning to Barry, who stood behind her.

"In the carriage with the King? Yes."

"'T is a strange fashion of headgear," murmured Julia, reflectively. "Strange, but very pretty— I would I could copy it!"

Barry made no response. His feelings at the moment were rather complicated, chief among them being a speculation as to where he would be most likely to find a replica of the pearl scallop-shell. It was a shame the poor little thing should lack a trinket—she who was certainly the prettiest woman in Paris, or indeed in all France.

CHAPTER XXII

THE RUE DU SAPIN ROUGE

BARRY FITZULICK, riding from Corbeil into Paris between twelve and one of a warm May night, chose the route which must take him past the Hôtel de Louysnes.

He took this course for no more sentimental reason than that the only alternative route had brought down half a dozen horses in the past week, but having made the choice, it followed almost inevitably that he should think of Julia. The moon, high in the vague steel blue sky of a summer night, silvered the roofs of Paris, and threw black silhouettes of gable and turret across each whitened street. Barry, looking down the river from the high back of the Pont de Sully, recalled that Lady Lisronan had on a similar occasion compared the moonlit water to a diamond chain, the shadowed arch of the bridges to a bat's wing, similes he thought at once original and beautiful.

The spell of her personality was strong on him when he presently turned into the Rue du Sapin Rouge, a narrow street of evil repute which lay at the back of the Place Royale and was connected with it by a narrow alley. He rode along in the warm malodorous shadow of old houses that nearly met overhead, neither seeing the occasional furtive figure that lurked here and there, nor hearing the sounds of revelry and quarrel from unshuttered casements above.

What roused him at last was the sudden bat-like flitting forth from a cavernous doorway of a slender cloaked form, which darted right under his horse's chest. It was feminine, by the rustle of its petticoats; young, by the swift grace of its movements, and it ran as a coursed rabbit runs across the Rue du Sapin Rouge into the moonlit space at the mouth of the Passage de la Lanterne.

As the strong white light fell on the girl Barry exclaimed aloud. The poise of the head, the slope of the shoulders, even the velvet cloak she wore were familiar to him with the familiarity that admits of no mistake.

"Julia!" he said under his breath. "Julia! Here—alone, at this hour!" The idea seemed too preposterously absurd on the face of it.

He drove the sorrel forward to the mouth of the alley that connected the Rue du Sapin Rouge with the Place Royale. The narrow passage, blocked against horse traffic by an iron bar, and lit midway by a latticed iron hanging lantern, gave absolutely opposite a postern door in the wall of the Hôtel de Louysnes.

Barry was in time to see the girl run through the

faint circle of lantern light, which showed her slimness, her gathered-up skirts, her little hurrying feet.

She reached the end of the "passage," stopped, peered anxiously up and down the Place Royale and then crossed it to the postern door of Madame de Louysnes's house. Barry saw the glitter of a key, a pair of white hands pushing impatiently against the heavy slow-moving nail-studded oak, a vista of three moonlit steps, and a door reclosed in a noiseless and furtive fashion.

He sat for some minutes staring thoughtfully along the black passage with its blur of smoky orange light, which did little save define the iron lattice-work of the lantern. The windows of the Hôtel de Louysnes winked blankly at the moonlight. The house was asleep—all save one inmate.

Barry glanced back at the building from which Julia had come. It was a place that suggested— and that had, as he knew, experienced—almost every vicissitude of squalor and vice. At the time of Nicholas de la Reynie's investigations, it had suddenly changed its sign, *Le Nain Blanc*, for the one it now bore—a blue fig-tree—the reason being, it was said, connected with certain answers extorted by the "question" from its then owner— but its character remained unaltered. A room might still be had there for half a louis for any purpose whatsoever.

FitzUlick remembered that Gustave de l'Afrie had mentioned it once to him. He recalled

Esmée's words. A wave of red fury possessed him
as he rode round into the Place Royale. What an
incredible little fool Julia must be!—he would not
admit even to himself the harder word. As for
Gustave—well Gustave, God be praised, could be
called out.

Under the Hôtel de Louysnes he drew up,
scanning the closed windows one by one till he
came to the casement of Julia's room. Even as
he looked the curtain was drawn cautiously back,
and he saw her standing by the lattice in the
bright moonlight tying her hair, which hung down
over her left shoulder until it swept the window-
seat. Evidently she feared to light a candle, and
feared still more to go to bed in the dark—poor
little coward!

That she who was so timid, so devoid of initia-
tive, should have crept out at midnight to keep a
tryst, argued some very strong inducement.

Again Barry recalled Madame de Louysnes's
words, "She has chosen of all people to admit to
the intimacy of friendship—Gustave de l'Afrie!"

"That hound! How may any woman endure
such a fellow?" he thought savagely, still staring
up at Julia where she stood framed in the dark
woodwork, a white-robed moonlit figure like some
pictured saint. His feeling for her, hitherto hardly
acknowledged even to himself, flamed up as he
looked, fed by jealousy of Gustave de l'Afrie, and
a cynical reflection that if she were capable of all
that a midnight tryst in the Rue du Sapin Rouge

with Gustave de l'Afrie implied, the man who supplanted Gustave would not be greatly injuring Dermot.

It was not a nice thought—not one that he cared to dwell on. In fact, he wondered afterwards how it had forced its way in on the tumult of rage, surprise, and disgust which surged through his brain. The idea that Julia might have acted out of pure ignorance only occurred to him when he was back in his quarters, and had somewhat relieved his feelings, after the logical masculine fashion, by rating his servant.

Then he remembered her extreme youth, her childlike appeal to him for advice on the simplest matters. He would speak to her on the morrow. He would also—an infinitely more agreeable prospect—put an abrupt termination to Gustave de l'Afrie's career of rascality.

He went to sleep meditating pleasantly on the insult he proposed to offer that gentleman, and wondering which of his friends would best act as second.

CHAPTER XXIII

SAINTE SIDONIE

BARRY FITZULICK stalked across the Place Sainte Sidonie in a very bad temper. Gustave de l'Afrie was out of Paris—had left unexpectedly the previous day, and would not return until to-morrow evening—a circumstance sufficiently aggravating to a man who had spent several hours in fabricating pretext for a quarrel.

Gustave de l'Afrie was out of Paris and—further matter for grievance—Julia, with whom he desired a few words, was in church. Her sedan-chair, with men in Madame de Louysnes's livery, was awaiting her at the western door.

After a second's hesitation, Barry went down the steps into Sainte Sidonie. Julia had only gone to confession, and would not be long.

The church seemed to him very silent, strangely dim and cool after the heat and noise of the street. It was a small, ancient building of great beauty, perfect in every detail, from the crucifix of marble over the high altar to the bas-relief above the western door. Every window glowed with jewelled lights, green and purple, sapphire and amethyst, burning ruby and royal blue; and the reflection of them lay in softer tints across carved column and narrow dusky aisle. A faint smoke-soft haze of incense haunted each archway, veiled each grey fretted scroll.

That indescribable atmosphere that comes only to a place where men for centuries have felt themselves to be in the actual presence of God lay like a spell on the little church.   Those devout, ancient craftsmen had done more than make Sainte Sidonie a poem in stone. The passionate exaltation of spirit which had inspired their hands, lingered still about their work, and all who stood among its dim glories were subtly touched thereby.

Barry, waiting near the doorway, was very conscious of this.   Though Art and Nature failed to reach him, he responded to Sainte Sidonie's appeal. He even began to reflect uncomfortably on. his own deficiencies—a most unusual proceeding for him.

While he was meditating, Julia slipped out from the confessional and went across to the altar of the Blessed Virgin. Barry, like Dermot, was moved by the exquisite grace of her reverence as she passed the high altar. He had known in a vague way that she was devout, but among all the devout women of his acquaintance, not one possessed her air of profound simple piety.

The side altar to which Julia made her way was in a niche between two grey slender columns.

Centuries earlier a reverent master hand had carved it out of yew-wood, and inlaid it with jasper and ivory and fine gold. Mary's robe was of silver, marvellously wrought with little jewelled flowers, and edged and girt with worked gold. Her face and hands, and the Child in her arms, were all of ivory, fine as the most perfect sculpture, delicate as a cameo. A little lamp of silver and ruby glass burnt at her feet, and on either side of it some recent worshipper had laid two great bunches of cream-coloured roses, which scented the cool still air.

Barry, after a single glance at Julia's kneeling figure, looked away. The supreme earnestness of her, the unquestioning faith and utter whole-hearted devotion she showed, touched and embarrassed him. He felt that he of all people had least right to watch her prayers. It was impossible to reconcile anything so beautiful to the squalid nastiness of an illicit intrigue with Gustave de l'Afrie. He moved noiselessly into the doorway, and stood looking up the sunlit steps to the level of the street, until a faint rustle of brocade made him turn.

Julia came slowly from her prayers as if she were loath to leave. When she had made her genuflexion to the high altar, she stood for a second looking wistfully up the church, and Barry realised all at once, that whatever might befall her in after life she would always find consolation in religion, would always feel it to be the most real thing in life, more near and intimate than husband or lover or child.

She walked past him up the steps without seeing him, and when he spoke her name she turned with a start.

"Barry! Have you been in the church? I did not notice you."

"Do you ever notice outside matters in church?" he asked, with a smile.

"Not often, i' faith!" she responded, glancing back to the brass-bound pointed door. "Is it not beautiful, Sainte Sidonie? There is nothing in all Paris pleases me so vastly as her churches."

They were at the top of the steps by now. Her chair stood ready for Julia on the hot flagstones.

"Walk with me as far as the end of the street, Madame," said Barry in a rather low voice. "I— I would say a few words to you."

"*Bien!*" returned Lady Lisronan indifferently. She was fast picking up both the phraseology and the manner of Esmée de Louysnes's friends.

There was a ring of very ancient walnut trees round Sainte Sidonie, which ninety years later were to provide the *sans-culottes* with means to burn and batter the building. Julia paused under one to gather her pale blue brocade skirt up from her little silver-heeled, silver-buckled tan shoes. Then holding a fan in the Spanish fashion between her and the sun, she began to pace sedately along the worn old pavement, over the dancing checkers of sunlight and shadow.

Barry walked beside her in silence for a full minute. He found it very hard to put what he had to say into words.

"I was in the Rue du Sapin Rouge last night between twelve and one," he began suddenly, stammering a little over the curt sentence, and growing red.

Julia's rare rose-pink blush flew into her cheeks at mention of the street, but she neither spoke nor raised her eyes.

"I—saw a girl there—she passed into the Hôtel de Louysnes," continued Barry in profound and growing embarrassment. "She—she wore—" the words "your cloak" died on his lips.

He stole an agonised glance at Julia, now very white. She did not speak nor answer as she walked along with bent head—one might almost have imagined she had not heard.

Barry, horribly confused, went on: "She wore clothes—a cloak that made me think she might—be your tire-woman, Madame," he said hurriedly. "And—and—and—well, the Rue du Sapin Rouge is a place no decent woman would go to at that hour. A wench seen there would be undone—I mean——"

Again he paused in hopeless dismay, choked by a sense of his own impertinence and the difficulties of the position.

Julia gave him no help. The hand that held up her painted Spanish fan was shaking visibly, but she remained silent.

"Doubtless 't is pure ignorance on the girl's part," Barry continued, wishing passionately he had never been fool enough to broach the subject. "Doubtless, did she but know the risks she runs and the character of the street, she 'd—she 'd be vastly horrified. She should be warned that any one—woman or man—who would lure a wench there, after nightfall, on any pretext whatsoever, is a scoundrel."

There was a heavy and embarrassed silence after the last word. The rustling of the walnut leaves overhead, and the tapping of Julia's high silver heels on the uneven old pavement, sounded preternaturally loud to them both.

"You are not angry, Julia? You do not take what I said amiss?" he asked nervously as they walked out from the shadow of the last tree into the blazing sunlight, where Julia's chair waited.

She glanced up at him with eyes of panic fear, her childish face white and quivering.

"Don't tell Dermot!" she whispered. "I—I trust you."

The plea, and the tacit admission it conveyed, took Barry's breath away as effectually as a sudden immersion in ice-water.

"God! Julia!" he said, with horror in voice and expression.

Lady Lisronan's only answer was to walk swiftly away to her chair. Further speech before the servants was impossible.

"May I come to the Hôtel de Louysnes, Madame?" he asked in a low voice, as he settled a cushion at her back.

Julia shook her head.

"*Madame ma tante* does not receive to-day," she returned without looking at him, "nor do I. *Bon jour, Monsieur.*"

CHAPTER XXIV

"HUGUENOT! HUGUENOT!"

THE hour of twelve two nights after—the evening on which Gustave de l'Afrie was to return to Paris—found Barry once more on his way to the Rue du Sapin Rouge. His intention was to intercept Julia, to take her home, and afterwards himself to keep the tryst with De l'Afrie. Happen what might, the girl should not wreck her life for such a fellow. There were men almost worth the sacrifice, men who would honour and cherish her— or at least display as good an imitation of these attributes as the superior sex can be expected to show a female sinner—but Gustave de l'Afrie belonged to a very different type.

At this stage in Barry's reflections a singular sound caught his attention. He stood a second listening. Obviously it came from the region of the Rue du Sapin Rouge, and obviously it was a street row of some sort.

The thought of Julia stealing unattended to her tryst made him slip his sword out of its sheath and break into a run.

As he turned into the Rue du Sapin Rouge, he saw a little knot of people gathered in front of the squalid house in which Lady Lisronan and Gustave held rendezvous. They were a small and ragged crowd, but fiercely hostile, as was demonstrated by their cries and gestures.

Barry, hurrying along in the shadow, heard a single word, "Huguenot! Huguenot!" The narrow street echoed with it.

He had come within a stone's throw of the group, when a hand clutched frantically at the skirt of his long coat, and looking down he saw a small figure huddled against the carved post of a closed door.

"Well? What is it?" he asked sharply, his sword point towards the clutching hand. In the Rue du Sapin Rouge it was well to be wary.

"Barry," whispered the figure with a little sob of pure terror.

Barry, without a word, slipped his sword into its sheath and took her up in his arms. The crowd was swaying towards them. At any moment it might surge into the doorway. He lifted Julia higher, until her head lay on his shoulder, and then pushed the door, against which she had been crouching, with knee and elbow.

Like most doors in that ill-conditioned quarter it was unlocked, unlatched even. Barry stepped into a long panelled room, with one window at the farther end and a dim lantern burning in a cresset on the wall. Julia, weeping as usual, clung to him like a child. He could feel the sobs shaking her

slender light little body, and the terrified clutch of
her hands when he took his right arm from round
her to bolt the door.

"For mercy's sake, my dear, do not cry!" he
protested, pushing the hood of her cloak back.
"Not a man of those damned scoundrels shall
harm you, on my word—not a man of 'em. See,
I 'll carry you across the room, so shall we hear
less of their infernal noise. Now, are you
happier?"

He propped her on the window-seat, and then,
filled with a sudden fear that she had been
hurt, fetched the lantern the better to see her
face.

"Oh, I was so frightened!" she whispered as he
came back. "I was well-nigh dead of fright—
Barry, you won't let them——"

Her trembling lips refused to finish the sentence.
She put out a hand and clutched at him.

"Only frightened—not hurt—not hurt in any
way?" he asked with the curtness of curbed
emotion, looking down at her white face. "Sure,
Julia?"

Julia nodded. "I—I ran into the doorway
when I heard them coming," she said, letting her
hand lie in his. "Why—I mean what annoys
them? Why do they call "Huguenot?"

"Some poor devil of a Protestant lies hid in the
street, doubtless," he answered drily. "A Huguenot here fares rather worse than a Catholic at
home. One can only hope that the Deity, in

whose name it is done, gets as much satisfaction out of the matter as His followers."

Julia, who was wiping her eyes, stopped.

"Do you mean—would they kill the—the—Huguenot?" she asked breathlessly.

"If he's fool enough to be caught. Yes."

"What house were they attacking? Not one two doors from here—the Sign of the *Sapin Bleu?* Oh, say it was not the Sapin Bleu!"

Barry glanced sharply at her. There was sudden poignant anxiety in her voice and eyes.

"So Gustave de l'Afrie has turned Huguenot, has he?" he said, stung by a jealousy so fierce that it made him careless of whether he hurt her or not. "Good quittance for us, say I!"

"Gustave de l'Afrie!" repeated Julia. "Nay, I know nought of Monsieur de l'Afrie's religion—and care less. 'T is for my brother Willy I fear. He lies in that house, wounded—a Protestant!"

"Your brother Willy!"

"Yes. Ten days ago I learnt of his plight. He made shift to send me word. I creep out by stealth to visit him and to nurse him at night. 'T was I you saw—not my tire-woman, last Tuesday at the postern door."

"Your brother. Egad!" muttered Barry.

Bitter shame of his past suspicions and a relief, illuminating in its intensity, kept him silent for a moment, and Julia went on.

"I dare not mention Willy to Dermot or Madame de Louysnes—I feared to——"

"Why did you not tell me? I would have assisted you right gladly."

The warmth of his tone brought a faint colour into Julia's cheeks.

"I—I did not like to trouble you," she said shyly.

"Trouble!" he retorted with a short laugh. "Nay, Julia—you know—you must know—that I ask nothing better than to serve you—nothing in life."

He made an effort to speak lightly, to keep the feeling he had no right to express, out of his voice, but the attempt was not successful. Julia, preoccupied though she was, glanced up at him with a startled, almost terrified air. Since her arrival in Paris various men had essayed to declare, or at least insinuate, undying devotion for the newly-come Irish beauty. Ninon de l'Afrie told her it was the fashion, and Lady Lisronan had accepted their homage gently, without the smallest comprehension of what it meant, just as she accepted a new shape in gowns.

But Barry's tone, Barry's expression as he stood looking down at her now, was an enigma. She understood nothing—except that she felt an unaccountable vague dismay—almost a fear.

And then suddenly the clamour in the streets, which had lulled for a moment, broke out again. With a scream she clutched at him. She was a panic-stricken woman, he a man, some one strong to cling to—some one who would protect her, and possibly Willy, from the enemies outside.

"They will kill us!" she moaned, hiding her eyes on his sleeve. "They will kill us all three— we shall be murdered! Oh, *mon Dieu!*"

She cowered against him like a frightened child, deaf alike to his assurances that neither she nor Willy should suffer, and to certain protestations which in a saner moment he would have kept to himself.

It was not until an interval came in the noise outside that her paroxysm of terror began to subside.

"Willy!" she whispered, freeing herself from Barry's arm. "Can you save Willy?"

Her evident unconsciousness of the sentiment which shook him both relieved and vexed her companion. He had, he felt, made an infernal fool of himself, never a pleasing conviction.

"I can go to the Sapin Bleu, of course," he answered rather irritably. "But I must take you home first."

"No—no! I will come with you. There's no time to lose. Listen! Oh, those terrible people— how they shout!"

She clapped both hands over her ears with a gesture of distraction. Barry bit his lip.

"Any back door to the Sapin Bleu?" he asked after a second.

Julia between her sobs nodded emphatically.

Captain FitzUlick, anathematising all religious differences from the bottom of his soul, leant past her and forced open the crazy window.

As he had hoped, it looked into a very narrow
alley which ran directly behind the Rue du Sapin
Rouge—a dark well-like passage-way, with an
occasional wilted fig tree making it yet more
narrow. By hanging the lantern out, Barry was
able to gauge the depth from the window-sill to
the ground—a space of six feet or so.

He drew in again and looked dubiously at Julia.
To leave her alone in this house, of which he knew
nothing save that it doubtless shared the usual
characteristics of the street, was impossible.

"Listen, my dear," he said, laying a hand gently
on her shoulder. "Listen. You must get through
this casement—I 'll go first and lift you down—
and, Julia, if you could control your fears—I suppose 't is impossible, but—could you try?"

She cast an anguished glance at the street door.

"I—I will be quite brave," she whispered,
clasping her ears again with a gesture of agony.

"Heroic," said Barry, laughing in spite of himself. "Now, Madame!"

He lifted her off the window-seat, swung himself
onto it instead, and a second later was standing
in the alley under a narrow strip of star-strewn
sky, with the crowd's angry roar—most horrible
of all noises—echoing dully above the black roofs
overhead.

The Sapin Bleu was only a pace away. It did
not seem worth while to put Julia down on the
damp slimy flags.

Two figures loitering near the back door, which

stood open to the alley, slunk off at sight of Barry
and his burden.

"Where lodges your brother? Which room?"
he whispered, as he carried Julia over the threshold.

"The back attic."

"Ah—well, you 'll have to walk upstairs, child—
I must e'en have my sword-arm free. Give me
the lantern. Every scoundrel in this rat-run is
awake and anticipating his last hour."

The Sapin Bleu was indeed in a ferment, but a
ferment, like its inhabitants, of a furtive nature.
Faces peered from doorways as Barry and Julia
climbed the steep dark staircase; doors shut with
a rasping of shot bolts; golden threads of light disappeared all in a second out of the cracked wall
panelling on either hand.

On the top step Julia paused.

"Do but hearken to the blows on the street
door! 'T will never hold!" she gasped, looking
back into the well of darkness below.

Barry listened for a moment. Her words had
been hardly audible above the uproar of voices
and the clang of steel on wood, but he guessed
their import.

"Has your brother a pistol case?" he asked in
a sudden lull.

"Yes!"

"Fetch it out to me—and afterwards bolt yourself in his chamber. Quick!"

He thrust the lantern into her hand, pushed her
towards the door of the back attic, and then turned

18

again to the stair-head. The flight was a narrow
one, so very narrow and so very steep, indeed, that
to hold it even against a score of men must prove
a comparatively easy task.

Barry, always self-confident, ignored the fact
that there was nothing to prevent the crowd wearing him down at last by sheer force of numbers,
since the authorities were not likely to notice a
street row in the Rue du Sapin Rouge.

"Courage, Madame!" he said with a smile, as
he took lantern and pistol case out of Julia's
trembling fingers. "No one shall harm either you
or him. *V'là!* There goes the street door! Away
with you, my lady!"

Julia needed no bidding. The crash and the
roar of triumph that accompanied it sent her
helter-skelter into the attic, where Willy stood,
half-dressed, holding feebly to the bed-post.

Barry hung his lantern from a carved griffon on
the banister rail, and then set to to prime Willy
Van der Wynykt's pistols—listening keenly all the
time to the noise of the human torrent as it surged
tumultuously from room to room.

The dilapidated old building seemed to rock
under the noise. Dust and screams rose and
sounds of cracking wood, and the never-ceasing
cry of "Huguenot! Huguenot!"

Barry, standing at the top step, one elbow on
the griffon's broken wings, listened, smiling grimly.

"'Huguenot' here—'Papist' at home! Everywhere men doing the devil's work in the name of

God, and all well satisfied that thereby they might gain heaven!"

Before long he saw signs of the invaders—first one head, one hesitating figure; then two, then a string that ran upstairs noisy and thoughtless as a pack of hounds.

Barry let the foremost man come within six steps of him before he fired. He had no particular desire to kill any of these silly yelping rogues, but to gain a hearing one must inspire fear.

Silence, sudden and complete, followed the crack of the pistol.

"Oh, *mon Dieu*, I am shot!" screamed a voice, shrill with pain and terror. "*Sacré nom*, I perish!"

Barry, enveloped in smoke, heard a confused clatter, as of bodies thudding downstairs, and guessed that the leader, in falling, had knocked over his immediate followers. A crack of breaking wood, a yell and a dull thump suggested further that some one had gone through the banisters.

Clamour broke out again on the landing below. No man would venture upstairs, but each impartially cursed his neighbour for his poltroonery.

It was clearly a case for offensive tactics, and Captain FitzUlick lost no time. With his pistol in one hand and the lantern in the other, he came down to an elbow of the staircase from which he could be seen.

He had turned out the guard before starting for the Rue du Sapin Rouge, and his unbuttoned greatcoat showed a gleam of red, as he stood looking contemptuously down at the mass of upturned faces. The lantern lit his sword-hilt and the pistol's long barrel, and hid the void behind him.

"Soldiers!" shrieked the wounded man from where he lay on the bottom step, "A regiment! A battalion!"

His cry put the finishing touch to a general uneasiness. Panic in its most violent form seized the invaders to a man—and the "battalion," watching their headlong flight, which the steepness of the stairs at once reduced to a helpless yelling descent *en masse*, like a human waterfall, was bent double over the banister-rail with laughter.

He was still laughing when he pushed open the door of Willy Van der Wynykt's room, but his mirth died abruptly at sight of Julia trying to lift her brother's body off the floor.

"He has fainted!" she gasped, "I would get him back into bed."

Barry crossed the room in a stride and pushed her away.

"Sit down," he said shortly. "I will see to him."

"Let me aid you, Barry."

"You! Sit in that chair or I do not touch him!"

Julia obeyed. She was the type of woman to worship a man who did not defer to her.

"I'll send my servant to attend him," said Barry shortly, when he had managed to haul Willy

on to the bed—no light task. "Come, my lady,
I must take you home before all else."

"Oh, no—no!"

"Yes—most decidedly yes. And see here,
Julia, there must be no more of this." He
nodded at Van der Wynykt lying inert among
tossed blankets. "I 'll see he lacks for nothing,
but you must keep away from the Sapin
Bleu."

"Oh, Barry, I cannot—I will not! Pray—pray,
Barry!—Can I leave him to die here alone?"
Julia got up as she spoke and came forward. "I
will not do it!" she ended, passionately.

"Dermot must be told then."

Julia melted into tears.

"Dermot will prevent my coming hither—
Dermot hates all of our name!" she sobbed.
"Oh, Barry, if you were truly kind, you would—
would——"

"Well?"

"Would bring me here yourself. Then I could
come to no harm."

Her voice dropped to its softest note.

She put out a hand and laid it on his sleeve.

Barry shook off the little trembling fingers with
a curious violent gesture.

"You—you misjudge Dermot!" he said harshly.

"I would not come very often. I—I hoped you
would not mind escorting me," she went on in a
rather crestfallen tone, ignoring his remark. "An'
you dislike it, of course——"

"Dislike it! Egad, child, don't you understand?
I mean——"

He looked at her helplessly, irritably, anathematising her innocence.

"I am sorry—but, indeed, you have been more
than kind as it is," she murmured with a little
wistful sigh, "kinder than any other."

Barry looked down at the lantern which he still
carried.

"I think you would do well to trust Dermot,"
he said stiffly, "but that's your concern. For
your brother, I promise you he shall lack nothing—
and as to visiting him—well, would every other
night satisfy you?"

"Does that mean—you will? Oh, how good
you are—I—I have been so frightened traversing
that dark alley and this terrible street all alone!"

CHAPTER XXV

STOLEN WATERS

THERE are few things on earth more dangerous
than a shared secret. Almost always it acts
either as a bond to draw the participators in it yet
closer or as a weapon to cleave them irrevocably
apart. Those midnight excursions from the postern door of the Hôtel de Louysnes to the Rue
du Sapin Rouge were a very forcing-bed for the
sentiments. Though no word to which Dermot
could have taken exception was spoken, though
neither Barry nor Julia ever tried to prolong
the journey, both had come, by the third occasion, to regard that stolen walk through the
warm ivory-tinted moonlight as the main incident of the day.

The evening that saw Willy Van der Wynykt set
out for Ireland was a gloomy one to both. They
stood together by mutual consent in the mouth of
the Passage de la Lanterne, looking back at the
dingy Sapin Bleu with unveiled regret.

"I shall miss him," said Julia tearfully, hardly
appreciating the fact that what she would really

miss were these minutes of intimate and happy companionship.

"You have been more than good in the affair, Barry," she added. "No one has ever been so good to me as you—I can never thank you enough."

Barry made no response, though the speech certainly demanded one, and Julia went on speaking in a soft reflective way.

"You might so easily, so naturally, have declined to aid an enemy—a——"

"Willy is your brother," put in FitzUlick shortly, as she hesitated.

His tone made Julia's heart jump strangely. The night of the disturbance she had been too thoroughly terrified to realise what he said, or indeed anything save the fact that in his arms there was safety from the yelling crowd. All through she had accepted his help with as little thought as a child, and it was only to-night, when the realisation of her own pleasure in those midnight walks reached a climax, that the question of his feeling the same began to dawn on her.

"Without you Willy must have—died," she stammered awkwardly, conscious that it was a banal thing to say, yet more afraid of the silence than of words.

"Willy be hanged! What I did I did for your sake—solely for your sake. I would do anything for you, Julia—anything on earth—good or bad!" FitzUlick answered with a savage abruptness that had in it something of anger. "In fact," he added, "in fact, things being as they are, I wish to God I had never seen you!"

In the tense little silence that followed, sudden enlightenment came to Julia. She was not a person of many or very subtle ideas. She realised only the bare shadow, as it were, of her feeling for Barry and Barry's feeling for her, but even that sufficed. At last she was of value to some one— at last she might claim first place in a human heart, might know the warmth for which all her life she had pined. A grand passion she did not desire— would not indeed have comprehended—but she craved affection.

No one else cared for her—not Madame de Louysnes—not Dermot—not her fickle fashionable newly-made friends. No one else appreciated her intolerable loneliness. The silly ever-ready tears welled up in her eyes, but she could find no words. Stress of emotion held her tongue-tied.

When Barry moved a step towards her she shrank nervously away. He stopped with an angry shrug of his shoulders.

"Nay, you need not flinch from me, my lady," he said, still in the passionate undertone which seemed to Julia to have no connection with the light-hearted jesting Barry of her acquaintance. "Right well I know it means nothing to you! Come! 'T is time you were home."

He turned abruptly to the "Passage," but Julia did not move. Under cover of the darkness in which they stood she put out a trembling hand and supported herself against the wall.

"You misjudge me," she whispered slowly, as if the words were forced from her by some power outside her own will. "It means a good deal—to me."

Barry's sword clanked suddenly on the stones. He had been gathering it up and had let it drop.

"Is—is that the truth, Julia?" he asked with a sharp note of suspense in his voice.

"Yes."

He turned swiftly to her and caught both her hands.

His touch sent a little warm thrill through her, but the tightened pressure of her wedding-ring brought with it remembrance.

"Oh," she whispered, trying to draw her fingers out of his, "this is wrong! There 's a gulf between us that neither you nor I dare forget."

"I know that—I know that!" Barry retorted impatiently, stung by the poignant truth of her words and by the fact that she had remembered when he did not. "Let 's forget it for a moment— only a moment! I cannot put this from me all in a breath. It means too much to me—I——"

"Hush, oh, hush!"

The sound of hoofs coming along the Rue du Sapin Rouge broke the moonlit silence. In a second Barry had twisted round and put himself between Julia and the street.

The approaching horseman hardly noticed the

one dim figure in the alley's dimmer shadows. He rode by slowly, with a single careless glance, his own features fully displayed by the ivory light, his sword-hilt and silver coat buttons agleam.

Barry felt Julia shiver, and for a second his own heart seemed to stop, for the rider was Dermot Lisronan. The whole position, the impossibility of explanation, flashed through his mind like a hideous picture.

Julia was the first to break the long silence that followed.

"Oh, if he had seen us!" she gasped. "Oh!"

She clasped her hands together and looked wildly down the Passage de la Lanterne, to where a turret of Esmée de Louysnes's house loomed grey against the night sky.

"Will he ask to see you? Will he come to your rooms?" asked Barry quickly, any delicacy he might ordinarily have felt about the question merged in consternation.

"No—no! Let me get home!"

She gathered up her skirt with a little moan and began to creep along the "Passage."

"He saw nothing," said Barry.

"Yes, but if he had! Oh, it won't bear thinking of. We must not meet again ever—ever!"

"Come, Madame—you don't expect me to agree to that," he said. "Why, even to travel into Ireland—as I must next week—seems exile. Do not make bad worse, I pray you."

"What takes you to Ireland?" asked Julia, and

an anxiety too poignant to conceal rang in her
voice. "It is not safe," she added.

"The Colonel is sending me on a matter privy
to his interests," said Barry indifferently. "I
shall be gone under a sennight."

Julia walked a pace in silence and then stopped.
They were at the mouth of the "Passage," with
the Place Royale and the postern door just before
them.

"Stay here," she whispered peremptorily.
"Some one might see you if you crossed in the
moonlight. Good-bye—I hope the journey into
Ireland may prosper with you."

She would have darted away, but Barry caught
her.

"Julia! Of course I shall see you again before
I go?"

"'T were better not."

"Oh, nonsense, sweetheart! Why——?"

"Do not call me that," she interrupted nervously. "I—mean—I mean——"

"What *do* you mean, Madame?" he demanded,
his hands on her shoulders.

"I mean that already we have said too much—
you and I," retorted Julia with the relentlessness
of extreme youth. "I as Dermot's wife—you as
his friend. Remember your own words—that you
would you had never seen me—and think of the
reason of them."

"Nay, the reason's gone now—I thought then
that you did not care a rush," he answered shortly.

"We 've been friends up to this—why should it make any difference?"

She glanced up at him doubtfully, as if his sophistry and the obvious flimsiness of his argument troubled her.

"Will it—not—make a difference?" she asked. "Do you really think that, Barry?"

"On my soul I do."

Julia hesitated.

"You know best," she said after a second. "I am indeed very ignorant. Do not come until you return out of Ireland, Barry. I had rather you did not."

"Why?"

"Oh—because—because I—I——"

"Well?"

She hung her head muttering something of which Barry only caught one word—the name of her confessor.

"Père de l'Ecrillon!" he repeated impatiently. "What has he to do with it?"

"That is a silly question," she returned in a pettish tone. "You know I must ask Père de l'Ecrillon—and tell him of to-night—and I dread to, for he is strict—oh, very strict. I pray you do not seek to see me, Barry, until you are come out of Ireland."

She laid her hand on his for a brief instant, and then slipped across the street with the speed and silence of a cat, and had opened the postern door almost before he realised that she was gone.

CHAPTER XXVI

JAMES TAAFFE'S STORY

THE woods of Slieveronan dated back to the days when Conchobar reigned in Connacht. Carew's destroying axe had passed them by, Cromwell had forgotten or never known them. They stretched along the hillside, mile upon mile of holly and hazel, and little native Irish oak, waist deep in trackless undergrowth or overhanging precipitous ravines, where hidden waters plunged and splashed eternally behind a curtain of swaying fern.

It was a sanctuary for all hunted things, that wide green dim territory uncrossed by path or trail. The red deer lived there, and the wolf and his human compeer, those outlawed sons of the land who would not follow King James abroad and could not serve Queen Anne at home—a landless, altarless tribe, whose hand was against every "settler" and every settler's hand against them.

One of their many camps lay in a furzy hollow, so fenced by dense thickets of holly and bramble and alders that no one but the initiated would

286

either have suspected its existence or found a way in.

There were a dozen of them gathered here this May afternoon—ten playing cards, one doing sentinel, and the twelfth lying under an oak gasping out his life with every hard-drawn breath.

Barry FitzUlick, on his way down from the hillside above, came on this twelfth man and stopped abruptly.

"Good God, Taaffe! What's happened?" he exclaimed, glancing aghast at the livid, blood-stained face that showed so grey against the tree's moss-green roots.

"Father Talbot!" gasped James Taaffe. "For the love of God, fetch him!"

"Bus-an-appagh!" called Barry, turning and signalling with his chin to the leader of the Grey Dragoons, who was at the moment dealing.

Bus-an-appagh dropped the last card into his own pile, grabbed the hand up in a manner more significant than complimentary to his fellow-players, and rose reluctantly.

Thirty-six years earlier his birth had enmeshed two of the highest of the old Norman-Irish families in a hideous scandal, and it was in tribute to this exalted origin that the Grey Dragoons had elected him chief. The feudal feeling dies hard in any clan people. To them a ruler is an even more vital necessity than to the average man, though he, heaven knows, makes a poor enough display without one.

Bus-an-appagh had come in ten years to ride roughshod over his outlaw crew, and it said much for Barry FitzUlick's power of taking a lead that he, a chance outsider, could assert himself at all against the tyrant.

The pair met half-way across the moss-grown space.

"What befell Jimmy Taaffe?" asked Barry shortly, with a backward jerk of his head.

Bus-an-appagh gave his huge ape-like mouth a twist. He had shot Taaffe in a moment of temper.

"The boys quarrelled," he said. "Jimmy was making for safety when a chance ball found him. He's done nought since but cry upon Father Talbot."

"The fellow's dying."

Bus-an-appagh looked down at his cards.

"Is he so? The fool!" he said indifferently.

"Have you sent for the priest?"

"No."

"Why not? You don't want the poor fellow to die unshriven, do you?"

The leader of the Grey Dragoons shrugged his shoulders.

"Father Talbot's away to Lisronan. To bring him across the bog in open daylight were too risky. There're two score scoundrels scouring the countryside for you. 'T is surely better Jimmy Taaffe should burn than Father Talbot lose his life. Eh?"

The logic of this, if somewhat brutal, was beyond dispute. FitzUlick pushed his hat on to the back of his perukeless head and swore softly.

Bus-an-appagh, without waiting for a further opinion on the subject, returned to the circle of players, who greeted him by a hasty shutting together of their cards as he passed behind them.

Barry's inclination was for flight. He hated the unpleasant with all his soul, dreading it as only the sensitive and kind-hearted can; but this man was Julia's uncle—a poor derelict devil—and he knew how very little he himself would like to die alone, neglected and deserted—he who was no coward.

He spread his coat over James Taaffe, fetched a saddle to support his head, and pulled away a large stone that was pressing into his side. The wounded man whimpered weakly all the while, and plucked at the bracken on either side with restless fingers.

"Father Talbot!" he panted. "Father Talbot!"

His eyes, staring up at Barry, who stood over him in his shirt sleeves, a picture of impatient perplexity, were the eyes of a terrified animal.

"Father Talbot!" he whispered again.

"What of Father Talbot?" asked Barry.

"I—I must see him—I cannot die without. Oh, for God's sake, fetch him before it is too late!"

The last word rose to a note of panic-stricken despair. Cravenly as James Taaffe had feared death, horrible as he had always anticipated it to

19

be, the idea of meeting it unsustained by the Church had never entered his worst imaginings.

"Father Talbot—Father Talbot!" he gasped, the tears hopping grotesquely down his blood-stained cheeks.

Any sympathy Barry might have felt was chilled by the sight of so much abjectness. Common humanity, and the knowledge—unpleasant though it was—of his relationship with Julia alone kept him by the dying man. His strong desire was to walk away—far enough to neither hear that whimpering voice nor see those frenzied eyes.

James Taaffe seemed to read the thought.

"FitzUlick! Stay! The—others have all gone," he begged, trying to clutch at the young man's boot. "Don't leave me too—for the love of God do not leave me!"

"I had no thought of leaving you," said Barry in rather an irritable tone. Taaffe's cowardice and his own repulsion from the whole scene—also a species of cowardice, as he ruefully admitted—made him hot with shame. "So much talk will assuredly start that infernal bleeding again," he added, dropping, reluctantly enough, on one knee beside Taaffe.

"Send for Father Talbot!" reiterated the wounded man. "Send him word that I am dying, I pray. He will come—assuredly he will come!"

"And lose his life in doing so. Listen, Taaffe—we can send and, as you say, he'll come—but it's a thousand chances to one Wynykt's men get him.

There 's a ring of them outside these woods. Can you understand me?"

Taaffe began to pluck again at the young bracken which curled all about him.

"He will come an' he 's told," he whispered. "God! to die without a priest!"

Barry bit his lip. On one point he was perfectly clear, namely, that to risk Father Talbot's life that one shivering wretch might die the easier was folly.

"It 's your need or his neck!" he said brusquely, after a second's silence.

"Send for him! Send for him!"

"'T is your need against the interests of all Lisronan. Have you weighed that?"

James Taaffe had weighed nothing, could consider nothing, save the fact that the Church to which he had clung all his life was failing him now. He broke into a weak tempest of sobs, and what Barry had prophesied happened—the hemorrhage began again.

FitzUlick watched it a second hopelessly, and then got up and strode across the hollow to where the group of Grey Dragoons sat playing spoil-five beside a small fire.

"Taaffe 's dying," he said shortly, standing outside the ring.

The players one and all glanced at him. Taaffe had long ago forfeited their esteem, such as it was, and not one cared how or when he came to his end; but Barry, by his very masterfulness, his indif-

ference to Bus-an-appagh, had won an unwilling
admiration from the most democratic—even Bus-
an-appagh himself, who was as savage in his denun-
ciation of "the gentry" as he was vehement in
asserting his right to rank amongst them.

It was he who spoke now. "Ah, poor James,
I'd be sorry anything would happen to him.
Indeed, I'd not wish it for a hundred guineas."

Barry's set, angry face relaxed for a second into
a smile not flattering to the speaker.

"You're the readiest man at a lie in Ireland,
Bus," he said in his nonchalant fashion, adding:
"Where is Brother Ignatius?"

"Gone hence this sennight," answered Bus-an-
appagh sulkily. He might cow his circle into
silence, but he could not stifle their grins—and
FitzUlick was always eliciting a grin at his
expense.

"Gone hence—um—well, will any here bear a
message to Father Talbot—praying him come to
Sir James Taaffe, who lies at the point of death,
and praying him at the same time remember that
Lisronan needs him bitter bad, and that Taaffe will
not in an hour's time need him at all. Will one of
you bear him that message? Craoibhin dhun,
hang me if I saw you before! Will you go?"

The hedge-schoolmaster, who had been sitting
on the roots of an oak half hidden by bracken,
rose up, ink-horn in hand.

"Aye, will I, your honour," he said simply.

"Belike Jimmy hath somewhat on his conscience," sneered Bus-an-appagh, looking again at his hand.

"Like enough—seeing the company he has kept," returned Barry, and went back across the glade.

Taaffe lay just as he had left him, his face, ghastly in its blood-stained pallor, upturned to the sky, his eyes still full of tears, but Barry noticed a change.

Turning, he summoned Bartley with a jerk of his head. The hedge-schoolmaster understood. He came quickly across the moss and paused behind a holly-bush, mouthing a silent question.

"Father Talbot!" moaned Taaffe.

"I 've sent for him," answered Barry, kneeling down.

"Have you ought special to tell him?"

Something in his tone told that which he hesitated to put into words.

"You—you think—he will be too late?" whispered James Taaffe.

Barry nodded.

A shudder ran through the wounded man.

"Oh, my God—and I have sinned—I have sinned!" he sobbed. "I have sinned grievously—I am lost! FitzUlick, are you there? There is something that I should tell Lisronan—about Julia. It lies on my conscience——"

The voice tailed off in a whisper. Barry, his heart beginning to thump suddenly, bent closer.

"Yes—go on—I will tell Lisronan," he said unsteadily.

For a second there was no response. Then Taaffe, fighting feebly for breath, turned his head.

"I promised Margaret—her mother—to tell," he went on in tones hardly audible to the man bending over him. "Lisronan should have known when first he married her—but I—I feared Wynykt—Julia is—is——"

"Not his daughter. Eh?" put in Barry curtly as Taaffe paused gasping.

It seemed to him that the answer would never come. He laid an arm across the hands that crept upon and plucked at the outspread coat, and looked down straight into Taaffe's eyes.

"You guessed?" whispered Julia's uncle. "Oh, I should have told—I promised Margaret to tell. There are papers will prove it—here."

He drew his right hand from under the restraining arm and tried to feel about his breast.

"Take them," he added. "Take them now."

"I will take them—later." Barry's voice had a decidedly tense note.

"No. Now—now!" James Taaffe shivered as he gasped the words, adding, "I feared Wynykt. My God, how I feared him!"

"I will tell Lisronan," said the young man, groping tentatively and with extreme care at the blood-stiffened buttonholes of Taaffe's waistcoat.

He got them undone at last, and heaved a sigh of relief when he saw that the shirt underneath had no fastenings.   Under it, on James Taaffe's chest, beside his scapular, lay a flat leather bag.

Barry slipped a knife from his pocket and cut both the string of the bag and the fine chain of the scapular.   The bag he took, feeling through the thin leather as he did so the rough edges of folded parchments.   The scapular he put into Taaffe's hand.

The dying man began a muttered prayer—an act of faith.

Barry, who could think of nothing but the news he had just been told, glanced over his shoulder at Bartley Sullivan, and stumbled to his feet.

At once the little hedge-schoolmaster came forward, knelt where FitzUlick had knelt, and took up the prayer.   It was not the first time he— God's second priest, as the Irish idiom calls the teacher—had had to guide stumbling feet down the last steep steps of the river-bank.

Barry watched him for a second doubtfully and then turned away.   There was nothing more he could do, and he was glad to escape.

He walked straight off out of the camp and on into one of those fairy places that exist still where civilisation has not set its destroying foot.   It was a grove in which ancient, very ancient, nut trees, broad-limbed, twisted, draped with fringes of emerald moss, stood sentinel round a sunlit spring, fern-ringed and diamond clear.

Barry, who never consciously observed nature, used in after years to wonder why he had a vague

dislike for the sparkle of water and the transparent
green of a young sun-warmed leaf.

His hands shook as he unfastened the little
leather bag and drew forth its contents.   One fact
alone filled his thoughts.   If Julia was not Van der
Wynykt's daughter no barrier existed between
her and Dermot.   He tore the tindery old parchments in his haste.

The story they set forth was very simple.   Margaret Taaffe, at the time of her marriage to
Albrecht Van der Wynykt, had loved and been
loved by another man—Conor Connel of Bally
Kilconnel in Mayo.   Wynykt, tired of his wife
before their union was a week old, soon developed
a habit of sending her home for months at a time,
and during one of these periods the news of his
death came from Holland on some side-wind.

The rest hardly needed words.   Barry, blessed
—or cursed—with imagination, was able to picture
very vividly Albrecht Van der Wynykt's descent
upon the newly married couple—his shooting of
Conor Connel—the treatment meted out to his
wretched wife.   Margaret had indeed set forth
the facts with extraordinary vividness, consider-
ing her natural stupidity.

In a letter to James Taaffe she had prayed him
to take charge of Conor Connel's child should Van
der Wynykt cast it forth.   In a later letter, written on her death-bed, she had besought him as her
only relation to enlighten the girl's future husband
"since none would wed with one believed to be this

monster's daughter," adding: "Yet be wary that
he is not acquainted of this fact, the which I have
never dared to tell him, lest he should wreak his
vengeance upon the child."

Barry shook his head when he came to this
sentence. That Van der Wynykt was ignorant
seemed curious, for Margaret and Conor had been
ten weeks married at the time of his return, but
doubtless the unhappy woman had lied. The fact
of her having been Julia's mother made him lenient
to her faults.

He turned over the other papers—a certificate of
the marriage that was no marriage—some letters
of Conor Connel's.

The name recalled to Barry a vision of a handsome, fair-headed, brown-eyed young man—also
a Connel of Bally Kilconnel, and also a "Conor"—
whom he had met in the Low Countries. Julia's
cousin, beyond question! He remembered now,
and could at last explain, a likeness which had
often puzzled him.

He thrust the parchments back into the bag,
and stood frowning and staring fiercely ahead.
Dermot would welcome the news which bridged
this gulf between him and his wife. And Julia——?

Until that moment Barry had never appreciated
the fact that he almost subconsciously counted
on and hoped for the moment when Dermot's
unnatural attitude would drive Julia to revolt.
He had imagined that he wanted to "play the
game." He had believed sincerely that he *was*

playing it, and since he enjoyed the discovery of flaws in his own nature as little as any other man or woman, it gave him a decided shock to realise that, though he would not act the part of tempter to the woman whom Dermot had married, he yet anticipated the day when she would, of her own free will, turn to him. This course seemed on reflection only a fraction less dishonourable than that which he might—probably would—have pursued if Julia had not been the wife of a friend.

Barry was under no delusion as to Dermot's present feelings for Julia. He knew a fact of which Lisronan was ignorant; he had noticed a subtle change from indifference to unwilling interest— a reluctant pleasure in her society, unadmitted as yet by Dermot even to himself. He had, indeed, even while he wondered contemptuously that any man should allow a mere sentiment, however strong and reasonable, to outweigh affection, thanked God for the existence of that sentiment.

And now he must, with his own hand, raise up a gateless barrier between himself and the woman he loved. He knew just what Julia would do— how she would weep, how unhappy she would be, how tearfully obstinate in what she considered the "right." The Church would support her—the Church and the iron virtue of the Irishwoman. She would make Dermot an excellent wife, even though she loathed him—if she were capable of loathing, which Barry doubted.

Doubtless her mother had done the same. Doubtless Conor Connel had striven unavailingly to supplant the man whom Margaret hated and feared, long ere that false news came from Holland.

No. To tell Dermot, to show Dermot the papers, was to lose Julia surely—nay more surely— than if she were in her coffin.

Barry had no intention of losing Julia. All along, hand-in-hand with his intention strictly to play the game, had gone an unadmitted belief that one of those miracles on which youth alone relies would intervene in his favour. About the nature of the miracle he did not speculate. In fact, since it premised Dermot's demise, he carefully abstained from any thoughts thereof, but he counted on it nevertheless.

And now this infernal revelation upset everything, altered everything, save and except the one great fact of his feeling for Julia and Julia's feeling for him. Exactly at what point of his bitter cogitations the thought that it was, after all, possible not to tell Dermot occurred to him, he could never subsequently decide. He put it away with all conceivable speed. But it returned; in spite of his efforts it returned. Even while he stood frowning in the warm sunshine, it crept back, insidious as the water filtering through the sand. If Dermot remained in ignorance he would continue to treat Julia after his present fashion—and if he continued to treat Julia after his present fashion, the day must come when she would——

He shook himself free of the idea again—rather less resolutely this time.

"I 'll tell him the first opportunity that serves," he thought, and turned back towards the camp.

CHAPTER XXVII

"LOVE THAT SINGS AND HAS WINGS LIKE A BIRD"

MADAME DE LOUYSNES had a little *pied-à-terre* at Fontainebleau—a very small thirteenth century "château" in a glade of the forest—to which she generally moved from her Paris house when the Court went to Marly.

Barry FitzUlick was riding thither this June morning, down an aisle of silver-stemmed giant beeches, riding slowly and morosely, with an unwonted shadow in his blue-green eyes. The thought of what he was about to do preyed on his mind like the remembrance of a wrong—but so far he had not wavered. Dermot must be told—must be given Margaret Wynykt's letter. After that—? Barry so far had contrived to avoid the thought of what would follow the revelation, but this morning it rose up and insisted on being faced.

It went with him like a shadow along the sun-flecked shade-dappled ride, where last year's leaves lay rust-coloured in every hollow of the emerald moss. It blinded him to the flickering pale green

arches over his head, and to the far-flung blue fire
of the wild hyacinths in shadowed places between
the great grey stems.

It even made him oblivious of a lady who sat on
a bright bay cob at a turn in a bridle-path, though
he was rarely unobservant of his fellow man.

She watched him in silence for a moment, as he
rode towards her in the gold gorget, the scarlet
uniform and dark facings of Galmoy's regiment.
The dancing sunlight caught his sword-hilt, his
spurs, and the long ends of the bit.   Bright ripples,
like the sheen of satin, ran down every line of his
sorrel's golden-brown coat.   Her white-streaked
forehead, her one white hind leg, stood out with
startling vividness against the green-gold shadows
of the wood.

Madame de Louysnes, that enthusiastic worshipper of all that pleased the eye, looked her fill
before she spoke.

"Whither away, Sir Launcelot?" she said at last,
when Barry was almost within hand's touch.   His
start was not lost on her.   "I interrupted a dream,
I fear," she added remorsefully.

He shook his head, with a smile which struck
Esmée as strangely rueful—for him.

"I never have dreams so good that you would
n't be welcome to dispel them, Madame," he said,
pulling up.

"Dermot?   No bad news?" she queried hastily,
seized by the fear that always beset her in her
nephew's absence.

"Bad news! No. Is n't Dermot here? I came to see him."

"Dermot is at Valence, with the regiment. He left us three days ago."

Barry was conscious of a relief almost too poignant to conceal. Never until this moment had he realised how intensely he hated the task before him. Now—unless he wrote—Dermot would have to remain unenlightened for at least two months. Valence lay a good week's journey from Corbeil, and there was not the remotest chance of his being granted another fortnight's leave to go there. His spirits raced up like quicksilver in fine weather.

Esmée de Louysnes, watching him, wondered why the shadow had gone so suddenly from his over-expressive face. As yet she had no inkling of how affairs were between him and Julia Lisronan. Dermot filled her horizon, and that any woman honoured by the position of Dermot's wife, should—however Dermot treated her—have eyes or thoughts for another man was to Madame de Louysnes simply beyond conception.

"We had Dermot here for the past sennight laid up with fever," she said suddenly. "The King's chief physician, whom I summoned, would have it 't was smallpox at first. A nice fright he gave us with his head-shakings and his pomander box, silly old man! I 'm glad to say Julia showed herself of better metal than I should have expected. Nothing would do her but to nurse Dermot. She had no fear of infection."

"You did not allow it, surely?"

The wrath and haste in Barry's tone made Esmée raise her eyebrows.

"A wife's first duty is to her husband," she said drily, with a sharp glance at the young man's agitated face. "Of course I permitted it. 'T was not the smallpox after all, but a camp fever, and she proved an excellent nurse. Indeed, Dermot——"

"Well, what of Dermot?"

But Madame de Louysnes left the sentence unfinished. She was thinking of the little drama which had unfolded itself before her eyes during the second half of Lisronan's illness—of his growing interest in his wife, of the way he had come to watch her when present and listen for her step when she was away.

Esmée, whose feeling was all for her nephew, hated to remember, as she had hated to watch, a process which could only mean more unhappiness to him. Dermot had not told her in so many words that in no descendant of Albrecht Van der Wynykt should his mother's blood run; but she knew his mind. Bad as it was that this most misguided marriage should cut him off from the average man's birthright, a son to perpetuate his name, it would be worse were he called on to endure the added misery of loving a woman debarred by such a barrier. Esmée would have hated Julia if it had been possible to hate a creature so sweet-natured, so gentle, and so infinitely pretty.

"You are very silent, Madame, on a sudden,"

said Barry, who had been watching her impatiently
and reading her thoughts with an accuracy of
intuition unusual in the mere male.

"Your pardon, Barry! My mind had gone to
Dermot's illness."

Barry bent to straighten a holster strap, already
quite straight. He was meditating a remark which
would, he knew, probably earn him a rebuff, but
it was not the prospect of this that made his heart
beat all at once unusually fast.

"What terms are they on now—he and Julia?"
he asked abruptly. "Better—or worse than—
when I was last in Paris?"

Esmée de Louysnes hesitated a second.

"Much better. I think Dermot is greatly
drawn to her—now," she answered at last.

"He 'd be a cold-blooded fish of a fellow if he
was n't," said Captain FitzUlick, with elaborate
indifference. "There 's no prettier woman in
France."

"No—more 's the pity!" sighed Esmée bitterly.

"Why, Madame?"

"Why, Barry? Do you really ask why? What
benefit would it be to poor Dermot to love the
pretty little goose when—when there 's what
there is between them? Far better that he
should hate her! You know as well as I that
he is not so light as to forget all that has been
for the sake of a beautiful face. He could
not—no man could! An' he really cared for
Julia he 'd be miserable."

20

"And Julia?" Barry's voice had an edge as he asked the question.

Madame de Louysnes gave her shoulders a shrug.

"Julia!" she returned, "Julia will never suffer overmuch through her feelings."

Barry opened his lips to contradict her hotly, and then thought better of it—an action quite foreign to his nature.

They had let the horses follow their own inclinations during the conversation, and those inclinations being set stablewards, they were now within sight of Esmée's château. Barry glanced at its pepper-castor turrets, dark against the blue June sky. They represented a temptation.

"Does Lady Lisronan receive this morning?" he asked, as indifferently as he could.

"I think so. You'll find her in the pleasance. We may count on your society for at least a few days, I hope, Barry?"

He shook his head.

"No such luck for me, Madame—I rejoin this afternoon," he said with a downward glance at his regimentals. "Otherwise I should have been only too glad. Are you not coming into the château?"

"No—I have but just come out—stolen out, I may say, without as much as a groom to spoil my enjoyment of nature. To see the sun on the blue-bells this morning is worth a year of life—not that you understand that, Barry."

"I think I do, Madame."

Esmée laughed and shook her head. "And I
know you do not," she answered lightly. *"Au
revoir. Viens! mes enfants."*

She turned her cob, whistled to her dogs, and
rode back into the aisles of gold and green without
another glance.

Barry went on across the steep backed bridge
that spanned the moat. The pleasance lay behind
the château, and he made his way there as soon as
he was rid of the sorrel.

It was a small place, medieval as the house itself,
divided into strange plots by yew-hedges and over-
run with roses. At the end farthest from the
château the ground had been levelled away to the
edge of the moat, giving a glimpse of dark green
waters and a gold-spangled meadow beyond.

Barry, who had found Julia at this particular
spot once before, headed instinctively for it. A
thrush pouring out his whole heart "in a rain of
silver laughter" drowned the light clink of his
spurs, and on the moss-grown old turf his steps
made no sound.

He stopped when he came round the hedge of
yews that sheltered this low-lying terrace. Julia,
in a white dress with a filmy mantilla of black
Spanish lace over her head, was indeed there,
sitting on an old stone seat close to the water.
She had a book on her lap, but her eyes stared
dreamily out across the moat and the field that
bounded it, to where the outposts of the forest
stood, grey beech-stems that loomed through the

heat haze like the pillars of a temple.   Barry could
see her delicate profile outlined against the smooth
waters with their dim reflections of the blue overhead, their flat lily leaves, their fringe of yellow
fleurs-de-lys.   She sat so still that a green lizard
had stopped in his rush along the narrow flagged
pathway to gaze at the white sweep of her skirts.

"Julia," said Barry very softly.

Julia gave a violent start and glanced round.

"Barry!" she cried, with an eager delight that
defied concealment.   "Barry!"

She sprang up and ran to meet him, careless of
effect as any joyful child—and Barry, who had come
into the pleasance full of most excellent resolutions,
caught her in his arms and kissed her passionately.

For a second Julia clung to him.   There was no
uncertainty now in her mind about the nature of
her feeling for Barry.   His absence had dispelled
any possible doubt.   In her ecstasy at his sudden
advent, she forgot Dermot, her position, Père de
l'Ecrillon's exhortations, everything save that here
was the man she loved and from whom she had
been parted.

But in a second the sense of her guilt assailed
her.   She had all youth's crude horror of wrong-
doing as wrong-doing, all youth's inability to
realise the existence of extenuating circumstances,
even for itself.   Father Moran and Father Talbot
had never failed to impress on her the necessity of
virtue, the utter heinousness of vice—she knew
no half measures.

"Oh, Barry—no," she whispered piteously, struggling to escape; "this—this is n't right!"

"I know that," he answered morosely.

Julia drew back from him.

"You promised last time," she said, midway between tears and laughter.

He stood silent, staring at her with sombre eyes.

"I—I—cannot see you—if—unless——"

Her voice tailed off into incoherence.

"It is n't right," she added, clinging to the one definite point in the chaos of emotions that surged round her.

Barry made no response. He was wishing definitely and viciously that Dermot had not recovered from that fever of a month earlier.

"It is wrong really, Barry," said Julia, in the tone of gentle protest which was her nearest approach to anger. "It—it is a sin."

"An awful thing that," he retorted with an angry smile. "Oh, you baby—do you think I don't know right from wrong as well, aye, and better than you! Listen—and answer me truly. If one of us—Dermot or I—had to go from your life for ever, which should it be?"

The colour went suddenly out of Julia's face, leaving it white to the lips.

"Barry! You are not going away—not really?" she asked slowly, in a terrified undertone, her eyes wide with distress. "You—you—have n't come to tell me that?"

"Would you care?"

She flung out both hands with a gesture of passionate dissent.

"You asked me that once before—and I answered you!" she said fiercely. "It is cruel to ask again—when you know what—what I ought to say."

Her voice broke on the last word. She motioned Barry away when he would have taken her hand.

"No!" she said, breaking in on the protestations he was beginning. "Words are easy—and you men think all is healed by a kiss and an 'I am sorry.' You are cruel, Barry—you hurt me! You lower me in my own estimation. You, who ought to be strong, are—are——"

"Weak—miserably weak!" he put in, as she hesitated for a word. "I admit it—God knows I cannot deny it—but—" He broke off and shrugged his shoulders hopelessly, adding, "As you say, words are of no use. There exist none to fit any situation out of the ordinary."

A silence fell between them. Barry stared down at the grass and Julia watched him, and occupied her mind by profitable reflections as to how much handsomer, nay, how much more desirable in every way he was than Dermot. She recalled with bitter contempt her interest in Lisronan after their first meeting by the nut-grove in Poulnoe. It seemed the mere ghost of a sentiment now.

Barry's look of morose concentration distressed

her. Like most women, she could face personal
misery with more equanimity than the thought
that she had entailed unhappiness on one dear to
her heart.

"I spoke in haste, Barry—forget what I said,"
she begged suddenly. "You would never hurt me
willingly, I know. 'T was the remembrance of
Père de l'Ecrillon's words stung me to over-ready
speech."

"Père de l'Ecrillon is right—more 's the pity,"
said Barry with a sigh. "Say I may come here
sometimes, Julia. The regiment's at Corbeil—
only fifteen miles off."

Julia hesitated a second over the answer—
hesitated, and looked away across the placid moat
and the golden fleurs-de-lys to the sunlit meadow
with its veil of buttercups. Somewhere far overhead a lark, pouring forth his pæan of joy, almost
drowned the deeper notes of the thrush among
the roses. Who, given a choice on such a morning,
could have declined the chance of happiness,
however brief, however ill-gotten?

"'T is unwise, Barry," she faltered at last.
"'T is vastly unwise of us both—but——"

"I may?" He snatched the words from her lips
in his eagerness. "Say I may, Julia."

"Would you stay away at my bidding?" she
asked with a little smile.

"I should try," he returned. "It 's possible—
being only mortal—that I should fail."

She answered his words by a glance which proclaimed her feeling for him more eloquently than she realised.

"Do you ever ride in the forest?" he went on hurriedly, fearing lest she should repent of her decision. "We might go there together, time and again, you and I?"

The look of pleasure that lit her face was eclipsed almost at once by one of dismay.

"I have so great a fear of horses," she said plaintively. "There is a horrid yellow palfrey here—I had to ride it on Wednesday. It did dreadful things!"

"I 'll find you a mount that will do nothing 'dreadful,'" said Barry with a laugh. "My Major's wife has a white Spanish jennet, which she would fain have kept for a month or so while she is away. You would not fear her—no one could. I 'll bring her here for you to try on Saturday next. Now I must be shortening the road. There 'll be a devil of a to-do if I 'm late in reporting myself. Good-bye, my lady,—until Saturday."

"I wonder if 't is wise," she said dubiously.

"Doubtless not—since 't is so pleasant. The wise course is invariably the detestable one," he answered, taking her hand. "Oho—a new ring, Madame. What a little person you are for baubles!"

"Dermot gave it to me," said Julia, with an almost angry glance at the ruby and pearl marquise upon her slim third finger. "It was his mother's."

Barry's face hardened. There could be no doubt about Dermot's feeling for his wife if he had voluntarily given her any of Ethna's personal belongings. More than ever he realised the baseness, the absolute dishonesty of his own part, and the imperative need for revealing what Taaffe had concealed. It was useless to try and stifle conscience by reflections on his own unhappiness or Julia's.

"He 'll have to be told," he thought ruefully, as he kissed the girl's hand. "But—six weeks hence will be time enough."

CHAPTER XXVIII

"ARROWS THAT MURDER SLEEP"

"WEEPING again, Julia? My dear child, you will have no eyes left—and 't is so vastly bourgeois!"

There was a hint of impatience in Madame de Louysnes's tone. That any one should cry anywhere but in the privacy of an empty chamber, behind locked doors, was to her incomprehensible.

"I—I want to go to Ireland," sobbed Julia, with a fresh paroxysm of tears.

Esmée raised her eyebrows. Dermot, having been granted leave in lieu of the furlough cancelled five months earlier, had set out straightway to complete his mission of vengeance, and it seemed to her that Julia in wishing to accompany him had shown a strange lack of delicacy.

"You would have vastly incommoded your husband," she said drily.

Julia looked out of the deep-set window. A mid-August storm was playing havoc with the pleasance. The moat waters leaped under

314

sheets of tropical rain and little whirlpools of
torn leaves spun and danced in every corner.

"I was n't thinking of Dermot, I was thinking
of Ireland," she said drearily.

"Ireland!" repeated Madame de Louysnes.
"Surely you hate Ireland! You were very
unhappy there."

Julia remained silent. She had no words to
describe that nostalgia of the bogs which goes with
Ireland's children to the uttermost ends of the
earth. She hardly understood the curious dull
yearning towards the far silver horizons, the solitary wind-swept shadow-haunted hills of her
native land, but she knew that Fontainebleau at
its brightest, Paris at its gayest, could never
quite still that ache.

Fresh tears came into her eyes at the thought,
her lips trembled. Madame de Louysnes gave
her shoulders an impatient shrug. There were
times when she longed to shake this meek child
for the very meekness that made it impossible
even to speak roughly.

"I think you Irish are all a little mad, my dear,"
she said. "Your land appears a place of infinite
discomfort, a place from which the major part of
you must fly, and where the remainder live in perpetual strife, and yet you can all of you do nought
save bemoan your absence from it. Dermot 's the
same—and if you want to see Barry FitzUlick in a
rage you have but to abuse Ireland. Truly, you 're
a wayward people!"

Julia's only reply was to wipe a tear off her cheek.

Esmée, drawing on her gauntlets, looked down at the fair, uncontorted face, the long wet eyelashes, with a certain envy. A disposition that provided so ready and easy a vent for all emotions was not entirely to be despised.

"I trust you won't be lonely, child, during my absence. 'T will be at most but for two days," she said more gently. " *Au revoir, mignon.* Pray for my poor friend, Elise de Montjours, will you not?"

"But of course, Madame—I will pray that you may find her vastly better on your arrival," answered Julia rising. "La! I fear you will have a terrible ride!"

Esmée glanced carelessly out at the driving rain-veil. It seemed to her too trivial a thing even to notice when so old a friend as Elise de Montjours had summoned her, possibly to her death-bed.

She kissed Julia in a rather perfunctory manner, gathered her riding coat about her, and moved towards the house-steward, who was waiting by the door to assist her in mounting.

Lady Lisronan from a narrow window watched the little cortège across the bridge, Esmée sitting straight in her saddle, indifferent to the storm, the two men-servants bent over their horses' necks.

The tears, momentarily dispelled, gathered again in Julia's eyes. To her longing for "the fair hills of holy Ireland" were added other woes which

she might confide to none.   Memories of the past
ten weeks with their hours of exquisite stolen
bliss—and a blistering remembrance of what Père
de l'Ecrillon had said to her two days earlier.
Père de l'Ecrillon was not over-lenient to any
sinner, from his most Christian Majesty downwards.

His words had induced a tempest of remorse and
dismay in Julia's young conscience.   He refused
her absolution so long as she continued to see
Barry, he ordered her to join Dermot forthwith and so put herself outside the sphere of
temptation.

Julia had crept out from the confessional feeling
as if every minute spent in Barry's society were a
deadly sin, had hailed with feverish eagerness the
news of Dermot's impending arrival at Fontainebleau and subsequent departure for Ireland, had
begged him in a passion of tears to let her accompany him—and had been told very gently, by
a man only too obviously delighted that she should
so desire his companionship that the risks were
too great.

To the girl, with her bitter consciousness of an
even greater danger, his refusal had seemed like
the withdrawal of a rope from a drowning man.
The position into which she had gone so light-
heartedly, with a child's ignorance of the forces
invoked, threatened to overwhelm her.   A touch,
a word, and the slender barrier of honour which
divided her from the man who cared for her as

much, or more, than she cared for him would fall.
And then——

Julia covered her face with her hands and shivered. Such imagination as she possessed showed
her a crude and lurid picture: Barry and Dermot
face to face in a duel *à l'outrance*.

Julia was not made of strong enough elements
to face the cold, sordid disgrace that envelops a
woman who permits a man to lure her from the
path which an all-wise society had ordained shall
be so much narrower for her than for him. She
was capable neither of the callousness nor of the
supreme devotion needful for such a state. Moreover, her woman's intuition told her that Barry
also lacked these attributes. Reckless as he was,
he would face the dishonour, the cackle of mali-
cious tongues, with even less equanimity than she.
And the onus of saving their three lives from open
and obvious shipwreck lay on her shoulders.

At last she realised this fact—realised too that
further association with Barry, even on the "good
friend" footing of the past ten weeks, would inevitably lead to catastrophe. Each unfrequented
moss-grown track of the forest held memories of
long golden summer afternoons passed there with
him. This very window-seat on which she now
sat, was a post of vantage chosen because it commanded the path from Corbeil. There remained
only one sure remedy—escape to some place
where Barry was not.

To forbid him the château was useless. He

would plead for another ride together, and another
—would argue that neither had overstepped the
bounds of friendship in word or deed since that
June morning in the pleasance. She knew just
what he would say and how she would eventually
yield to his importunity and the impulse of her
own feelings and permit one last meeting—which
would never be the last.

No. Flight alone spelt safety. But where to
fly? There was the conundrum. She turned it
over desperately in a mind quite unused to conun-
drums, as she sat staring out across the wet bridge
to the storm-wracked forest. It was all Dermot's
fault, of course. Dermot ought to have taken her
to Ireland when she so besought him. A wife's
place was with her husband. Père de l'Ecrillon
had said so.

"I wonder if I could follow him, could pass him
by night on the road and board the ship ere he
arrived at Havre de Grace," she muttered, smooth-
ing a fold of her brocade skirt. Dermot, pleased
at her interest in his expedition, had drawn her a
rough map of his route. She slipped off the window, whisked across the hall, and found the scrap
of paper.

From Fontainebleau to Havre de Grace was,
roughly speaking, a five days' ride—more for a
lady—but, since Dermot proposed to spend two
nights near Grainville at the château of a friend,
Julia thought it just possible that she might keep
ahead of him on the road—assuming that she left

Paris before he did. Once in Havre de Grace, she would find his ship, demand a passage into Ireland under an assumed name, and not show until they were off the Land's End. He could not send her back then.

She had fifty guineas upstairs. She would take two men, send the white jennet and Madame de Louysnes's horses back from Paris and post on. Her heart beat tumultuously as she thought out details. It was a most audacious proceeding of course—one for which Madame de Louysnes and Dermot would doubtless scold her soundly—but desperate diseases needed desperate remedies.

CHAPTER XXIX

A WOMAN'S WAY

LADY LISRONAN stood by the door of the deck-house of the Havre brigantine *L'Espérance* and looked nervously about.

For the first forty-eight hours of the voyage she had been glad enough to lie in her berth, dozing off the utter exhaustion induced by her five days' ride. Now, a longing for fresh air and society drove her on deck. She wanted to meet Dermot when there were few people about. He would no doubt be angry with her—as angry as Dermot was capable of being with any woman—and it was better to have the storm behind than before one.

A following wind just strong enough to fill *L'Espérance's* sails swept the deck, wrapping Julia's skirts about her and ruffling her hair. All round stretched the wide wrinkled grey-green sea, its furrows reddened by an August sunrise. To the imaginative, there was something curiously arresting in that rose-tinted east, that far-flung waste of restless, desolate waters, but Julia of course saw in it only the elements of a shipwreck.

The brigantine's deck was almost empty, for the fo'castle hands were at breakfast and the "quality" had not yet appeared. Julia, as she walked over to the taffrail, heard a single step behind her and turned, expecting to see the captain —an amiable Kerry man—or possibly her husband. The figure she did see brought a cry to her lips.

"Barry!" she gasped, "Barry!"

FitzUlick, one hand on the corner of the deckhouse, stared at her for a second incredulously.

"Julia! By all that's wonderful!" he exclaimed, crossing in a single impetuous stride to where she stood with the dawn-light full on her troubled face. "Dermot told me he'd left you at Fontainebleau?"

"So he did," she answered dully.

"Then——?"

Her obvious dismay puzzled Barry. She had no smile for him—no joyful greeting. He left his question unasked and looked down at her perplexedly.

"I followed him—to get away from you," she said with the fierce curtness of dismay and embarrassment.

"You remind me of Garrett Fitzgerald when Harry the Seventh, prompted by the Archbishop of Cashel, asked him why he'd burnt Holy Cross Abbey," said Barry laughing. "'My liege,' quoth Garrett, 'I thought the Archbishop was inside.' What wrong have I done, Madame?"

Julia glanced up miserably.

"No wrong," she stammered, "at least—I—I——"

"Père de l'Ecrillon has been worrying you again!" he said angrily, as her sentence died into incoherence.

"It 's wicked to speak so of him, Barry. You know he 's right and that we are in fault," said Julia breathlessly. "Oh, 't is hard when I try to—to do my duty that you should jeer. Go—Go away, pray."

She turned her back on him with so pettish a movement that it nearly stirred him to mirth, perturbed though he was.

"What brings you into Ireland—and why did you depart without a word to me?" she demanded a second later.

"I rode to Fontainebleau to see you last Monday —only to learn that you had journeyed to Paris after Madame," he returned crossly. "As to what brings me into Ireland, 't is a plaguey business of the Colonel's and no pleasure of my own, I promise you! He could not go himself and so hath sent me. If you 'd but written me a word you 'd have known 't was unnecessary to fly the contamination of my company."

"I' faith then I wish I had," she exclaimed with weary bitterness. "Where is Dermot? I would fain see him. Send him to me, please."

Barry, his face flushed and his mouth set in a grim line, swung round, but before he had gone a foot Lisronan stepped out through the deck-house door.

"Here's a surprise for you, Dermot," said Barry with rather ill-judged haste. "My lady would not be left behind after all."

Dermot for a second made no response. The confusion and distress in the faces of both wife and friend were unmistakable. He looked from one to the other perplexedly, shaken for the first time by a strange intolerable suspicion.

"How did you come here, Julia?" he asked, ignoring Barry.

Julia explained—that is she began several incoherent sentences and left them unfinished.

"I—I—will go back from Ireland an' you wish," she ended tearfully.

"Why did you come?"

Julia looked helplessly at the spot where Barry had stood a moment earlier. He was gone now— had slipped away when she began her tale.

"I—I was lonely—I did not want to stay at Fontainebleau," she stammered. "No one desires my presence there—save as your wife. But I am sorry—I will go back from Ireland."

"You cannot, more's the pity," said Dermot gloomily. "We are not making for Cork but for Tratullig Bay in Clare. I do not wish my return to be known before I reach Lisronan. *L'Espér-ance* will run on to Galway and lie there awhile. No, you must e'en remain with me, unless mayhap 't were possible to leave you in charge of Brian

Betagh at Tratullig. I 'm sorry you should have
this hardship, child, but indeed 't was only the
thought of it made me decline your request at
Fountainebleau. You might have known that."

"I wanted to be in Ireland," muttered Julia.

She avoided his quick, wistful glance. The
prudent thing, of course, would be to say that
she wanted to be with him—but she could not
compass the lie.

"I 'll try and leave you at Tratullig," he answered. "Brian has a sister who 'll no doubt
make you welcome."

There was a little silence after his words. Julia
broke it.

"How long till we sight the Clare coast?" she
asked abruptly.

"Five days more—if this wind holds."

"Five days! Well, I shall keep to my cabin
I—I—do not care for the deck. 'T is cold and
hath nowhere to sit. *Au revoir*, my lord—till we
make Ireland."

She turned abruptly, ignoring Dermot's hand
outstretched to assist her, whisked through the
deck-house door, and was gone.

Her husband stood for some minutes after she
had departed, with his back against the taffrail
staring across the brigantine's deck. One question repeated itself in his brain maddeningly. Had
Barry known when they left Havre de Grace that
Julia was on board—and if so what did it portend?

Suspicion did not come easily to Lisronan.

Those who had his esteem had it without any reservations. He trusted Barry, his friend, as implicitly as he trusted Madame de Louysnes. The mere thought of anything else seemed impossible. Yet if Barry had known that Julia was on board—and what else did their palpable confusion when Dermot appeared mean? Well, things wore an ugly look.

He shook himself free of the idea at last by mere force of will and walked away to breakfast. But a shadow worse than "the fear of death" went with him, haunted him, stood between him and Barry—erstwhile his boon companion—and both knew it.

CHAPTER XXX

"FRUITS **FULL** FEW AND THORNS ENOUGH"

BEHIND Brian Betagh's house on Tratullig
Bay there was an old rath, almost levelled
by the passage of centuries, on which gorse held
undisputed sway. Bushes tall as thorn trees
towered to heaven, their dry twisted stems rising
like a miniature forest out of a sea of dwarf furze,
olive green, gold tipped, spangled on autumn morn-
ings with the fairy lace of wet cobwebs. It was
a place of perpetual summer, always sheltered,
always sweet, always cheered by the little song of
a stream a few yards away and the secrets whispered by the west wind to the gorse.

Julia Lisronan had discovered it the evening of
L'Espérance's arrival, and on this, the ensuing
morning, she and Barry were sitting there encircled
by high green ramparts still flecked with an occasional spike of apple-scented blossom, yellower
than sunlight. They fitted into the scene as well
as any two mortals ever fitted into a purely pagan
setting, but their faces wore no reflection of the
earth's summer mood.

Barry was speaking. Fitfully, in short, uneven sentences he was telling Julia what James Taaffe had confided to him in Glaunateeragh. He expected tears, and it surprised and rather piqued him that she should take the news so quietly, should watch him so unflinchingly with her dark soft eyes. The development of Julia's character was a fact outside his comprehension. To him she would always be the meek, gently obstinate child who half a year ago had wept at a word.

"Three months," she said slowly, as he stammered through the last curt sentence. "You have known this three months, Barry?"

He nodded.

"And you have not told Dermot?"

Barry bit his lip. "Do you blame me for that, Julia?" he asked in a voice rough to aggression.

Julia looked down at the piece of embroidery that lay on her lap.

"He—he—ought to be told," she muttered.

"Ought! Ought!" retorted FitzUlick passionately. "God, Julia, I think sometimes that you 're not flesh and blood—that you feel nothing! Nothing!"

She lifted her head and gave him a sudden, startling glance. "Feel!" she answered, her gentle tones vibrant with emotion. "Feel nothing—I? Barry, why say such things? You know them to be untrue! No. Do not touch me. Let me think."

She pushed away his hand, and her gesture as she held him off had something of repulsion in it.

"You make it all very hard for me," she said breathlessly, averting her eyes from his.

Barry sprang up, his face white and twisted.

"Hard—for you!" he cried furiously. "Hard for you!" Words seemed to fail him. He stood looking down at her with a tragic vehemence curious in so light-hearted a man. "Doubtless you think it easy for me," he ended, and the short savage laugh that rounded off the sentence made her shiver.

"Barry—Barry—pray!" she stammered. "We —we—have spoken of this before—and to no end."

"The end lies in your hands!"

Julia drew a long shuddering breath.

"Oh—you 're cruel!" she whispered, and then added some words of which he caught only one— "sin."

"Sin!" he repeated with bitter contempt, dropping on one knee beside her and seizing both her hands. "The old cry! Julia, speak from your heart—not as Père de l'Ecrillon's mouthpiece. I 'm weary of parrot words! You *shall* speak as you feel."

"You know how I feel," she answered, making no effort to draw her hands away, though his fingers sank into her flesh, "as well as you know the tie that binds me to Dermot—as well as you know, that were I to break my vows and go with you, you 'd despise me for it within the hour!"

Her voice faltered on the last word. "Nay, you but hurt us both by this, dear," she said very gently.

For a second they looked at one another in silence and her eyes, wistful as they were, held the greater resolution.

"I wish to God I had never told you!" he exclaimed, tightening his grasp until she could have cried aloud from sheer pain. "Dermot! Do you think if Dermot cared for you as I care he would weigh the matter of whose daughter you were for an instant?"

The colour flew into Julia's cheeks.

"Leave Dermot's name out of the matter!" she said sharply, wincing under the sting of Barry's words. "Or, better still, remember that he is your friend—that he saved your life. Methinks you 've not given these things overmuch thought."

"I have—upon my honour I have. But they can't weigh against you, Julia." Barry paused for a breathing space, and then added, in a curiously dull tone, "Nor will I believe you want them to!"

Julia saw that he was shaking from head to foot, and the fact and his change of voice suddenly overthrew her much-tried self-control.

"Go—go and tell Dermot," she whispered, beginning to cry. "Go at once!"

Barry let her hands go and stood up.

"Is that your last word, Julia?" he said huskily.

"Y—yes."

"This is to be the end of it?"

"Yes."

She had covered her face with both hands, but the word came clearly, even firmly.

FitzUlick stood for a moment looking at the high spikes of blossom, burning gold against the blue of the August sky. In the face of her resolve, his own part in the matter seemed all at once incredibly base, but he was too sore and angry to care much for this. A galling sense of double defeat stung him. He had not been strong enough to prove either a loyal friend or a successful lover.

"We should n't be happy—either of us—if we took the easy road," sobbed Julia.

"Oh yes, we should, my dear," he answered with the bitterness of great anger. "We should be very happy—for a time—probably as long as most people are happy—possibly longer. Why talk of it when you do not hold the happiness worth what it would cost?—The world's esteem! The favour of women whose own lives, God knows, are not so white that they should cast mud at others!"

"Your esteem," she amended quietly. "The favour of the man who—who cared for me because I was not as those other women. Barry, your very look, your very tone when you speak of them refutes your words. I should not be happy—no, not for an hour—if the price of that happiness was —was sin."

He remembered that she had used the same

argument, even the same words, once before, and
the old impatience of the Church's iron laws
surged through him again—but this time he
said nothing.

Silently he kissed the hand she held out in token
of dismissal, silently turned and walked off towards
Brian Betagh's house, leaving her among the gorse
—and Julia, looking after him through a mist of
tears, knew that this time he had gone for ever.

She did not break again into weeping in her
usual fashion. This thing went too deep for any
ordinary display of grief. The tears dried on her
lashes, leaving her hot-eyed and strangely numb.
That fire of enthusiasm for the right as right which
had fortified her against Barry, died down suddenly in her heart, and what remained was passing
bitter.

"He loved me—and there would have been
some good months," she said just above her breath.
"There might even have been many good months
—and there will be none now—none! None!"

She put a hand to her throat, as if the very
thought of those barren, bitter years ahead came
near to choking her. Père de l' Ecrillon's solemn
edicts on the sacredness of marriage, the blessing
of virtue, seemed all at once as cruel a mockery as
pictured bread displayed before a starving man.
Rebellion surged up suddenly in her heart. She
held the pagan creed, pathetically common to
youth, that happiness is man's birthright, mis-
fortune an intolerable injustice, and the feeling,

like most primeval instincts, once aroused over-
whelmed the teachings of civilisation as the sea
overwhelms man's barriers.

A new spirit woke in her while she sat, white-
lipped and dry-eyed, staring down to the Betaghs'
dilapidated old house. Barry, had he come back,
would have carried his point without much difficulty—but Barry at the moment was scrawling a
disjointed account of the affair for Dermot's perus-
al, and sealing it up with Margaret Wynykt's
letters. To face the friend whom he had wronged
in intention if not in actual deed, was more than
he could compass.

Julia, still motionless in the semicircle of gorse,
saw him presently take leave of his host on the
doorstep and mount his horse. A murmur of
laughter drifted to her. Captain FitzUlick and
Mr. Betagh were making a joke of something—
presumably their relative chances of the gallows.
It hurt her, though she knew that Barry would
have jested had his neck been on the block.

As he rode off her fortitude gave way. She
sprang up with outstretched arms, crying aloud a
broken protest which the wind carried away across
the rath. But Barry never looked back; it was
not his way.

The girl turned blindly to the high maze of
bushes, prompted by the stricken animal's desire
to hide. The mere fact of pushing a passage
through the furze, which pricked her ankles and
tore her gown, was a relief.

On the top of the rath she threw herself down, moaning inarticulately and rocking her body to and fro like a mourner at a wake. It was one of Madame de Louysnes's complaints of her, that her grief was the grief of the peasant—crude, outspoken, displayed for all to see.

How long she sat there she had no idea. The patter of dog-feet roused her at last, and looking up she saw one of Brian Betagh's wolf-hounds— saw too that the sun, which had been high overhead when she and Barry parted, was now far down the western sky.

A second later her husband came breasting his way through the sea of gorse.

"Julia! What is amiss? These three hours past I have been seeking you!" he exclaimed, looking perplexedly from her white, haggard face to the rents in her pearl-grey gown. "How came you here, pray?"

"I came here to rest," she answered listlessly, without moving. "The place pleased me. 'T was peaceful."

Her tone puzzled Dermot even more than her expression. Hitherto he had always found her eminently responsive, eager for conversation with him, anxious to win his approval.

"You look troubled," he said, walking across the rath's green moss-grown circle to where she sat.

Julia volunteered no reply.

"You are not ill, Julia?" he asked with a solicitude that was obviously sincere.

She shook her head.

Dermot, after a second's troubled scrutiny of her limp figure, sat down beside her.

"I 've news, sweetheart—the best news in the world!" he said, a note of exultation such as she had never heard before in his voice. "Doubtless I should prepare you for it. But I know 't will rejoice you as it rejoices me. In a word, Van der Wynykt is not your father—you have no kinship with him!"

He leant eagerly towards her, expecting joy, incredulity, tears of thankfulness. His hand touched hers, tried to close on it. Julia drew away. She was looking eastwards across the land and hardly seemed to have heard his words.

"Don't you understand, dear?" he asked in obvious disappointment and surprise.

His wife glanced coldly at him.

"You are long in coming to your news—your good news!" she said with a sneer.

"My news!" he repeated. "That *was* my news. Barry writ it to me—though why write when he might have spoken, the stars alone know. It appears he had it from your uncle who died three months back. I confess I do not know why Barry kept the secret so long. 'T was a strange act. Scarce the part of a friend—or even of an honest man."

A wave of colour flushed Julia's pale cheeks.

"'T was not to Barry the blame should be laid," she said sharply, prompted by the woman's instinc-

tive desire to defend those she loves at any sacrifice
of justice or truth. "Doubtless he thought I
would tell you."

"You! Then you knew? You have known for
three months?"

"Yes."

The light went out of Dermot's face, leaving it
grey and blank.

"You knew—and you never told me," he said
in a curiously hard dull voice.

"Why should I tell you?" she demanded with
sudden passion. "To my mind it made no
difference."

"No difference! No difference that you should
not be that man's daughter. God! Are you
mad, Julia?"

She laughed bitterly.

"I am the woman you married—the woman
you have treated as—as something unclean,
abhorrent, for six long months. Why should
I tell you? The change of my name has not
changed *me*."

"It has thrown down the barrier that held us
apart—and you knew—you must know how much
you have become to me of late—how much I love
you."

Julia gave her shoulders a contemptuous
shrug.

"Love knows no barriers," she said scathingly,
"no barriers i' faith!"

"Except that of honour," he retorted. "And of

vows made. God! to think that you should have known and never told me!"

"You give me credit for scant pride, my lord," said Julia with a little angry smile. "Am I—a creature spurned, barely tolerated,—to creep to your feet and beg favour so soon as I learnt that that which made me hateful in your eyes is removed? What of me—the woman? Do I, myself, count for nothing?"

Her voice broke on the last word. Barry's impatient cry, the echo of what her own heart told her, rose instinctively to her lips.

"Dermot, do you think an' you really cared for me you could consider for an instant the question of whose daughter I was?" she exclaimed. "Do you know so little of true affection as to think that?"

She had turned to him with cheeks turned suddenly rose-pink and a look that was almost pity in her star-like eyes.

Dermot, staring morosely ahead, bit his lip.

"You speak as a woman," he said slowly. "There are some things in life that no love can obliterate. An' you choose, you may say that I have not in me as great a love for any woman as I have hatred for your—for Albrecht Van der Wynykt. But such love as I am capable of is yours, Julia—now and always."

There was a little silence after his words had died out on the warm afternoon air. Julia, her head averted, her eyes fixed on the moss, was con-

scious that he was looking at her with wistful
intentness, that he was hoping, hoping desperately
for some response. The seconds seemed to her
endlessly long.

"Julia, you understand?" he said at last in a
voice of appeal. "You believe in my love? Tell
me you do, dear."

"I believe you care—now," she said stiffly.
"Oh, yes—I do not doubt it at all."

"Then—Julia, what is amiss? Why are you
so—so unlike yourself?"

Julia laughed unsteadily.

"Mayhap 't is to match you, my lord," she
answered. "You also are 'unlike yourself.'"

Her eyes met his for a second.

"Is that all you can find to say to me?"
he asked very quietly, in the manner of a man
desperately hurt.

Julia nodded.

"You are certain?"

"Certain."

Lisronan got up, walked a step, and then turned
and offered her his hand.

"It grows late," he said, "and you look tired.
Come down to the house. I will excuse you to
Brian if you 'd rather keep your room this
evening."

His instinctive consideration for her needs
touched Julia. She knew, however much she
might wound or disappoint him, that he would
never, if he could avoid it, wound or disappoint

her by word or deed. It was one of the points
in which he far outdid Barry.

"Dermot, I am sorry—I will try to be a good
wife to you," she stammered, using in her embarrassment the same bald phrase she had used on
the evening of their marriage.

"Nay, my dear—an' 't is a question of 'trying'
I had rather you let it alone," he answered, and
then after a second of hesitation, added gently,
"I will never reopen this—matter again—save by
your express wish and suggestion. I would have
you understand that clearly, dear."

Julia drew a long breath.

She avoided his glance as she took the hand he
proffered and got stiffly to her feet. What was
there to say? To tell him the whole truth was
impossible.

She would have been considerably startled could
she have read his thoughts at the moment. He
had guessed how things were between her and
Barry in the very second when she quoted Barry's
indignant comment upon his own coldness. He
hardly realised as yet what this new knowledge
meant, but it was characteristic of him that he
should weigh it well before he allowed it to affect
his actions.

"I have been talking with Brian Betagh about
leaving you here, Julia," he said suddenly, as they
walked one behind the other through the gorse.
"He does not advise it. He thinks that something
he has done has rendered him suspect, and, as you

heard last night, he has sent Kathleen, his sister, into France for greater safety. I fear there's nothing for it but to take you to Lisronan."

Julia picked a handful of gorse blossoms and let them drop through her fingers like sand.

"As you please," she said listlessly. "Where you go I will go."

They walked the rest of the way in silence.

CHAPTER XXXI

" HE WHO TAKETH TO THE SWORD —— "

" I AM tired—I can ride no farther," said Julia, with a little dreary sob.

Lisronan made no response for a second. His inclination was to retort that since her own foolish action had brought her into her present predicament she must make the best of it.

"Pouldarrig is only thirteen miles away now," he answered after a moment's silence. "Could you manage that?"

"No! If I cannot lie down and rest I shall die."

The words were a wail, and having spoken them Julia dropped her reins and gave way to unrestrained tears.

Dermot with a muttered oath dismounted. Knowing the uncanny fashion in which news flies through Ireland, he had taken every precaution to keep his return to Lisronan a secret lest his quarry should again escape him. Their journeying had all been done by night, and now, when his wife's fortitude so inconveniently gave out, the ruined tower which had sheltered them during the previous daylight hours lay a bare mile behind.

"Would a change of horses help you?" he asked.

"I could not ride your horse—it is cross and wild—I go in terror even riding beside it," sobbed Julia. "No—I must rest—I must! 'T is cruel to force me on!"

Dermot looked about him helplessly. They were on Monadarrig bog, enveloped in hot, heavy darkness, and out of the way of any cabin or house.

"I can't leave you alone in the old Castle of Clashkill, Julia," he said. "I am sorry, dear, more than I can say—but I fear we must push on to Pouldarrig."

Julia was not listening. A low distant rumble had caught her ear.

"Thunder!" she whispered in a tone of horror.

"Oh, miles away—it won't come here," said Dermot hastily, with a dismal recollection of her ungoverned hysterical panic during a storm in Paris. "Would you be afraid to stay in one of the cabins in the long glen? Noreen Dwane would take you in. 'T is only a mile from here."

Julia's answer was a scream. A flicker of lightning had quivered along the eastern horizon— and lightning to her was equally terrific whether twenty miles off or close at hand.

Dermot with a shrug of his shoulders turned both horses' heads to the long glen. Noreen Dwane was a sister of Shaun Ronan and old Anne. Her assistance might be relied upon in any emergency, and there could surely be no danger in leaving Julia in this out-of-the-way place. If anything, it was safer than bringing her to Pouldarrig.

. . . .

Precautions were as little observed by Dermot as by Barry—though not for the same reason. Where FitzUlick neglected them because they were irksome Lisronan neglected them from an inability to realise their necessity. He did not possess that animal quickness of observation common to most country-bred men and when, having laid Julia in Mrs. Dwane's box-bed, he emerged again into darkness, a rustle among the hollies near Noreen's isolated cottage escaped his notice.

He had no consciousness of eyes that watched him, paid no particular attention to his horse's raised head and sudden alert air. His whole mind was centred on reaching his enemy's house.

The thunder muttered again as he rode up onto the bog, and another stab of steel-blue light went flickering across the eastern horizon.

"Lucky I found shelter for Julia," he thought, shaking up his mount into a rapid trot.

His plan was simple. To get in at the still-room window, to confront Wynykt, to settle the score. What happened afterwards would matter little. Madame would befriend Julia—or Barry—if, as he fully expected, Wynykt's men took a life for a life.

The thought of Barry carried its sting—a surprising sharp one—which went with him persistently through all the long dark miles.   He had
himself to blame—himself and the cursed barrier
that had made him neglect Julia against his own
inclination.

He recalled the whole sequence of his feelings
for her; first indifference tinged by dislike; then
an unwilling, almost unrealised, appreciation of
her beauty and her gentleness; and finally the
sentiment against which he had struggled and
steeled himself, only to be the more completely
vanquished in the end.   The thought of it ousted
the thought of his vengeance, as he rode ahead
steadily and speedily across Monadarrig.

Away in the east the thunder was still muttering,
with now and again a flash which showed where
dark earth and dark sky met, but the storm had
come no nearer as yet.

He had gone more than two thirds of the way
when his horse stopped suddenly dead short, and
swerved aside with a violent snort.

Instinctively Dermot's hand went to his sword-
hilt, but before the blade ran clear of the scabbard
a voice whispered from the shadow of the giant
gorse-bushes that bordered the track.

"'T is an craoibhin dhun, your honour," it
said.

Dermot slipped back the weapon.

"What do you want, Bartley?" he asked, peering down with annoyance at the little dim figure.

Ireland was an impossible country to do anything in of a private nature! The stars alone knew how the hedge-schoolmaster was cognisant of his carefully concealed movements.

Bartley came very close, putting a hand on the bridle.

"Wynykt's men have the word, your honour," he whispered. "They're waiting on ye below in Ballaghnarney, in a dark narrow place where ye'd not escape them."

"Damnation!" muttered Lisronan angrily. "How the devil did they know I was coming, Bartley?"

"Sure I couldn't rightly say, sir. Is it to Lisronan House ye'd go?"

"Yes. Is Wynykt there?"

"He is so. Sitting above in the long hall—Cromwell's curse on him!—waiting till they'd bring him in your honour's head. That his black soul may never know rest! That the flames of hell may be salt in his throat!"

"Damnation!" said Dermot again, thinking of the narrow pass where the sloe-bushes grew thickly and the path wound between walls of rock. Ambushed there a man would have no chance—and on each side of it lay stretches of green morass almost impassable for a horse.

"I must get round Ballaghnarney somehow—could you guide me, Bartley? You know every yard of the bogs."

"Deed aye," answered Bartley dubiously.

"We 'll get a passage if we go west two miles from the pass—but sure it 's a backward place an' a crabbed.   Ye 'll get delay there, sir, an' maybe trouble with the horse."

"I must chance that—confouna tne curious nature of people!   How did you learn of my coming, Bartley?"

"I heard tell of it, your honour, this two days back.   There was them in it said the young master would be in Bally Ulick too any night—but I got no account of him yet."

Dermot shrugged his shoulders irritably.   He was not really surprised—no Irishman ever is on his native soil—but he was intensely aggravated. Wynykt warned, would mean Wynykt fenced round with precautions, would mean in all probability death without any possibility of settling the score.   However he was not going back now. Nothing more should come between him and his vengeance.

.   .   .   .

"Curse this darkness and that infernal track!" grumbled Lisronan some two hours later.

They were within a stone-throw of his home at last, but the passage through the bog had been, as Bartley said, "crabbed," and had involved considerable delay.   The storm was working momentarily closer now, bringing with it heavier darkness, broken at intervals by the sudden blinding glare.   Twice in a minute Dermot had seen the house sharply revealed, with the lightning flash mirrored in every window.

It had no appearance of life, but this, Bartley whispered, was due to iron inside shutters lately put up.

"You 'll see to her ladyship, Bartley, if they kill me," he said. "She 's at——"

The hedge-schoolmaster's hand gripping his arm cut the sentence short.

"Horses, your honour! Horses crossing the ford!" he whispered.

Dermot listened. The sound of splashing and loud laughter came clearly to him through the silent night.

"One would almost think they *were* bringing home an enemy's head," muttered Lisronan.

Before the words were said a flash zig-zagged from horizon to horizon, illuminating the river and nine dark figures that were cleaving their way through its waters.

"Egad! why should n't I await these fellows at the big door and slip through it amongst them? 'T is worth trying!" exclaimed Lisronan, seized by a sudden inspiration.

He snatched a pistol from the holster, thrust the rein into Bartley Sullivan's hand, and was gone before the little schoolmaster could protest.

The story of Siveen's curse recurred to the young man's mind as he groped his way along the house. He too would wait behind the white rose-bush near the door. To go in by the still-room window had savoured too much of the thief in the night. He was glad to escape the necessity.

By this means—granted an interval of darkness just when he was emerging from the bush—he might come straight into Wynykt's presence before his own was realised. He reached his goal some minutes in advance of the riders, and listened between the rumble and bang of the thunder to their noisy hilarity. One was singing *Lillibulero* the others laughing and shouting like men well pleased.

Dermot, behind the rose-bush, now grown to a substantial shrub, heard them speculating in Dutch as to what the "old devil" would do and whether there was any hope of largesse. A flash of lightning played over the party while they dismounted. One who rode a grey horse, carried with care something round and white like a large turnip, and Lisronan, watching through the branches, noticed that wherever it touched the horse it left a dark smear.

He had no difficulty in following the men's movements. Three led away the horses, six stamped up the one low step and banged upon the arched door. At the sound a sudden ray of light shot out into the darkness, obviously through some small grille, the shutter of which had been withdrawn.

"The word?" demanded a voice.

"Lisronan, you d—d fool," answered the man who had ridden the grey horse. "Let us in out of the storm!"

The ray of light disappeared and a rasping of bolts warned Dermot that the moment had come to muffle his face in his cloak and slip from behind the bush.   It was a dark interval, so dark that he could see nothing at all until the door, creaking reluctantly open, let out a smoky glimmer.   Even then the entering men were featureless black shadows, and Dermot, treading close on the heels of the sixth, passed in unchallenged in the gloom.

The only light inside came from an unsnuffed dip in an ill-cleaned horn lantern, heavily latticed with iron.   To distinguish more than a grey glimmer from the wide steps and the vague bulk of human forms was impossible, but Dermot realised that a barrier had been built at the top of the stairs—a wooden wall which divided them from the rest of the long gallery.

He stood a little apart, unnoticed among the shadows, while the six men marshalled themselves in a semblance of order on the bottom step.   The lantern was carried up before them by one of two janizaries, whose duty was apparently to scrutinise all comers through the grille.

This warder unlocked and threw open a narrow wicket in the partition, and Lisronan noticed that though he was a small man he had to stoop to get through.   Plainly Wynykt had neglected no precaution that might safeguard him in an invasion by the grey dragoons.

The young man, anticipating a sudden flood of light, had been careful to edge off to the side instead of venturing upstairs in the wake of the others. The necessity for caution and silence made him slow of movement, and before he could reach the wicket the last man through slammed it.

A curse rose to Dermot's lips. He pushed at the panel recklessly. A cracking rattle of thunder right over the house drowned the noise of his onslaught, but though the wicket shook it would not give.

As he stood in the dark, baffled and furious, feeling aimlessly about the rough surface of the partition, a golden bead of light fell suddenly on his fingers. It came from a small Judas hole— a hole hardly larger than a human eye—cut in the woodwork.

He bent to it, keeping one hand still on the wicket. The long gallery was a blaze of light. Looking through at it Lisronan could see that there were candles everywhere—candles on every stick and rushlight-holder the house possessed, candles stuck in their own wax upon the floor, upon the wide window-seat, even upon chairs. It was as though the occupants of the room would not tolerate the merest hint of darkness.

And in the middle of this glare, huddled upon a settle, with an armed serving-man at either elbow and Minna Viebert beside him, sat Albrecht Van der Wynykt. His bestial face was flushed with wine and lit by excitement.

He kept looking from the advancing men to

something which lay huddled against his legs and half hidden by them—something which Dermot took to be a bundle of clothes.

A wave of fury violent as a tropical storm seized the young man. It was the first time he had seen Wynykt since the night of horror. He had straightened himself for another onslaught on the wicket when the man who had ridden the grey horse spoke.

"We caught him, Mynheer, in the pass—I have brought—" Van der Wynykt's roar of laughter drowned the rest of the sentence.

"Good! D—d good!" he cried, getting stiffly to his feet. "Did you bring the blackguard's head as I bade you, Conradd? That's it you're carrying, is it? Good! Come, my lady—get up! Here is a sight should interest you."

He bent, caught the bundle of clothes, hauled it up roughly. It swayed in his grasp like a limp figure of straw, and Dermot saw that it was a woman—a woman whose head hung forward on her chest and whose unbound hair gleamed yellow in the lamplight.

A horrible fear shot through him. Had Bartley been mistaken? Had it been Barry they were waiting for—and was that inert form Aideen's? He turned again to the wicket and drove his shoulder against it with all the savage force of desperation.

This time it burst open, and he half fell, half stumbled, through it. No one of the company

looked at him—no one even turned, though
the splintering sound had echoed all up the
gallery.

Every eye was fixed on what Conradd carried
in his hands—a human head, held up by the hair.
The light of the many candles showed it in all its
horror; showed the green pallor, the twisted blood-
splashed features, the open mouth, the half-closed
eyes.

A sudden horrible silence had fallen. One
thought ran through every mind, showed in every
paling face. The livid dead countenance was
familiar to all—but—it was not Lisronan's.

There was no sound in the long room except
a noise of large drops falling slowly on to wood.

Then, all at once, Wynykt loosed his hold of
the woman, who fell with a heavy limp thud at
his feet. He kicked her aside as he stepped forward, his neck craning, his eyes fixed on the ghastly
thing which Conradd still held out to him. His
face had begun to work horribly.

"More light—curse you all—more light here!"
he said in a strangled voice, still staring desperately
at the head.

Some one thrust forward one of the many
candles, bringing the full warmth of its glow on
that grey dead face.

A shriek burst from Minna Viebert.

"Willy!" she screamed. "*Lieber Gott!* Willy!"

Van der Wynykt put out a hand—withdrew it—
put it out again.

"God!   God!" he said stupidly, and then broke into a long howling inhuman cry.

In his whole life Willy was the only person for whom he had ever felt affection, the one being whom he had trusted.

"He—he—came—through the pass," said Conradd in a broken whisper.   "He—he came through the pass!"

The head slipped from his fingers as he spoke— he turned and made blindly for the door.

Minna Viebert got up, whimpering, and stood irresolute, looking at Wynykt, who had the appearance of a man on the verge of a fit.

No one took any notice of Dermot   Horror— and fear of the consequences—had robbed them for the moment of their wits.   Even when he moved past them up the hall they glanced at him unseeingly.

It was Wynykt who first realised his presence.

"Lisronan!" he cried, lifting both arms as if to ward off a blow.   "Lisronan!   The   witch   spoke of   his   coming—and   of   blood—my   own   blood wrongly shed—and—and—after that—after that —God!"

The last word was a gasp.   He stood staring at Dermot with panic terror in every line of his face, and twitching lips that muttered inaudibly.

For both the past twelve years were wiped out. Their thoughts went to the last time they had stood face to face on the evening of the taking of Lisronan.   Every detail of that scene came back to Ethna's son. He saw the white stairs; his mother's slim form as she stood, hesitating and terrified, by the wall; the monstrous figure clutching her in its arms—and the sight made him oblivious of everything else. Of the mutilated head, of the fainting woman who lay near it, of the eyes that now began to watch his movements with such savage menace—of everything but the sentiment which the Celt long ago crystallised into one pregnant sentence:

"Revenge! Revenge! To-day for revenge and to-morrow for mourning!"

Wynykt—insane fear in his bloodshot eyes—shrank from him as a beaten dog shrinks from the whip. For the space of perhaps a yard he backed away, with both arms raised above his head—then, as if his terror had suddenly overwhelmed him, he turned and ran—ran madly, blindly, like a panic-stricken horse, screaming horribly all the time—ran with such violence straight into the wall that the crash of his fall shook all the house.

Dermot saw a convulsive spasm twist his features and contort his whole gigantic form, saw sudden blankness in the livid upturned face, and knew that the vengeance for which he had waited so long had been taken out of his hands.

As he stood looking down at the dead man, Minna Viebert's voice came shrilly to him.

"Kill the Irishman, some of you! Run him through!" she shrieked in Platt Dutch. "The

girl is stirring, too.   Raise her that the slut may
see him killed!   Her turn will come next!"

Lisronan swung round, his hand on his sword-
hilt.   He had forgotten the yellow-haired woman,
once recognition of the head drove the fear that
she might be Aideen FitzUlick out of his mind.

But he looked at her now—he ran to her—and
as she lifted her head feebly the hair fell away
from her face, and he saw that she was Julia!

CHAPTER XXXII

" THE WAY OF MANY FEET "

THAT which, for want of a better word, is
called the subconscious mind has a curious
habit of asserting itself in crucial moments—
moreover, when it takes charge of the body, it
guides its actions with an unerring precision the
normal brain seldom achieves.

In the same second that Dermot recognised his
wife, he remembered that the one and only means
of communication between the rest of the house
and the long gallery was the door at its western
end—the door through which he and Julia had
come on the night of Barry's rescue. He caught
her up and turned towards it, spurred to haste by
Minna Viebert's shrieks.

The men who had been indirectly responsible
for Willy's death were slow to follow her orders.
They hardly realised yet that Van der Wynykt
was dead, and the fear of his anger paralysed
them.

Dermot had reached the door before a pistol was
fired or a man stirred. He stumbled through,

356

with the cracking echoes of the shot in his ears,
half carrying, half dragging Julia. The door was
a heavy one, fastened on the inside by crossbars of
iron, which ran into holes in the wall. He leant
against it when he had flung these bars home, to
recover his breath and his wits.

Julia, thrown down in the exigencies of the
moment, was moaning at his feet. He could hear
her whispered words, her faint sobs.

"Barry! Barry—they have killed Barry!" she
gasped. "They said it was Dermot—but the hair
was yellow. Oh, Mother of Heaven! Oh, had
I but gone with him he would be alive now!"

"Good God, Julia!" cried Lisronan sharply. A
man is seldom too obsessed by extraneous circumstances to resent the idea that his wife has been
tempted by another.

But Julia took no notice.

"Barry would never have deserted me in
Noreen's cottage," she went on in a heart-broken
whisper. "Barry would have saved me from
those terrible men who came in and bore me away.
Oh, Barry, Barry, Barry! why did n't they kill me
when they killed you?"

The utter despair in her voice touched Dermot
in spite of his hot anger, and his conscience smote
him for having left her. Heaven alone knew what
she had suffered, what agonies of mind and body
had been inflicted on the unhappy child.

A blue fork of lightning zigzagged past the
narrow stairhead window, lighting for a second her

huddled figure where it lay inert upon the floor. He saw the flash reflected in her wide eyes, which gazed up at him with the vacancy of panic terror— that her face was scratched, as if she had been dragged head downwards through gorse, and that her clothes were torn to ribbons.

"They did not kill Barry, Julia," he said with an effort, bending to lift her to her feet. "Barry is safe—safe. Can you understand?"

The last word was drowned in the hideous clamour of wood battering wood. Their enemies had begun an attack on the door with the nearest weapons available, stools, logs from beside the hearth, fire-irons.

Dermot put an arm round Julia and then, feeling how limply she swayed against it, gathered her up like a child. She hid her face against his shoulder and clung to him with feeble hands, while he stumbled up the stairs, but though the instinct of consideration for her womanhood had prevailed over his natural feelings a moment earlier, every minute brought with it fuller realisation of what her words meant—fuller realisation of the intensely bitter fact—that had the mutilated head been his she would have felt relief. He could think of nothing else—not even of the strange mischance which had led Willy into the ambush set for him. The rattle of thunder and the racket that rose from the long gallery made speech impossible, at least as long as they were on the staircase. Besides, what did it matter? He knew the truth now.

He carried her into the first room they came to—
a small panelled bed-chamber near the head of the
stairs—and bolted the door behind him.

"Now, listen, Julia," he said imperatively in
the comparative silence. "Your only chance of
safety lies in obeying me and keeping calm. Do
you take that in? Wait—I will make a light."

He withdrew his arm from about her to grope
in his coat pocket for a tinder-box.

The sparks, when it at last caught, showed him
that her eyes were still vacant, still terror-stricken.
She had the air of a sleep-walker. Her lips moved
noiselessly. She signed herself twice, with apparently no idea of what she was doing.

Desperate as their plight was, Dermot put a
hand on each shoulder and looked down into her
face.

"Julia—he's safe—he's alive," he said, driven
by an overwhelming desire to comfort her.
"'T was Willy they killed. Doubtless he learnt
by chance of the plot—aye, and rode through the
pass to warn me, and was returning when he fell
in with them. Darling, don't you hear? Don't
you understand?"

Her hands strayed aimlessly over the front of
her tattered riding-coat.

"My pearl scallop shell is gone," she muttered,
"the trinket he gave me. I wore it always—
always!"

Dermot let his hands drop and shrugged his
shoulders with a sudden savage wonder why the

human race went on when life held such possibilities of pain.

"That door below still holds—they'll have to burn it or blow it down with gunpowder," he said abruptly, turning towards the shuttered window.

It looked out to the shrubbery where Bartley waited. It was only fifteen feet above the ground, and a projection of the house hid it from general observation.

Julia watched in the same vacant fashion while Dermot stripped the bed of its strong handspun linen sheets, and knotted them into a rope twelve feet in length.

"You know the yew tree in the shrubbery, Julia," he said very slowly as he worked. "I'm going to let you down from the window, and you will make your way there at once—at once, mind—as quick as you can run—and tell Bartley, who is waiting under it, to take you straight to Bally Ulick. He must make all possible haste."

"I wonder how much of that she takes in—poor little thing," he added desperately to himself.

"My pearl shell—my scallop shell," muttered Julia, but she glanced at the white coils with a certain fear which suggested that some part of Dermot's speech had penetrated to her overwrought brain.

Downstairs the attack on the door was being carried on with unabated vigour. Echoes of it rose fitfully to them, dulled by intervening walls, and drowned now and again in a crackle of thunder

Julia apparently realised its significance, for she kept turning her head incessantly from side to side, with an air of almost insane terror.

Dermot's heart sank as he looked at her. Would she ever have sufficient wit and self-control to find the yew or to give Bartley the message? He glanced about despairingly for an ink-horn, or even a pin with which he might prick a few words on the back of a letter he had in his pocket, but neither were to be seen, and there was no time for search.

Julia made no protest when he fastened the sheet-rope round under her arms.

"Don't try to unknot it when you are down. Gather it about you and run," he said as he led her to the window.

She stood silent beside him while he unbarred the shutters. She even held to his coat, but it was evident that she hardly realised who he was and cared less.

"You don't wish to be again in the hands of those who brought you from Norween Dwane's cabin—do you, child?" he asked, anxious to rouse her at any cost.

Julia gave a convulsive shudder.

"Barry!" she cried suddenly, with a little scream, hiding her face in her hands.

Dermot looked hopelessly out into the night, lit just then by a flare of lightning. There seemed to be no one about—no one on the grass path below the window—no one between house and shrubbery. He lifted Julia out on to the sill.

"Bally Ulick, dear—and with all speed—remember that," he said in her ear as she slipped inertly
into space.

He could not watch her descent, for he had to
lean back and brace himself against the rope—
no easy task even with as light a weight as Julia.
It seemed to him an age before he reached the
last inch of sheet, and must perforce lean out over
the sill so that she might reach the ground with as
little jar as possible.

As he did so the lightning flared once more from
horizon to horizon, giving him a momentary glimpse
of his wife standing forlornly among white coils of
twisted linen.   Before it went he saw her move
feebly away, trailing the sheets as though she were
too dazed and weary to remember their existence.

Lisronan, groaning at her slowness, swung his leg
over the sill with the intention of lowering himself
from the window-ledge to the full extent of his arms,
and then taking his chance in the nine feet or so of
drop that would remain; but before his foot had
left the floor a shout from below chilled his heart.

He heard the clatter of heavy steps running,
the clink of a scabbard hitting a stone—and then
the lightning blazed out again and showed him two
of Wynykt's men right under the window—and
Julia a few yards off pushing irresolutely into the
hollies that fringed the shrubbery.   On the instinct
of the moment he gave a cry.   As he had hoped,
it drew both men's eyes to him, and before they
could look elsewhere the light was gone.

"Well—that ends my chance of escape," he thought grimly, while their calls echoed through the darkness. A momentary flash of that doubt from which even the most devout cannot wholly escape—the doubt whether any life exists beyond the grave—shot through his mind. But it was of short duration. Somewhere at the very heart of the Irish race there lie two instincts that dominate all the rest—faith in a God and lust of combat. Both were called on now and both responded.

As he sat on the window-sill waiting for the next flicker of lightning, his hands were busy with his sword-hilt and his thoughts with the coming fight. They should not take him easily, these Dutchmen.

The blue glare came again, illuminating earth and sky. He saw it reflected in the swords of the men below, and looked down at them, not as Barry would have done with a laugh and a sneer, but steadily and defiantly. Julia's figure had disappeared—she must be near the old yew by now.

Sounds echoing through the house told him that some one had been sent in by the stairhead window to unlock the big door. He could hear it grating on the stone floor as it was dragged open. He could hear Minna Viebert's voice shrilly urging on the men with promises of gold and hideous references to Julia.

Instinctively, driven by the savage impulse aroused in the human heart by savagery, he took up the rushlight which he had lit and deliberately set fire to the bed-hangings, deliberately scattered the contents of his powder-horn about the room. The old house should not be for this hag and her base-born sons.

He watched the creeping tongues of flame with relentless satisfaction. His enemies were at the door now. A very few seconds would see them inside.

. . . .

The ever-strengthening light was showing out every detail of the room. There was a little lace-edged handkerchief on the floor which Julia had dropped. As he picked it up mechanically a sudden silence fell in the passage where some new tool was being requisitioned, and a sound came drifting in to him through the utter stillness of the night—the faint but unmistakable noise of a horse crossing the ford.

He stood with the little scented bit of cambric in his hand, listening to it. It was his last message from the outer world. It meant that she was safe —it meant——

Dermot let the handkerchief drop. The realisation of how intensely he hated Barry, of how little he could face the thought of her in Barry's arms, surprised him even at that moment.

And then the door gave.

THE END

www.ingramcontent.com/pod-product-compliance
Lightning Source LLC
Chambersburg PA
CBHW021214090426
42740CB00006B/213